POSTAGE

1898.

"PIRE THAN HAS BEEN"

2¢

THE AMERICAN RESPONSE TO CANADA SINCE 1776

THE AMERICAN RESPONSE TO CANADA SINCE 1776

Gordon T. Stewart

Michigan State University Press
East Lansing
1992

All Michigan State University Press books are produced on paper which meets the requirements of American National Standard of Information Sciences—Permanence of paper for printed materials ANSI Z23.48-1984

Michigan State University Press
East Lansing, Michigan 48823-5202

Printed in the United States of America

00 99 98 97 96 95 94 93 92 1 2 3 4 5 6 7 8 9 10

Library of Congress Cataloging-in-Publication Data
Stewart, Gordon T. (Gordon Thomas), 1945-
   The American Response to Canada since 1776 / Gordon T. Stewart.
   p   . cm. — (Canadian Series; #3)
   Includes bibliographical references and index.
   ISBN 0-87013-312-8
   1. United States—Foreign relations—Canada. 2. Canada—Foreign relations—United States. I. Title. II. Series.
E183.8.C2S74 1992
327. 73071—dc20

Contents

Acknowledgements

I wish to express my appreciation here for support from the Canadian Studies Grant Program in the United States for a Senior Fellowship which helped defray the cost of research in Washington, Ottawa and London. Additional funding for my research was supplied by the All-University Research Initiation fund of Michigan State University. Throughout my career at Michigan State, the Director of the Canadian Studies Centre, Victor Howard, has been unstinting in providing support and encouragement. At a critical stage in the writing of this book, I received trenchant but constructive commentary from Jack Granatstein of York University which helped clarify my thinking. Professor Robin Winks of Yale University provided insightful observations with respect to the general approach of the manuscript. I would like to acknowledge here the support of Jeffrey Simpson, the national political correspondent of the *Globe and Mail*, who provided such a generous reception to my work on the origins of Canadian politics and thereby encouraged me to think that there was some place for outsiders to write on Canadian topics. Finally, while I would not wish another book to be condemned by the company it keeps, *The American Response to China* by my friend and former colleague Warren Cohen (now at the University of Maryland) was the model for this study.

A Note on Terminology

The term "Canada" is used throughout this book even though the Dominion of Canada was established only in 1867. From 1608 to 1760, Canada was a French colony. Following the conquest by Britain in the Seven Years' War and the migration of English speaking settlers (most of them loyalists fleeing the American revolution) into the region west of the Ottawa River in the 1780s, the old French colony of Quebec was divided in 1791 into two separate colonies— Upper Canada (corresponding to modern southern Ontario) and Lower Canada (corresponding to modern Quebec). Between 1841 and 1867, Upper Canada and Lower Canada were rejoined to form the Union of the Canadas. These colonies along with the maritime British possessions of Nova Scotia, New Brunswick, and Prince Edward Island were collectively referred to by contemporaries as British North America. With the exception of Prince Edward Island, they came together to form the Canadian Confederation in 1867. By 1873, the new Confederation included Prince Edward Island, British Columbia, Manitoba, and the vast northwest territories previously held by the Hudson's Bay Company. Canada now stretched from the Atlantic to the Pacific and was the largest settlement colony in the Victorian empire. Newfoundland remained a distinct British colony until becoming a Province of Canada in 1949. Where it is necessary to make sense of the evidence, the specific entities in this array of colonies are singled out, but in general the usage "Canada" has been adopted to make for easier reading.

I
Introduction

Canada is an odd case in the scholarly field of United States foreign relations because much more has been written by the Canadian side than the American. A basic characteristic of the U.S. foreign relations field in recent years has been the shift from American-centered research and interpretations to multiple perspective approaches. Research in the foreign country or countries, and incorporation of interpretations from those countries, are now viewed as essential elements in the scholarly analysis of U.S. foreign policy. The topic of Sino-American relations is perhaps the best-known example of this new approach as scholars such as Michael Hunt have called for a comprehensive effort to develop knowledge from the Chinese perspective. The journal *Diplomatic History* eagerly prints interviews given to select American scholars by Chinese diplomats who were involved in the diplomacy of the late 1940s when the great break in relations took place. Scholars keep hoping for better access to Chinese archives and libraries.

In the case of the cold war in Europe, much of the weakness in the literature stemmed from the fact that the major interpretations were based almost exclusively on American and western sources. George Kennan remarked that such an approach was akin to describing a boxing match with only one participant. Scholars such as Gaddis Smith are now committed to a systematic recovery of sources on the other side, and there is great hope that recent developments in the former Soviet Union and eastern Europe will lead to a cornucopia of telling sources that will make our understanding of the 1940s and 1950s more sophisticated and complete. While relations with China and Russia stand out because of their status in the modern system of international relations, the multiple perspective approach is now considered commonplace and essential in studies of American foreign policy. In all cases, there has been ample documentation and interpretative richness on the American side but very little on the other end. The task of modern scholars has been to provide balance by bringing into play knowledge and perspectives from the foreign countries under examination.

Canada does not fit this pattern. In fact, it presents the opposite problem. Modern scholarship on Canadian-American relations has produced a torrent of writings from Canada but only a trickle in the United States. The subject has been of consuming interest to Canadian scholars since the 1930s. This attention reached a peak of fashion in the 1960s, when there was an outpouring of books and newspaper and magazine articles describing the manifold ways in which Canada had been on the receiving end of American imperialism. This theme became a central interpretative thread in modern Canadian history. In the aftermath of the 1914-1918 Great War, Canada began to disengage from the British Empire-Commonwealth and define her own identity and place in the international world. She became more assertive and autonomous in the 1920s and 1930s. Direct diplomatic ties with Washington were established in 1927 which enabled Canada to shape her own view of the relationship with the United States rather than have it mediated through Britain. Canada made her own declaration of war in 1939 in contrast to 1914 when she had entered as a colony of Britain.

Yet, as she was emerging as a more self-conscious North American state, Canada was becoming open to more influence from the United States in a range of economic, political, social and cultural spheres. At the outset, during the 1930s and 1940s, this interaction with the United States was seen as part of Canada's maturing process as she entered into bilateral policymaking and economic cooperation with the world's greatest economic and military power. By the late 1950s, however, many Canadians feared that American influence in, and over, Canada had become so intense that autonomy had been lost.

During the 1960s the United States was portrayed as an imperial power which had secured extensive control of Canada's economy and insisted on Canada following the American line in foreign affairs. The American influence on Canadian culture through radio and television and books and magazines was presented as an additional and dangerous dimension to the American empire's impact on Canada. While this view was popular in the 1960s and early 1970s, it relaxed in the 1980s. It is also worth pointing out that the more extreme views were usually made in non-scholarly works. But, it is still fair to say that a more carefully framed version of the American imperialism interpretation is still the dominant approach to the topic in Canada.

While this abundance of interpretation flourishes on the Canadian side, there is a dearth on the American. The analysis in this book seeks to restore some balance and perspective, which is required for a better and more complete understanding of the American response to Canada. In contrast to Sino-American relations, Canadian-American relations have the urgent task of further investigation of the U.S. position. In order to better understand that position, this analysis extends back to the founding of the republic to assess whether or not there are any deep structures to the relationship which run into modern times. For the late eighteenth and nineteenth centuries, the case made rests largely on evidence in the usual printed sources, above all William Manning's four–volume set of documents *Diplomatic Correspondence of the United States: Canadian Relations, 1784-1860*. The heart of the analysis is based on research in the State Department numerical file for the 1910-1953 years, the period during which the crucial reorientation in relations took place. For the recent period I have relied heavily on the work of Canadian scholars and on the printed sources in such series as *American Foreign Policy, Current Documents*. Since the focus of attention is on policy thinking at the federal level, the story begins and ends amidst the public buildings in Washington D.C.

1.

On the east wall of the old Treasury Building in Washington, D.C., there is a historical plaque intended to remind the American public about the nature of the United States' relationship with Canada. The plaque was placed there by the Kiwanis Club of Washington on 20 April 1929 to commemorate the signing of the Webster-Ashburton Treaty of 1842 and was one of several such projects undertaken in the 1930s. Six years later another historical tablet was unveiled on the site of the old British Legation to honor the Rush-Bagot Agreement of 1818 which had removed most British and American naval forces from the Great Lakes. This unveiling was marked by a dedicatory speech from Undersecretary of State William Phillips, who served as the first American Minister to Canada when direct diplomatic ties were established in 1927.[1] The purpose of these historical plaques and the accompanying ceremonies was to present a benign view of the U.S. relationship with Canada. Speeches in connection with the Rush-Bagot Agreement invariably turned into paeans of praise for the undefended border, a version of North American history that was at odds with the wars, invasions and border tensions throughout the late eighteenth and the first three quarters of the nineteenth century. The tablet on the old Treasury Building describes the Webster-Ashburton Treaty as having "developed and strengthened the friendship between the United States and Canada" thereby cheerfully ignoring the fact that Canadians regarded the treaty as a piece of aggressive land-grabbing by the United States.

This benign view of the American relationship with Canada was a construct of the 1930s and 1940s and was one cultural aspect of the cooperative relationship that developed as a consequence of the Depression and World War II. This rosy account is inadequate, however, as a view of the entire historical relationship since 1776 or even of the modern relationship since 1945. In spite of all the scholarly writing that can be marshalled to illustrate the shallowness of the good neighbor metaphor as the over-arching motif to describe the American response to Canada, this approach to the topic has proved to be remarkably resilient in the popular culture of the United States and even in political circles that should be better informed.

It must be added immediately that this popular, conventional wisdom about the Canadian-American relationship is not without some scholarly sanction. At the time these plaques were unveiled, there was a major scholarly enterprise underway which, when completed in 1945, gave support to the notion that the relationship between the United States and Canada (because of its peaceful and cooperative nature) was exceptional in the competitive world system. The enterprise was the twenty-five volume series on Canadian-American relations sponsored by the Carnegie Endowment for International Peace under the general editorship of James T. Shotwell.[2] The theme of the series was that the American relationship with Canada had been exemplary, providing a salutary lesson for the war-torn world of the first half of the twentieth century. If the proper lessons could be learned from this relationship, a brave new world of international relations would emerge in which rivalry and wars would be replaced by cooperation and arbitrated settlement of disputes. As Shotwell phrased it, the series would demonstrate "the way in which statesmanship and common sense have ultimately built up a technique for the settlement of disputes between the United States and Canada which can and should furnish a model to all the world."[3]

Within many of the individual monographs of the series, the conclusions were rooted in the view that U.S. relations with Canada were special because of the shared determination of both countries to develop a new kind of international cooperation. The final page of Charles Tansill's volume, which covered the 1875-1911 period, is a telling example of this didactic outlook. Tansill's account ends with a description of the Canadian outbreak of anti-Americanism over the issue of trade reciprocity in the 1911 election. The Taft administration had negotiated a reciprocal trade agreement with the Liberal government of Wilfrid Laurier. During the election campaign in Canada, the agreement was presented by the Conservative opposition as an attempt to break Canada's links with the British Empire and as a step in the direction of annexation of Canada by the United States. This opposition cry was helped by some careless speeches in the United States by President Taft (who talked about Canada being "at the parting of the ways") and by Champ Clark, soon to be elected Speaker of the House of Representatives, who declared that he hoped "to see the day when the American flag will float over every square foot of the British North American possessions clear to the North Pole." The fact that Canadians could be so agitated about American expansionist designs was an awkward fact for Tansill to deal with, especially since the 1911 reciprocity issue was the culminating topic in his narrative. But to keep in harmony with the overall direction of the series, Tansill preferred to end his book with the observation that such storms were bound to blow themselves out because there remained a fundamental convergence of interests and values between the two countries. Americans and Canadians shared the same dream of a new world order; they spoke a common language; they indulged in the same traditions in their public and private lives; they were knitted by ties of blood and by economic circumstances. It was inevitable, Tansill summarized, "Canadian-American discord would disappear when the two countries were challenged by forces that threatened their way of life."[4]

Tansill's book was published in 1943, and his view of Canadian-American relations was molded by the overwhelming fact of the war against Germany and Japan. The entire series was affected in its final conclusions by the development of cooperation between the two countries in the late 1930s and during the war years. The scholarship in each of the volumes was sound, but the series presented Canadian-American relations in teleological terms to illustrate the emergence of modern international cooperation. This theme was all the more compelling because several of the scholars who participated in the project and the general editor himself were the intellectual products of both countries.

There are numerous examples from the 1920s to the 1950s, including such well-known figures as the economist John Kenneth Galbraith, to illustrate the migration of Canadian scholars to the United States. James T. Shotwell was a typical example of this phenomenon. Born in Strathroy, Ontario and educated at the University of Toronto, Shotwell grew up in a culture heavily influenced by the

United States, noting in his autobiography that he had been an avid reader of "the great American magazines"—*Century, Scribners, Harpers,* and *Atlantic.* Part of his family lived in the United States (Michigan and Kansas) and thus presented an instance for the mingling of the Canadian and American peoples that had been taking place throughout the nineteenth century. (This was the theme of one of the basic books in the Carnegie series, *The Mingling of the Canadian and American Peoples,* 1940, by John B. Brebner and Marcus Lee Hansen.) Shotwell proceeded to Columbia for graduate study and from there entered government service. He was on Woodrow Wilson's team of experts at Versailles in 1919 and from that beginning became an influential figure in the 1920s in the movement which propounded the ideals of internationalism. In March 1928, he met with French Foreign Minister Aristide Briand to discuss a proposal for the "outlawry of war" as part of the background discussions which led to the signing of the Kellogg-Briand pact later that year. Following the signing of the pact, which would depend on the moral force of world opinion if it was to have any impact, Shotwell praised its significance in his *War as an Instrument of National Policy and Its Renunciation in the Pact of Paris.* He viewed his own career as a confirmatory sign of the new direction in international affairs because it also had successfully crossed a national boundary. He had joined the Canadian academic migration to the United States and the ease with which he and others became part of American society contributed to

> an awareness of the growth of a North American nationality in which old loyalties are cherished not for provincial exclusiveness but for the maintenance of the enduring virtues which embody the ideals of human rights and freedom expressed in the history and institutions of both Canada and the United States.[5]

In the preface to his volume, Charles Tansill fittingly remarked that Shotwell "symbolizes as no one else can, the essential unity of the Canadian and American peoples."[6]

It was in this social and intellectual context that the Carnegie series was conceived and completed. The lessons Shotwell drew from his own life, the influence of his commitment to internationalism, and the impact of World War II combined to make it seem obvious that mutual understanding and friendly collaboration were the hallmarks of U.S. relations with Canada. Shotwell and Tansill recognized that there had been misunderstandings and tensions but they concluded that this dimension to the relationship was outweighed by the fact that the United States and Canada had now become good neighbors and an example of how international arbitration could be routinized. Shotwell's own experience convinced him that nationalism (with its destructive impact on the world scene) had become outmoded. When his Ontario relations moved to Michigan and Kansas "we thought no more of it than if they had moved out of Middlesex into the adjacent county of Lambton."[7] Thus, for personal as well as idealistic reasons, Shotwell envisaged the Carnegie series interpretation of Canadian-American relations as a scholarly brief to prove the new internationalism had been born. It was a worthy goal but, in terms of scholarship, the results were tainted. The generalized summaries of the series were often at odds with the evidence in the monographs.

This was the case with the Tansill book on the 1875-1911 period. The volume ended on a pious note about the underlying harmony between the two countries instead of analyzing the results that the Taft administration had hoped to achieve by reciprocity and the related Canadian fears of American expansion. The same point can be made with respect to several of the most successful books in the series. A.L. Burt's account of the years leading up to the War of 1812—during which a United States army invaded Upper Canada and declared it a conquered country—did not fit the internationalist outlook.[8]

While the War of 1812 could easily be put into a separate category as the culmination of the post-revolution tensions between Britain and the United States rather than a pointer to the future, subsequent monographs also drew attention to the rivalries and tensions, and even threats of war, between the United States and the northern British colonies. A.B. Corey's *The Crisis in Canadian American Relations* describes the rebellions in Upper and Lower Canada in the late 1830s and early 1840s which led to border tensions and convinced the British and colonial authorities that there was a danger of American invasion on behalf of a democratic uprising.[9] Lester B. Shippee's account of the Civil War years showed how deteriorating Anglo-American relations and the activities of Confederate agents in Canada kept alive the old Canadian fears of attack from the south.[10] The post-war publicity given to the Irish-American Fenian plans for an invasion of Canada enabled Canadians to sustain such a view of the United States. So much so, in fact, that a perceived threat from the U.S. was one of the factors that led the British North American colonies to join and become the Canadian Confederation in 1867. Both periods of tension came to an end with treaties rather than war—the Webster-Ashburton Treaty in 1842 and the Treaty of Washington in 1871. Nevertheless, the tales told in these books show how the Shotwellian image of the relationship was limited by its own time.

If the contents of the Burt, Corey, and Shippee monographs were not in keeping with the idealistic picture of the American response to Canada, Donald G. Creighton's *The Empire of the St. Lawrence* was even more problematic. The basis for the optimistic view of Canadian-American relations in the 1930s and 1940s was the notion of a natural harmony of interests between the two countries. In the past, difficulties had occurred because of Canada's place in the British Empire. But, now that Canada was emerging as an autonomous nation, the geographical ties which pulled the two countries together would work their integrative influence on the relationship. The long, straight border cutting across the continent from west of the Great Lakes was taken to symbolize the artificial nature of the barriers separating Canada from the United States. Creighton's work was a powerful refutation of this approach. Far from portraying Canada as an awkward, northern extension of American geographical regions, Creighton held that there was a geographical logic to the origins and development of Canada which had led to the development of a distinctive economy and polity. In *The Empire*, he argued that the St. Lawrence River—with its easy access to the continental interior and with its fur-rich and lumber-rich northern hinterland—formed a natural geographic entity. In Canada, the history of the French in the seventeenth and eighteenth centuries and of the British in the late eighteenth and nineteenth centuries should be described in terms of the use and development of this region and of its impact on the European settlers.[11] In this view of North America, the history of the United States and Canada was the history of a continuing struggle over the trade routes and natural resources of the continent. In Creighton's scheme of things Canada and the United States were not natural friends but natural rivals.

Under the circumstances created by the Depression and World War II, the direction delineated by Creighton had little influence on American scholarship. On the other hand, it did have a significant impact in Canada, not only in terms of contributing to the Laurentian thesis which posited a geographical basis for Canadian history, but also in terms of anticipating the direction of modern Canadian scholarship on the topic of Canadian-American relations. However, the Shotwellian vision made a better fit with the times. Therefore, when the 1935 plaque was unveiled and Undersecretary Phillips made his speech about harmony and neighborliness, such sentiments could be seen not simply as another manifestation of the vapid speechifying common enough on such occasions, but as the considered judgment being brought to light by the massive Carnegie scholarly enterprise. Individual American scholars might turn for a different kind of knowledge to the separate monographs but, in American popular culture, the good neighbor rhetoric has stuck as the most fitting way to describe the relationship. The concept that Canada and the United States had always been good neighbors became firmly embedded. Canadian scholars might write books and articles to expose the undefended frontier as a myth but, at the annual celebrations of Canada-United States Friendship Day, the good neighbor myth has held sway.[12]

Scholars inside the United States understood the limitations of such a rendition of the American response to Canada but the subject was of such marginal interest that no collection of scholarship similar in scope to the multi-volume Carnegie series was written to provide a new interpretation. By the 1960s and 1970s, it was possible to piece together the writings of various American historians as a revisionist view of United States policy toward Canada. The work of scholars who focused on U.S. continental expansion and who built their interpretation of American foreign policy around the expansionist needs of the maturing industrial economy in the United States provided the twin bases upon which a model could be constructed that would finally expose the good neighbor version as a relic with no analytical validity.

The interpretations of American expansionism presented by Richard Van Alstyne, William Appleman Williams, and Gabriel Kolko in the 1960s, best represent the themes in this revisionist view. They portray the U.S. as an imperialist power pushing for territorial acquisitions in the west and the north in the nineteenth century and for access to Canadian raw materials and the investment and consumer markets in the twentieth. The argument made by Kolko and other revisionists—that the United States was working in the 1920s, 1930s, and 1940s to break up the British empire and the sterling bloc in order to prepare for American control of the world economy—had obvious relevance to U.S. policy toward Canada during that period. But none of these scholars placed Canada near the center of their thinking—it is rather that U.S. relations with Canada could be viewed within the framework they proposed for a general explanation of American expansion. One interesting attempt was recently made to make the link more specific. In his 1982 article in *Diplomatic History*, Robert Hannigan made the case that the Taft administration's reciprocity policy toward Canada in 1910-1911 could best be understood

11

as an aspect of the open-door policies the United States was pursuing with respect to China and other potential foreign markets in the late nineteenth and early twentieth centuries.[13]

In Canada the Carnegie series interpretation had much shorter innings than it did in the United States. Even before the series began, a Canadian book had been written which gave a less celebratory view of the relationship. Hugh L. Keenleyside's *Canada and the United States: Some Aspects of their Historical Relations*, published in 1929, while paying homage to "the accomplishments and intercourse of peace," presented an account that tended to emphasize rivalry and American threats toward Canada. Among the causes of the War of 1812 was "an imperialistic lust for the conquest of Canada"; President Andrew Johnson talked complacently in 1866 of the ease with which the United States could conquer Canada—"a military promenade"; and by the first decade of the twentieth century, Keenleyside explained American interest in Canada was a consequence of a "growing American demand for markets and raw materials."[14]

Keenleyside's book is also more complex in its approach than the Carnegie series. It draws attention to the traditional Canadian view that, as long as her diplomatic relations had been controlled by Britain, she had suffered from the British willingness to succumb to aggressive American bargaining. Thus, for example, the Webster-Ashburton Treaty of 1842 is regarded by both American and British scholars as a sensible solution to the northeastern boundary dispute which had troubled Anglo-American relations since the revolution. Coming at the end of a tense period—the loss of British investments in the U.S. in the wake of the 1837 panic and the border incidents in the aftermath of the 1837 Canadian rebellions—the 1842 treaty seems to be an unambiguous diplomatic success. But, Keenleyside reminds his readers that for Canadians the Webster-Ashburton Treaty represented an abandonment of Canadian territory to the United States. Canadians viewed the treaty as the first example of a loss of Canadian rights due to the aggressiveness of the United States and the supineness of Britain when it came to defending Canadian interests. This view of the United States was part of Keenleyside's intellectual outlook in the 1920s and 1930s during which time he rose to become the Assistant Undersecretary for External Affairs.

The interpretation advanced by Keenleyside in 1929, while couched in workmanlike and friendly language, was one in which Canada was portrayed as vigilantly attempting to defend her territory, resources, and autonomy against the ever-expanding United States. When discussing the 1911 reciprocity policy, for example, Keenleyside emphasized quotes from the *Congressional Record* which revealed an ulterior American purpose. Senator Porter McCumber of North Dakota declared, "Canadian annexation is the logical conclusion of reciprocity with Canada," and the Speaker of the House announced, "we are preparing to annex Canada."[15] Keenleyside, in pursuing this vein of evidence, was also the first modern writer to draw attention in a systematic way to American investment expansion inside Canada. Keenleyside explained the rapid increase of U.S. capital investment in Canada as driven, above all, by the need to gain access to Canada's mineral resources. "American industry, the greatest economic and technical organization that the world has seen," he reasoned, "was in need of raw materials and of these Canada was an amazing storehouse." This investment led to significant influence by Americans in entire sectors of the Canadian economy. By 1920, American investors owned 49 percent of the electrical appliance industry, 42 percent of the rubber goods industry, 54 percent of the petroleum and natural gas business, 61 percent of the automobile industry, and about 41 percent of the steel furnaces and rolling mills.[16]

As befitted his career as a diplomat, Keenleyside drew only cautious conclusions from his evidence. He admitted to an "unease" about the extent of American economic expansion in Canada, but he made no claim that this was a form of imperialism. During the 1930s he established very friendly ties with top State Department officials, especially the key figure in relations with Canada, John D. Hickerson, Assistant Chief of the Division of West European Affairs. The prefaces in both the 1929 and 1952 editions of Keenleyside's book emphasized friendliness and cooperation as the themes that mattered.

There is, therefore, a tension in Keenleyside's views. On the one hand, in the 1930s and 1940s as a dedicated diplomat, he was determined to end Canada's colonial treatment by Britain and to establish closer, friendlier ties with the United States. On the other hand, he was troubled by the historical and contemporary evidence that the United States often acted toward Canada in ways that could be described as aggressive and overbearing. This latter view of the relationship was presented in a 1941 Department of External Affairs memorandum on "Recent Trends in U.S.-Canada Relations." Keenleyside warned his masters that the United States seemed intent on managing plans for economic warfare entirely by themselves "not only for the United States and Canada but for the remainder of the hemisphere as well." "The Americans," he continued, "were ready for Canadian 'cooperation' so long as that meant that Canada would follow the American lead and subordinate the policies of Ottawa to those of Washington." Keenleyside pointed out with restrained vehemence that it would "hardly be a satisfactory phase of Canada's national development if, having acquired our rightful place as a free and separate nation in the British Commonwealth, we accepted something less than the equivalent of that position in our relationship with Washington." "The United States," he concluded, "consider us almost a colonial dependency."[17]

In his published work Keenleyside was more circumspect. The 1952 revised and enlarged edition of *Canada and the United States* praised the Carnegie series. Showing his shared Shotwellian idealism, Keenleyside agreed that the Canadian-American relationship was exemplary. "In a war-racked world, Canada and the United States must continue to prove that peace is not an impossible ideal, that states can best maintain their national honor by not resorting to the law of the jungle but by reasoned and constructive friendship."[18] But it was Keenleyside's 1941 memorandum on American imperialism rather than his revised book that forecast the direction of modern Canadian scholarship on United States policy with respect to Canada. By the 1960s, the theme that Canada had ceased to be a colony of Britain in the 1920s and 1930s only to succumb to American imperialism in the 1930s, 1940s, and 1950s had become a common thought in Canada. Scholarly books and articles in Canada, as well as the writing in such magazines as *The Canadian Dimension* (which represented the mildly socialist New Democratic Party's viewpoint), criticized the American empire for its military adventurousness in Vietnam and its grab for markets, companies, and resources in Canada. Typical titles on these themes were Philip Sykes' *Sellout: The Giveaway of Canada's Resources* (1973), John Warnock's *Partner to Behemoth: The Military Policy of Satellite Canada* (1970), and Abraham Rotstein's and Garry Lax's *Getting It Back: A Program for Canadian Independence* (1974). Solid evidence to confirm the intensity of the American economic penetration of Canada was provided in the influential report of Melville Watkins, an economist at the University of Toronto. Watkins showed the extent to which Canadian industry and resources were controlled or influenced by the United States in a way unparalleled anywhere else in the world.[19]

Incidents in Canadian politics at the time helped sustain this view of American imperialism in Canada. Former Conservative Prime Minister of Canada, John Diefenbaker (in office between 1957 and 1963), contributed to the indictment by citing examples of rough treatment by the United States during his period in office. Diefenbaker further alleged that the State Department had actively connived to defeat him in the 1963 election because he had refused to follow the American line during the Cuban missile crisis. During the period of acute discord over the Vietnam War, Prime Minister Lester Pearson seemed to confirm Canada's dependent status by telling a Toronto audience that Canada must be careful before criticizing the United States because of the close military and economic ties that had developed since World War II.[20]

In this reading of the history of Canadian-American relations, the critical period began with the outbreak of the second world war. In the 1940 Ogdensburg Agreement, Canada committed herself to a permanent defense alliance with the United States. The Hyde Park Agreement (1941), which provided for joint economic planning during the war, began the process of economic integration that gathered pace in the next forty years. These two arrangements were seen as a turning point, marking the loss of autonomy Canada had recently attained within the Empire-Commonwealth and the beginning of a slide into a satellite relationship with the United States.

It was precisely at this moment in history that Keenleyside wrote his memorandum about America's treatment of Canada as a colonial dependency. The combination of close military ties with the United States and the integrative tendencies of trade and investment apparently left Canada with little room for independent maneuvering on the international stage. During the late 1940s and 1950s when western Europe and Japan were still recovering from the devastation of the War, Canadian officials looked forward to Canada playing a distinctive middle-power role in the world. By the 1960s and 1970s, however, this possibility was more doubtful, as Canada had been drawn into the American military and economic spheres restricting her world role. Canada, it seemed, was becoming part of the American empire.

It is important to make distinctions among those who developed such a view of the American relationship with Canada. Much of the work of the 1960s and 1970s in Canada was done in the context of the politics of the time, a context that was highly charged with controversy over the war in Vietnam and the threatening impact of American ways on Canada's culture and institutions. An anti-Americanism was fueled by the war and by the fear that Canada was being swamped by American books, periodicals, and mass media. Books and articles written in that context now seem dated and weakened by their obsessive approach. But there is scholarly work of permanent value which has made the case that Canada had indeed been worked into a dependent position with respect to the United States. Best known perhaps in this connection is the work of Donald G. Creighton (whose book *The Empire of the St. Lawrence*, as we have noted, struck a jarring note in the Carnegie series). Creighton was one of the great modern historians of Canada and the biographer of John A. Macdonald, a key figure in bringing about the confederation of Canada in 1867 and who served as Prime Minister for all but four years between 1867 and 1891. One of Creighton's books, *The Forked Road* (1976), in its very title stated the thesis that in the 1930s and 1940s, under the leadership of the Liberal Prime Minister William Lyon Mackenzie King, Canada took the fork in the road that led to a too-dependent relationship with the United States.[21] Beyond the general anti-American orientation characterized by Creighton, there have been first-rate Canadian scholars who have effectively used American and Canadian archives to make the case that Canada has suffered from American imperialism. The best example is R.D. Cuff and J.L. Granatstein, *Ties that Bind: Canadian-American Relations in War Time From the Great War to the Cold War* (1977). In the preface, Cuff and Granatstein argue that imperialism is indeed a category that must be applied to Canadian-American relations and criticize those scholars who concentrate on evidence for mutual understanding and friendly cooperation. They take a lead from the interpretation of modern America offered by Kolko with its emphasis on the American drive to make international policy fit economic needs. They argue that Canada has felt the impact of American territorial and economic expansion since the middle of the nineteenth century and that, since the 1940s, Canada has been faced with imperialism from the south in the shape of a deliberate American policy that forces access to Canadian resources and constrains her foreign policy options. Up until the 1930s, this approach was haphazard and, in economic terms, took the form of the spread of American branch plants in Canada. But, during and after World War II, American officials became self-conscious in their attempts to integrate Canada into American economic and strategic patterns.[22]

Thus, modern scholarship on the American response to Canada can be viewed as a spectrum, marked at one end by the idealistic interpretation of the Carnegie series and at the other by the model of imperialism advanced by Canadian scholars (supported, in general terms, by the work of American revisionist scholars like Williams and Kolko). Between those interpretations, however, the spectrum is filled with numerous monographs which treat different aspects of America's relations with Canada in rich and illuminating ways. In fact, it is difficult to draw the line in surveying this literature, since most books on American or Canadian domestic history have some bearing on Canadian-American relations. For example, J.C.A. Stagg's influential analysis of American politics and the origins of the War of 1812 draws attention to the fear in the Madison administration that

Canada was growing as a military threat to the United States. R.C. Brown's study of Canada's national policy in the 1880s and 1890s has as its central focus the impact of this domestic policy on Canadian-American relations.[23] Moreover, all books on Anglo-American relations have important relevance for a proper understanding of U.S. policies toward Canada. For example, Howard Jones' account of the Webster-Ashburton treaty, while concentrating on the forces which led the Peel and Tyler administrations to settle the northeast boundary dispute, helps us understand why Canadians might feel that their perspective was ignored by Britain as well as the United States. Canada being sacrificed on the altar of Anglo-American accommodation remained a characteristic Canadian view for the next sixty years. The 1871 treaty of Washington, which settled the tensions between Britain and the United States caused by the Civil War, was accepted with misgivings in Canada because Britain had not forced the issue of American reparations for the Fenian raids on Canada. During the period of Anglo-American rapprochement—between about 1900 and 1914—Canada claimed that she was cheated of her rightful claims in the dispute over the Alaskan boundary.[24]

In addition to pertinent work on American domestic politics and the literature on Anglo-American relations, there is extensive monographic literature covering special topics or periods. One of the most outstanding of these is Kenneth Bourne's *Britain and the Balance of Power in North America, 1815-1908* (1967) which traces the changing British policies through the nineteenth century with respect to the possibility of strengthening Canada to create a counter-weight to the growth of the United States. Another masterly account of an important topic is Robin Winks' *Canada and the United States: The Civil War Years* (1960),which provides a comprehensive and still authoritative analysis of the strained wartime period when Canada feared American invasion in retaliation for the Alabama depredations on Northern shipping. Excellent regional studies such as Alvin M. Gluek's *Minnesota and the Manifest Destiny of the Canadian Northwest* (1965) have shown the shape and significance of local and regional pressures for expansion into Canada. Thematic studies such as Donald F. Warner's *The Idea of Continental Union: Agitation for the Annexation of Canada to the United States, 1849-1893* (1960) have described the nature and extent of annexationist sentiment in nineteenth century United States. More recently, Reginald Stuart, in his *United States Expansionism and British North America 1775-1871* (1988), has provided a careful and comprehensive overview of American attitudes—official and non-official— toward Canada in the period from the revolution to the treaty of Washington in 1871.[25] For the period since 1945, the field becomes even richer. There is an extensive scholarly and official literature on a whole range of matters that have formed the basis of the modern relationship. A key figure in the scholarship on the recent period is J.L. Granatstein whose monographs, addressed to the specialist and to the general reader alike, have set the agenda for debate.[26]

The range of monographic literature on United States-Canadian relations demonstrates the variety of angles from which the subject can be viewed. Between the opposite polarities of the Carnegie series good neighbor approach and the imperialism approach in Canada during the 1960s and 1970s, the multiple, individual studies suggest the difficulties of agreeing that there are one or two over-arching themes that characterize the range of American attitudes and policies toward Canada. This book on the American response to Canada does not seek to replace any of these specialized studies in their interpretations of particular topics or periods. It is also less comprehensive than other general treatments of the topic insofar as it concentrates on American policymakers and those who influenced American policy-thinking rather than surveying the entire range of American attitudes. But the approach is comprehensive in terms of chronology because it tackles the entire period—from independence to the present—and has a narrow focus over a long time period. The task is to take a fresh look at the primary sources and assess whether there are some permanent features that have characterized the American response to Canada and to determine whether or not it makes sense to talk of an American imperialism, or even of an American policy, toward Canada. In short, this is an assessment of the historical evolution of American policy-thinking with respect to Canada.

Notes

1. Remarks made by the Hon. William Phillips, Undersecretary of State, 29 April 1935 at unveiling and dedication of tablet commemorating the Rush-Bagot Agreement, State Department Decimal File (SDDF) 1930-39, Box 4003, RG 59, National Archives.
2. All the titles in the series are listed on page 386 of the final volume by John B. Brebner, *North Atlantic Triangle: The Interplay of Canada, the United States and Great Britain* (New Haven, CT: Yale University Press, 1945).The intellectual context within which the series was written is discussed in Carl Berger, *The Writing of Canadian History: Aspects of English-Canadian Historical Writing* (Toronto: Oxford University Press, 1986 [1976]), 140-49.
3. Charles C. Tansill, *Canadian-American Relations 1875-1911* (New Haven, CT: Yale University Press, 1943), viii.
4. Ibid., 462-66; Brebner, 268; L. Ethan Ellis, *Reciprocity 1911: A Study in Canadian American Relations* (New Haven, CT: Yale University Press, 1939).
5. James T. Shotwell, *Autobiography* (Indianapolis: Bobbs-Merrill, 1961), 19, 291-93; Shotwell, "A Personal Note on the Theme of Canadian-American Relation," *Canadian Historical Review* 28(1947):42. Harold Josephson, *James T. Shotwell and the Rise of Internationalism in America* (Rutherford, NJ: Fairleigh Dickinson University Press, 1975).
6. Tansill, vx.
7. Shotwell, "A Personal Note," 36.
8. A.L. Burt, *The United States, Great Britain and British North America: From the Revolution to the Establishment of Peace after the War of 1812* (Toronto: The Ryerson Press, 1940).
9. A.B. Corey, *The Crisis of 1830-1842 in Canadian-American Relations* (New Haven, CT: Yale University Press, 1941).
10. Lester B. Shippee, *Canadian-American Relations, 1849-1874* (New Haven, CT: Yale University Press, 1939).
11. Donald G. Creighton, *The Empire of the St. Lawrence* (Toronto: Macmillan, 1937).
12. C.P. Stacey, *The Undefended Border: The Myth and the Reality* (Ottawa: Canadian Historical Society, 1960).Richard A. Preston, *The Defence of the Undefended Border: Planning for War in North America* (Montreal: McGill-Queen's University Press, 1977) is a masterly account of the military factor in Canadian-American relations.
13. William Appleman Williams, ed., *From Colony to Empire: Essays in the History of American Foreign Relations* (New York: Wiley, 1972), 39-202; James G. Snell, "The Frontier Sweeps Northwest: American Perceptions of the British American Prairie West at the Point of Canadian Expansion," *Western Historical Quarterly* 11(1980):381-400; Kendrick A. Clements, "Manifest Destiny and Canadian Reciprocity in 1911," *Pacific Historical Review* 42(1973):32-52; Robert Hannigan, "Reciprocity 1911: Continentalism and American Weltpolitick," *Diplomatic History* 4(1980):1-18; Norman A. Graebner, *Empire on the Pacific: A Study in American Continental Expansion* (New York: Ronald Press, 1955);

Reginald Stuart, *United States Expansionism and British North America, 1775-1871* (Chapel Hill: The University of North Carolina Press, 1988).

14. Hugh L. Keenleyside, *Canada and the United States: Some Aspects of their Historical Relations* rev. and enl. ed. (New York: Knopf, 1952), 48, 62, 263.
15. Ibid., 271.
16. Ibid., 277.
17. Memorandum of Assistant Undersecretary, Hugh Keenleyside, Ottawa, 27 December 1941, *Documents on Canadian External Affairs (DCEA)* (Ottawa: Government of Canada) 9:1131-36.
18. Keenleyside, *Canada and the United States*, 399.
19. In addition to the books referred to here, the 1960s are assessed in scholarly terms in A.E. Safarian, *Foreign Ownership of Canadian Industry* (Toronto: McGraw-Hill Co. of Canada, 1966); Kari Levitt, *Silent Surrender: The Multinational Corporation in Canada* (Toronto: Macmillan of Canada, 1970); Melville Watkins, *Foreign Ownership and the Structure of Canadian Industry* (Ottawa: Government Report, 1968).
20. J.L. Granatstein, "Co-operation and Conflict: The Course of Canadian-American Relations since 1945" in Charles F. Doran and John Sigler, eds., *Canada and the United States: Enduring Friendship, Persistent Stress* (Englewood Cliff, NJ: Prentice-Hall, 1985), 52-59; Peter Stursberg, *Lester Pearson and the American Dilemma* (Toronto: Doubleday Canada, 1980); Lester Pearson, "Canada, the United States and Vietnam" in Norman Hillmer, ed., *Partners Nevertheless: Canadian-American Relations in the Twentieth Century* (Toronto: Copp Clark Pitman, 1989), 121-25.
21. Donald G. Creighton, *The Forked Road: Canada 1939-1957* (Toronto: McClelland and Stewart, 1976).
22. R.D. Cuff and J.L. Granatstein, *Ties that Bind: Canadian-American Relations in Wartime from the Great War to the Cold War* (Sarasota, FL: Samuel Stevens, 1977).
23. J.C.A. Stagg, *Mr. Madison's War: Politics, Diplomacy and Warfare in the Early American Republic, 1783-1830* (Princeton: Princeton University Press, 1983); R.C. Brown, *Canada's National Policy, 1883-1900: A Study in Canadian-American Relations* (Princeton: Princeton University Press, 1964).
24. Howard Jones, *To the Webster-Ashburton Treaty: A Study in Anglo-American Relations, 1783-1843* (Chapel Hill: The University of North Carolina Press, 1977); Stuart, 238-61; John Munro, *The Alaska Boundary Dispute* (Toronto: Copp Clark Publishing Co., 1970); Norman Penlington, *The Alaska Boundary Dispute: A Critical Reappraisal* (Toronto: McGraw-Hill Ryerson, 1972); Alexander E. Campbell, *Great Britain and the United States, 1895-1903 (London: Longmans, 1960)*; Bradford Perkins, *The Great Rapprochement: England and the United States, 1895-1914* (New York: Athenum, 1968).
25. Stuart's analysis is particularly attractive because of the way in which he disaggregates the American response to Canada, showing, for example, how cross-border cultural and economic linkages continued even during periods of tension.

26. J.L. Granatstein, *Canadian Foreign Policy: Historical Readings* (Toronto: Copp Clark Pitman, 1986); Cuff and Granatstein, *Ties that Bind*, 1977; J.L. Granatstein, *Canadian Foreign Policy since 1945: Middle Power or Satellite?* (Toronto: Copp Clark Publishing Co., 1970); J.L. Granatstein, *Canada 1957-1967: The Years of Uncertainty and Innovation* (Toronto: McClelland and Stewart, 1986). Two important collections on the modern period are Doran and Sigler, eds., *Canada and the United States* and Hillmer, ed., *Partners Nevertheless*; Robert Bothwell, Ian Drummond, and John English, *Canada since 1945: Power, Politics and Provincialism* (Toronto, University of Toronto Press, 1981) is a general history of the modern period that is especially good on relations between Canada and the United States.

II
"Tendencies to Bad Neighborhood" 1783-1854

The United States and Canada began as bad neighbors. During the first seventy or so years after independence, the American response to Canada was characterized by suspicion and hostility. The War of 1812 (during which William Hull, Governor of Michigan Territory and Brigadier General in the Army of the Northwest, led an invasion and declared Upper Canada to be conquered by the United States) was the most dramatic manifestation of the tension and distrust between the two countries. The outbreak of war only served as confirmation to Americans that the Canadian colonies were a threatening and destabilizing force in North America. The constituent elements in this American view were a mixture of old and new attitudes. Throughout the seventeenth and eighteenth centuries, American colonists had interpreted French policy in Canada as one of encirclement.[1] From their base in Canada, the French design was to expand into the Great Lakes and Ohio country, travel down to the Gulf of Mexico, and keep the American colonies hemmed in between the Appalachian Mountains and the Atlantic Ocean. When the British replaced the French in Canada, the Americans saw the same geopolitical pattern repeating itself. While the boundary line had been established along the Great Lakes in 1783, the Canadians and the British continued to intrigue with the Natives of the Old Northwest in an attempt to block American settlement and maintain a British influence throughout the region.

The arrangements at the Treaty of Ghent in 1814 seemed to put an end to those particular Anglo-Canadian designs, but Americans remained suspicious of continuing British links with Native Americans inside the United States. Moreover, in the 1830s and 1840s, the presence of the Hudson's Bay Company in the Oregon country and British soundings toward Texas were worrying signs that Britain was still prepared to experiment with the old French policy.[2]

New concerns about Canada emerged in the difficult, first years of independence. Several leading Americans were convinced that the loyalists who fled to Canada during and after the revolution carried with them virulent, anti-American values, schemed against the new nation by encouraging internal revolts (such as Shays' rebellion in 1786) and attempted to dismember the United States through fomenting secession in the western territories. While these fears were most acute in the decade after independence—when the American federation felt particularly vulnerable—they persisted into the first two decades of the nineteenth century. There was also a clear American sense that Canada was playing an obstructionist role in trade matters throughout the period until the 1830s. This was especially so with respect to the vexing West Indian trade issue that bedeviled Anglo-American relations for fifty years after independence. The new United States wished to regain access to the British West Indies market, which had been such a source of prosperity during the colonial period.[3] The British excluded the now-independent United States from that trade, and American officials and politicians were convinced that the British colonists in Canada and Nova Scotia had influenced the imperial authorities to keep up the restrictive policies. The British colonies would then be able to replace the United States as the main supplier in the British West Indies. Canadian intransigence on the trade issue was seen as one factor cutting off hitherto profitable avenues of American trade.

Americans also developed a critical view of internal developments in Canada. In both Upper and Lower Canada there were armed uprisings in 1837, when radical reformers lost patience with the patronage-ridden, local ruling groups. These rebellions were interpreted in the United States as valiant struggles for independence and democracy—an attempt to follow the American example. There was widespread sympathy among Americans for the radicals' cause. Armed clashes broke out along the frontier between British and Canadian forces. Britain and the United States appeared on the brink of war over the "Caroline" incident when a small party of Canadians crossed the border to burn a ship that was carrying arms to the radicals. Such incidents heightened the American image of Canada as an undemocratic polity still very much under British imperial sway. In short, because of traditional fears of encirclement, resentment against loyalists, and a generally critical view of Canadian politics and society, the American perception of Canada in this period was negative.

1.

This American view of Canada was set firmly, almost from the moment Britain conquered Canada in 1759-60. The Treaty of Paris (1763), which formally ended the Seven Years' War, recognized British possession of the former French colony. Although the French population was concentrated in the central St. Lawrence Valley between Quebec and Montreal, French colonial claims and actual occupation, in the shape of trading posts and forts, extended into the Ohio country and included all territory between modern St. Louis and Montreal. The conquest of this French colony had a significant impact on British policy in North America over the next fifteen years. This was especially true with respect to all the land west of the Appalachians. The British discovered it was easier to administer this vast territory and maintain effective relations with the Native Americans from Quebec rather than from the old seaboard colonies. The natural and traditional trade routes ran from the Ohio and Great Lakes country back down the St. Lawrence. The fur trade continued to be centered in Montreal and Quebec. The Native American uprising in the region, led by Pontiac in 1763, convinced British policymakers of the dangers of allowing American settlers into the western lands. Britain prohibited settlement west of the Appalachians (Proclamation of 1763) and eventually decided to keep all the Ohio country under the jurisdiction of the new Canadian colony (Quebec Act, 1774).[4] Inside Canada itself which, of course, had a French-speaking, Catholic population, the British set up a colonial government which gave extensive powers to the governor and his appointed council but provided for no representative assembly. The British also recognized the existence of the Catholic Church in Canada at a time when Catholicism was still illegal in Britain and when anti-Catholic prejudice was common in her American colonies.[5] Americans viewed these developments in Canada as signs that Britain was embarking on a new, more authoritarian colonial policy which might be applied to the old colonies. Some leading colonists at the time thought that the deterioration of relations between Britain and her colonies began with the conquest of Canada. In his autobiography, John Adams recalled, "the memorable Year 1759 when the Conquest of Canada was completed by the surrender of Montreal to General Amherst" soon turned from a moment of triumph to an occasion of regret for American colonists. "This event," remembered Adams, "which was so joyfull to Us and so important to England if she had seen her true interest, inspired her with a Jealousy, which ultimately lost her thirteen colonies and made many of Us at the time regret that Canada had ever been conquered."[6]

Following the War of Independence, British policy was generally unfriendly toward the United States—the most immediately dangerous manifestation of that unfriendliness came from Canada. The retention of the Northwest posts, the strengthening of links with Native Americans living within the U.S. boundary, and a policy of military forwardness could only be implemented because of the British position in Canada. The very structure of the British colonies was seen as part of this aggressive policy. In 1791, Quebec was divided into two separate colonies. Lower Canada contained most of the old French population living in the lower St. Lawrence Valley; Upper Canada, stretching from the Ottawa River west to the Detroit River, had pockets of loyalist settlement along the upper St. Lawrence and the lake shores. The British had pressing reasons for this action, above all, to meet the concerns of the English-speaking settlers west of the Ottawa River who complained about living under French laws and Catholic customs.[7] But to American eyes this reorganization had less to do with the internal Canadian situation than with preparation to continue military pressure on the Northwest territories of the United States by establishing a colony whose government was in military hands. Upper Canada extended like a dagger into the heart of the Old Northwest.

As John Jay (then Secretary of Foreign Affairs to the Continental Congress) reviewed British policy in September 1785, he sketched the emerging pattern, "The Detention of the Posts, the strengthening of the garrisons in our Neighborhood and various other circumstances bespeak a language very different from that of kindness and goodwill." In seeking explanations for such behavior, Jay turned to the influence of the loyalists who had fled to Canada during the war. "I am well informed," he wrote to John Adams, "that some of the Loyalists advise and warmly press for the Detention of the Posts. It is strange that men who for ten Years have done nothing but deceive should still retain any Credit."[8] From his post as U.S. Minister in London, Adams endorsed the opinion that the loyalists were playing a role in this antagonistic policy. Adams wrote that he had confirmed reports

> of a general Confederation of the Indian nations against the United States, which the Refugees propagate, partly from the Pleasure they take in the thought and partly to persuade Government to build Ships and Forts upon the Lakes; Services in which they hope to get employment under the Crown and the fingering of some of its money.[9]

The British military buildup in Canada seemed designed to prevent effective American possession of territory in the Ohio and Great Lakes country. "The number of forces stationed in the province of Quebec . . . creates suspicions that they wish to see our Difficulties of every kind increase and multiply," reported John Jay to Congress in 1786.[10] British Prime Minister William Pitt's offer to mediate between the American administration and the Native Americans in the Northwest, Gouvernor Morris told George Washington, was simply a device "to constitute himself their Patron and Protector." Morris proceeded to make the case that this British activity—which kept the situation in the Northwest in a turmoil—was directly connected to the division of the colony of Quebec into Upper and Lower Canada. "It may be proper," he advised Washington, "to combine all this with the late Division of Canada and the present measures for the military organization of the Upper country."[11]

The actions of John Graves Simcoe, the first lieutenant-governor of the new colony of Upper Canada, supported the American view that the reorganization was directed toward long-term British interference in the Northwest territories. In 1775, Simcoe had served with his regiment in Boston and commanded the Queens Rangers, a loyalist unit, in the Revolutionary War. During his tenure in Upper Canada, he embarked on a vigorous campaign to attract settlers from the United States, extend contacts with Native Americans, and strengthen the British military presence throughout the region (for example, establishing a new fort on the Miami River).[12] This last action occasioned an exasperated complaint from Secretary of State Edmund Randolph to John Jay about the whole course of British policy in Canada. The irritation from the Canadian quarter, he summed up, "has been exceedingly aggravated." Lord Dorchester (the Governor-General in Lower Canada) had been making bellicose speeches that were followed by Simcoe's "invasion of the rapids of the Miami."[13] A series of military governors in both Upper and Lower Canada, until the 1830s, made it easy for Americans to view the Canadian colonies as military establishments, or "these commands," as Rufus King, U.S. Minister to Britain, described them in 1799.[14] The same perception was clearly prominent in Robert Livingston's mind in 1803. As U.S. Minister in France. Livingston described Canada to French foreign minister Talleyrand as "a martial Colony containing every means of attack."[15]

The intervention from Canada was viewed by Americans as part of a plan by the British to use her militarized colonies in Canada as a forward base from which she could impede the western growth of the United States—perhaps even dismember the new western territories from the thirteen coastal states. In 1794, Secretary of State

Randolph complained, "British influence has been tampering with the people of Kentucky and of the neighborhood of Pittsburgh, to seduce them from the United States or to encourage them in a revolt against the general government."[16] President Washington despaired of peaceful possession of the Northwest "so long as they [Native Americans] may be under an influence which is hostile to the rising greatness of these states."[17] In a report to the French Committee of Public Safety in 1795, James Monroe, then U.S. Minister to France, set out the case against Britain:

> With this view [of dismembering the west] she refused to surrender the forts, incited the Indians to make war on our Families, encouraged Spain to refuse our right to the Navigation of the Mississippi [and] improve it into an opportunity of separating the new from the old states and connecting them with her interests in Canada. . . . Next to conquest, separation would be the most advantageous for Britain [who would] become the ally of the western states and play them off against the eastern.[18]

This fear of separation of the west had been at work earlier when American leaders in the 1780s feared that Vermont might join Canada rather than the United States. "The English," Jay warned Jefferson in 1787, "are making some important settlements on the St. Lawrence—many of our people go there and it is said Vermont is not greatly inclined to be the Fourteenth state."[19] In another letter to Jefferson on this theme, Jay argued that the British authorities in Canada were promulgating, "the Interests of the Atlantic and Western Parts of the United States are distinct and that the growth of the latter will tend to diminish that of the former. . . . If Britain really means us harm she will adopt and impress this Idea."[20]

The extent to which the United States worried about the geographical fragility of the new nation and the destabilizing forces deployed from Canada can be seen even more revealingly when American leaders charged that Anglo-Canadian machinations were behind social and political unrest in the eastern states. The most dramatic outbreak of unrest, Shays' rebellion in Massachusetts in 1786, was attributed to interference from Canada. In December 1786, Jay was convinced, "a variety of considerations afford room for suspicion that there is an Understanding between the insurgents in Massachusetts and some leading persons in Canada."[21] Edward Carrington, a member of the Virginia delegation to Congress, told Edmund Randolph, the governor of Virginia, it is said a british influence is operating in this mischievous affair. . . . It is an undoubted truth that communications are held by Lord Dorchester with both the Vermonters and the insurgents of Massachusetts and that a direct offer has been made to the latter of the protection of Great Britain.

Once again British malfeasance was linked to the British position in Canada. "All her appointments to her Colonies," continued Carrington, "as well as her Missions into these States are calculated to this object."[22]

At times in the 1780s and 1790s, the initiative for this interventionist British policy seemed to lie in Canada rather than London. Edmund Randolph was puzzled by the warlike moves from Upper Canada at a time when it was reported from London that the British did not wish war with the United States. "They ought to be for peace," he wrote to William Short, the U.S. Minister to Spain, "for our courts proceed in the recovery of their debts, our trade is immensely valuable to them [but] they retain the old Posts within our limits, establish new ones and spirit up the Savages to make war upon us."[23] Edmund Randolph complained to Jay in 1794, "my pen is wearied by ineffectual remonstrances . . . on Governor Simcoe's perpetual encroachments, threats and indeed hostilities."[24] The mere possession of Canada seemed to encourage the British to foment domestic troubles and attempt to dismember the nation. As John C. Calhoun summed up—after repeating accusations that the Governor of Canada and Lord Liverpool, the British Prime Minister, had approved sending agents to the United States—"such is the conduct we have ever to expect from England while she retains possession of Canada."[25]

The treaty negotiated by John Jay in 1794 led to the withdrawal of British troops from posts in the Northwest, but British traders and agents continued to operate in American territory and Native American leaders remained in contact with British military authorities in Upper Canada.[26] Even as late as 1814, during the peace negotiations at Ghent, the British were still proposing the creation of an Native American buffer state between Canada and the United States.[27] Persistent British intrigues with Native Americans within the United States, along with the British maritime policy of impressing American sailors into the British navy, led the United States to declare war on Britain in June 1812.[28]

Historians have long debated the relative weight of the causes which led to the war, but there has always been general agreement that an attack on the Canadas was the only way for the United States to bring pressure to bear on Britain. This conquest of Canada would achieve the double purpose of forcing Britain to change her aggressive maritime policy—and of finally ending the interventionist threat from Canada. Jonathan Russell, the U.S. Charge d'Affaires in London, informed Secretary of State Monroe in February 1812 that the common opinion in Britain was, "we have not the energy and union to make efficient war." Russell urged that the United States should prove how wrong this view was "by calling forth the energies of the nation and pouring over Canada and Nova Scotia like a torrent [to] prevent the expense and bloodshed of a lingering and balanced conflict."[29] American war plans reflected this line of thinking and called for a three-pronged drive on Canada. General Henry Dearborn was to advance up the Lake Champlain route to assault Montreal; General Stephen Van Rensselaer was to attack the Canadians along the Niagara Frontier; and General William Hull was to invade Upper Canada from Detroit. All three invasions failed but the United States achieved some notable naval successes, especially the victory by Captain Oliver Perry at the Battle of Lake Erie on 10 September 1813. In spite of the failure to conquer parts of Canada, Perry's achievement and other local successes against the British, above all General Andrew Jackson's belated triumph at New Orleans, enabled Americans to view the war as a triumph. The United States had held their own and ended with a major victory over the world's mightiest military and naval power. This gave birth to a new sense of confidence that the young, decentralized republic—with no permanent military establishment on the scale of the European powers—could organize effectively to protect their rights and their territory. In the words of Congressman Israel Dickens of North Carolina, the War of 1812 became "this second war for our independence."[30]

On the Canadian side, the American invasion attempts and the defense against them by British regulars and Canadian militia gave rise to an anti- American ideology that became a permanent element in the nineteenth century. Canadians viewed the United States as an aggressive, expansionist military power.[31] The gulf between Canada and the United States was made evident by the fate of two capital cities during the war. During his campaign in the spring of 1814, General Dearborn seized control of York (now Toronto), the capital of Upper Canada, and burned all the public buildings, including the Assembly House and the residence of the lieutenant governor. The British thus had a pretext to justify the burning of Washington, including the President's House later in 1814. These two incidents symbolized the gulf of suspicion and fear between the United States and Canada. As he looked back on the troubled relationship between the United States and Britain since the revolution, John

Quincy Adams drew attention to this theme. Next to the British impressment of American seamen, Adams observed, "the most dangerous source of disagreement between the two countries arose in Canada. It had occasioned much mutual ill-will heretofore [and had led to] continued tendencies to bad neighborhood."[32]

But while this sense of bad neighborliness remained, the War of 1812 had settled a big issue from the American perspective. Since 1783, there had been fears that the British military presence in Canada would block American growth in the west. While the United States failed to conquer Canada, the naval victories on the Lakes and the victory at New Orleans were reassurances that the United States were now powerful enough to defend their western territories. Perhaps even more telling than this perceived military victory in the war was the American demographic victory in the Northwest. In the early 1790s, Lieutenant-Governor Simcoe had planned to attract American settlers to Upper Canada and make it the core growth center for the region. In 1814 the British were still forlornly trying to stem the tide of American settlement by proposing the creation of a Native American buffer state. But all the strength in this settlement war lay on the American side. By 1818, Ohio, Indiana, and Illinois had all become states carved out of the Old Northwest. In 1800, the population in the region had been just over 50,000; by 1820, it was almost 800,000. In an exchange with James Monroe in 1814, John Quincy Adams argued that while Britain, since 1783, had claimed she was only interested in the security of Canada, the real motive for the interventionist activities had been based on "a profound and rankling jealousy of the rapid increase and population and settlements in the United States; an impotent longing to thwart their progress and to stunt their growth." But this game, played by the British ever since the conquest of Canada in 1759-60, was now at an end—overwhelmed by the tides of American settlement flowing into the western territories. "It was," Adams continued in an almost exultant tone, "opposing a feather to a torrent. The population in the United States in 1810 passed 7 millions. At this hour it has undoubtedly passed 8."[33]

2.

While the War of 1812 and demographic power ended American fears of losing western territory to Canada, the negative image of Canada remained intact. Up through the 1820s, American officials (from territorial governors like Lewis Cass in Michigan to Secretary of War John C. Calhoun) made a series of complaints about continuing

Canadian interference with Native peoples from the Great Lakes to the Rocky Mountains. Some sense of the geographic scale of this concern can be gained from an observation Monroe made on the use of Fort Mackinac when the British occupied it during the war: "the commerce with and commanding influence of Mackinac over the several tribes of Indians inhabiting the country within our limits between the Lakes and Rocky Mountains has long been felt and known."[34]

In the years after the war, these contacts shifted to Fort Malden on the Detroit River at the western boundary of Upper Canada as Native American leaders made annual journeys to meet with the British officers in command. In the winter of 1819-20, Secretary of State Adams and Richard Rush, the U.S. Minister in London, exchanged notes on this vexing issue, Rush charged, "Indians inhabiting the country between Detroit and the Mississippi had repaired by invitation during the last season to Malden." Rush asserted that the British authorities in Canada were "systematically attracting" Native Americans from U.S. territory.[35] This view at the federal level was based on evidence provided by the territorial governor in Detroit, Lewis Cass, who saw for himself the traffic across the river to Canada. In one note to Secretary of War Calhoun, written in the summer of 1819, Cass pointed out that Sac Indians were then at Fort Malden and, "the greater proportion of Indians on this side of the Mississippi River make their annual visits there. The effects produced by such a body of men passing through the weak settlements of the Territory may be readily appreciated."[36]

Two years later Cass was even more convinced that the policy of inviting Native Americans to Canada was being "vigorously pursued." American agents who attended these meetings at Fort Malden reported the Amerindians were being told that as American settlers pressed in on their lands, they should remember that their real father "is living over the great waters."[37] In 1823 and 1826 British agents from Canada were reported to be working as far south as Arkansas territory.[38] Thus, while the issue of Canadian intervention with Native Americans never returned to the dangerous intensity it had reached in the 1783-1812 period, it lingered on as an issue to sustain a critical view of Canada.

By 1815, as John Quincy Adams' confident note on population suggests, there was no longer any fear of western secession due to British intrigue. Distrust of Canada remained, now in a less specific form that she might be built up as a rival power on the continent. Fears of a counteracting power emerging in the north was present before the War of 1812. In his comprehensive and insightful analysis of the war period, J.C.A. Stagg has drawn attention to American concerns about

Britain's strengthening of Canada.[39]   Back in 1801, when Louisiana
had been returned to French control, Rufus King, then the U.S.
Minister in London, warned of the dangers should France reestablish
links between her Mississippi colony and her old subjects in Canada,
thus, "realizing the plan to prevent the accomplishment of which the
Seven Years War took place."[40]   The prospect that Britain would use
the French reacquisition of Louisiana to extend her Canadian territories to the Mississippi concerned Secretary of State Madison who worried about "the anxiety which Great Britain has shown to extend her
domain to the Mississippi."   Madison's geo-political concerns covered
the entire continent as he ruminated about British expansionist possi-
bilities.   He pointed out, "the uncertain extent of her claims from
North to South beyond the western limits of the United States and the
attention she has paid to the North West coast of America," and
warned, "the evils involved in such an extension of her possessions in
our neighborhood and in such a hold in the Mississippi are obvious."[41]   In the early years of the new nation, when Jefferson had
taken stock of British moves on the Northwest coast and British hopes
of linking Canada to the upper Mississippi, he spoke in terms of a balance of power on the continent.   "A due balance on our borders," he
wrote to Gouvernor Morris, "is not less desirable to us than a balance
of power in Europe has always appeared to them."[42]

These American concerns about a rival power, expressed in the
period between 1790 and 1812, persisted after the war.   As Albert
Gallatin, Secretary of Treasury, explained to Monroe in 1814, "it is now
evident that Great Britain intends to strengthen and aggrandize herself
in North America."[43]   The post-war policies of the British in Canada—
which included government-sponsored emigration schemes to Upper
Canada along with elaborate plans for fortifications and military canals
along the border—Richard Rush told Secretary of State Clay in 1825,
were all signs "of a desire on the part of this government to cherish
their province of Canada."   Rush reported from London in 1825 on
British proposals to boost emigration to Upper Canada and of the
appointment of a commission of engineers "for the express purpose of
examining the whole line of frontier between the United States . . . to
report on the state of the posts and fortifications at every point."[44]
Kenneth Bourne, in *Britain and the Balance of Power in North
America, 1815-1908*, has shown that, during the Duke of Wellington's
long tenure at the War Office, the British did indeed commit substantial resources to the strengthening of Canada's defenses.[45]

These demographic and military measures were not seen by
Americans as based on Canadian and British fears of U.S. expansion
but were placed in the context of British imperial forwardness.   In an

1823 letter to Secretary of State Calhoun on this subject, Brigadier General Simon Bernard gave an overview of British imperial power and explained what Canada's role was. "The power of Great Britain," he began, "rests chiefly on her Navy, her Auxiliaries and her ultra-marine position." After listing British naval bases from Gibraltar to the Cape and from St. Helena to Singapore, Bernard argued that Britain had "completed her system of ultra-marine positions against the eastern hemisphere" and was now turning her attention to the western. He warned, "she will not suffer such a work of policy to lie unfinished in its relations with this continent." In this part of the world the West Indian bases were key, but now the securing of Canada meant, "Canada is a permanent and continental auxiliary of Great Britain."[46] Given the traditional, negative American orientation toward Canada and American fears about a rival power, the military consolidation in Canada was noted with concern.

Tensions did ease, however, in the post-war years. Two agreements between the United States and Great Britain marked this improvement in relations. The first was for mutual disarmament on the Great Lakes. In an April 1817, exchange of notes between Charles Bagot, the British Minister to the United States, and Acting Secretary of State Richard Rush, the two powers agreed to limit their naval forces on the Lakes to three vessels each, none of which were to exceed 100 tons or were to carry more than one 18 pound gun. This Rush-Bagot agreement later came to assume a fabled place in United States relations with Canada. In the 1930s and 1940s, speaker after speaker referred to the agreement as the beginning of the unguarded frontier and the starting point of good relations between the two countries. This modern significance of the Rush-Bagot agreement is a distorted one. First, the agreement did not lead to an unguarded frontier. On the contrary, it was during the three decades following the War of 1812 that a series of forts and canals were built along the frontier. As Kenneth Bourne has shown, these military preparations were pursued as part of a comprehensive plan by the British to keep up Canada's strength, in order not to surrender mastery of the North American continent to the United States.[47]

The agreement had, at the time, a narrow impact and was signed largely for fiscal reasons on both sides. After the war, both the United States and Britain were looking for ways to cut military expenses. In the United States the political culture of the young republic was not receptive to the idea of keeping up a large naval establishment. Besides, if hostilities were reopened, Americans assumed (as they had shown in the war) that they could quickly rebuild a force on the Lakes. On the British side, the troubled social and economic years following the end of the Napoleonic wars were the driving force behind the agreement to cut expenditures on a Great Lakes naval force. To contemporaries, then, the agreement was a much more restricted affair than it subsequently became in the modern mythology of the undefended frontier. The context, within which it might be more accurately viewed, can be glimpsed from a comment made by Gouvernor Morris to the effect that the Lakes were a welcome natural barrier between two hostile powers. "Those who made the Peace [in 1783] acted wisely in separating the possessions of the two countries by so wide a water," he wrote to Washington. "It is essential," he continued, "to preserve this Boundary if you wish them to live in amity with us. Near Neighbors are seldom good ones for the Quarrells frequently bring on wars."[48] The Rush-Bagot agreement then must be kept in perspective as a narrowly-based measure of economy that did little to alter the basic American suspicion of Canada.

The second agreement which eased tensions in the post-war period was the Convention of 1818 which, like the Rush-Bagot accord, was a sequel to the Treaty of Ghent. The convention fixed the boundary line between the United States and British North America along the 49th parallel, from the Lake of the Woods (west of Lake Superior) to the Rocky Mountains. This was critical because it kept the British and the Canadians north of the headwaters of the Mississippi River. One of the American concerns in the period up to the war, it will be recalled, was that Britain was scheming to join her Canadian colonies with the upper Mississippi.[49] This fixing of the boundary, along with the general impact of the War of 1812, ensured that the Old Northwest and the Louisiana Purchase territory could not be intruded upon by the British or the Canadians.

But the irritating British-Canadian pressure did not end—it simply moved further west. Under the terms of the 1818 convention, no boundary was fixed between the Rocky Mountains and the Pacific Ocean. The two powers agreed that the Oregon country would be open to joint occupation without prejudice to either American or British claims in the Pacific Northwest. The question now became which power would be able to establish the more effective presence in the region. Once again it was to be a struggle between the force of American settlement and the maneuverings of British imperial agencies based in Canada and London. The British presence was represented by the Hudson's Bay Company which, since its founding in 1670, had developed a vast fur-trading empire from its posts on Hudson's Bay across the continent to the Pacific. In 1821, the

Hudson's Bay Company united with the North West Company, a Montreal-based company that had inherited the old French trading networks. The joining of these two companies suggested a reinvigorated British-Canadian expansion into the Pacific North West. "The New Hudson's Bay Company," reported U.S. Special Agent William Slocum to Secretary of State John Forsyth in 1837, "have extended their enterprises over an extent of territory almost incalculable."[50]

This issue was not a pressing one in the 1820s and 1830s, but it bore watching as part of the old pattern of British imperial pressure on the United States. As John Quincy Adams remarked to Richard Rush in 1818, linking up the old and new pressure points (British claims to the Columbia country in Oregon as well as her past attempts to push the boundary south, beyond Lake of the Woods, to include the upper Mississippi) "manifests a jealousy of the United States, a desire to check the progress of our settlements."[51] Albert Gallatin added his forebodings along these same lines when he pointed out the advantages held by Canadians in the fur trade, then the dominant economic activity of white people in the west. Writing to Henry Clay in 1826 on the Columbia question, Gallatin (then U.S. Minister in London) noted,

> from Lake Superior to the Pacific, the intercourse is carried on in those canoes that are carried around portages. It is indeed to that mode of conveyance that the British are exclusively indebted for the extension of their commerce to the Western Seas. They have all that is necessary for it—the species of birch which does not grow in more southern latitudes and Canadians for canoe men.[52]

As John Quincy Adams tried to peer into the future, he expressed resentment that Britain with "her holds upon Europe, Asia and Africa and with all her actual possessions in this hemisphere" should push her claims in the far west. All this reflected "jealousy and alarm . . . to our natural dominion in North America."[53]

In these expressions of concern about British activities and claims in the Pacific North West, the old American fear of British intervention and the emergence of a counterweight power in North America were always near the surface. British presence in the Oregon country was linked to British approaches to the new republic of Texas and to fears that Britain might work for a cession of California.[54] All this, Louis McLane, the U.S. Minister in London, told Secretary of State James Buchanan in December 1845, was evidence of the British hope of "regulating and supervising the balance of power on the

American continent."[55] President Polk took a strong stand on the Oregon question, recommending in his first annual message that the joint-occupation agreement be ended and claiming all the Oregon country up to the border with Russian Alaska for the United States. This tough policy was summed up in the phrase "54 40' or fight" and was strongly supported by northern Democrats including Senator Lewis Cass of Michigan who, back in the 1820s, had complained so sharply about British intervention in the Old Northwest. A crisis was averted however because Britain wished to avoid war and because the United States was more concerned about the likelihood of war with Mexico. The settlement extended the 49th parallel boundary from the Rockies to the Pacific, dipping south to give Vancouver Island to the British.[56]

By 1846, the United States had secured its border against British North America. British-Canadian intervention in the Old Northwest had been repulsed by the War of 1812, the Mississippi Valley was kept in exclusive United States possession by the 1818 Convention; and, by 1846, the richest part of the Oregon country was won by diplomacy and the power of American settlement. All along the border the United States had held off British-Canadian pressure but, as we shall see, this success did not remove the complaint that Britain and her Canadian colonies were placing obstacles in the way of American growth. Running through this persistent American critique was the theme that Britain was attempting to create an artificial balance of power in North America with the corollary theme that the United States, as John Quincy Adams expressed it, ought to have a "natural dominion in North America." American expansion was deemed to be in harmony with nature and geography; British and Canadian expansion was viewed as artificially instigated by imperial designs to check American growth. This view of matters, formed in the early national period, remained a basic element of the American mind-set.

Another manifestation of this outlook occurred in the 1820s when Americans accused Britain and Canada of blocking passage down the St. Lawrence River. Navigation of the St. Lawrence had not been an issue at the 1783 peace conference because there was only a marginal American presence in the Lakes region. But by the 1820s settlement in western New York, western Pennsylvania, Ohio, Indiana, Illinois, and Michigan territory had created a need for additional trade routes in and out of the region. The St. Lawrence route was the easiest and cheapest. It had been the great French highway from the continental interior to the Atlantic during the seventeenth and eighteenth centuries and has remained into modern times the great northern river route into the continent. While the opening of the Erie Canal in 1825 and the coming of the railroads in the 1830s and 1840s meant that the United States was never dependent on the St. Lawrence route, it became a perennial issue of concern to American administrations.[57]

In 1823 Secretary of State Adams set out the American case for free navigation, basing his argument "upon the sound and general principles of the laws of nature." United States citizens from Vermont to Illinois, insisted Adams, had "a natural right of communicating with the ocean by the only outlet provided by nature." The Secretary also appealed to recent developments in international law on such issues, in particular the agreement reached at the Congress of Vienna in 1815 to open navigation of the Rhine, Necker, Main, and Moselle.[58] This dual base of natural law and international law remained the foundation of the American case, but another line of justification, more specific to North American conditions, was added. Richard Rush tried the ingenious tack that American colonists had helped to conquer Canada and that this "joint acquisition" gave Americans a share in Canadian river routes. This was a similar line of argument Americans used with respect to the North Atlantic fisheries—that in the colonial period the fisheries had been a joint British-colonial enterprise of discovery and exploitation. Such an approach to the St. Lawrence matter was quickly dropped when the British replied that if the joint-acquisition principle held, then Britain would still retain rights to the free navigation on the Hudson and Potomac and other rivers in the United States that had been acquired during the colonial period.[59]

American officials were able to move easily from these, sometimes treacherous, general arguments to claims based on the United States' superior strength of numbers. Richard Rush elaborated this argument to Adams explaining that the right of the United States to navigate through Canada rested on "the present interests of the United States [and was] yet more commanding because it rested upon their future population and destinies." This fact of American superiority in numbers was connected by Rush to the law of nature argument. As he explained to Adams,

> the immense regions which bordered upon the Lakes and north-ern rivers of the United States were rapidly filling up with inhab-itants and soon the dense millions who would cover them would point to the paramount and irresistible necessity for the use of the great stream as their only natural highway to the ocean.[60]

Rush presented this case to William Huskisson and Viscount Canning, the British negotiators:

> The river is the only outlet provided by nature for the inhabitants of several among the largest and most populous states of the American union. Their right to use it as a medium of communication with the ocean rests upon the same ground of natural right and obvious necessity heretofore asserted by the government in behalf of the people of other portions of the United States in relation to the river Mississippi.[61]

The St. Lawrence, which ran through Canada, was in this argument viewed as equivalent to the Mississippi, which ran entirely through American territory. This kind of argument was grist for the mill of Secretary of State Henry Clay, the great spokesman for western development, who declaimed in 1826,

> a population already exceeding two millions and augmenting beyond all example is directly and deeply interested in their navigation [the Great Lakes] which are united by but one natural outlet to the Ocean, the navigation of which is common to all mankind.[62]

These grand American pleas made no headway with the British or the Canadians. The local colonial authorities used their discretionary power to close ports or make special charges on American vessels that did venture into the St. Lawrence under limited terms set out in an 1822 Act of Parliament. The British negotiators also rejected the American case on the grounds that to concede free navigation of the St. Lawrence would establish "a perpetual thoroughfare through the heart of a British colony and under the walls of its principal fortress."[63] Thus, during the 1820s the St. Lawrence controversy merely developed another dimension to the American view: Canada was a martial colony of Great Britain from which local and imperial authorities pursued policies that ran counter to the natural trade and population patterns of the continent. As Secretary of State Henry Clay complained to Albert Gallatin, the United States asked only

> that the interests of the greater population and the more fertile and extensive country above shall not be sacrificed in an arbitrary exertion of power to the jealousy and rivalry of a small population inhabiting a more limited and less productive country below.[64]

American resentment over their exclusion from the St. Lawrence waned by the 1830s because the free navigation of the river was not important for the growth of the American economy. However, the St. Lawrence question was linked to the broader trade issue that rankled Americans through much of the period between 1783 and 1854. One of Richard Rush's complaints, during the exchanges over the St. Lawrence, was that Canadians were making difficulties to prevent American agricultural products from being shipped in American vessels to the British West Indies. The British North American colonies were "rivals in this intercourse, the only rivals, of the United States."[65] This trade issue remained a constant irritant in Anglo-American relations until the West Indian aspect was effectively settled in 1830, and a liberal trade agreement between Canada and the United States was signed in 1854. But even the 1854 reciprocity treaty, which ended seventy years of trade rivalry, was regarded by American officials (including President Buchanan) as another episode of Canadian chicanery.

From the winning of independence in 1783 to the signing of the Reciprocity Treaty in 1854, American trade goals with respect to the Canadas and the other British colonies were clear and unchanging. The United States wished to gain access to the British West Indies markets which had been supplied from the thirteen colonies throughout the colonial period. Beyond that specific goal American policymakers looked forward to the dismantling of the exclusive imperial trading system—which would give American merchants access to Canada and the other British North American colonies. Although until the 1830s and the economic collapse of the sugar islands (it was the West Indian market that was the more important one), the opening of the British North American market and the free navigation of the St. Lawrence were linked to that goal as part of a general American desire to see the entire British colonial system in the Caribbean and North America break up. As they negotiated with the British on these matters, American administrations saw the Canadians as playing a selfish and obstructionist role. The Canadians, it was argued, were determined to block any attempt at an Anglo-American accommodation over the West Indies so that they, in spite of their inferior resources and less favored location, could become the supplier of the sugar islands.[66]

In 1783, American negotiators tried to maintain access to the West Indies. Once the attempt failed, it became a fixed object of all administrations to make the British change their minds. This American position was set out by James Madison in 1806. "The permanent object of the United States," the Secretary of State reminded James Monroe and William Pinckney, "was to have the intercourse with them [the British West Indies] as free as that with Europe." In a characteristically realistic afterthought, Madison added that while such an opening of markets would be "an enlightened policy . . . it cannot be denied that it will give us a very great share of their carrying trade," and therefore, he could understand British and colonial reluctance to change the imperial system.[67] As free trade ideas began to make some headway in Britain, American policymakers looked hopefully to the center of the empire for signs of change. But on this side of the Atlantic, they saw only a continuing pattern of obstructionism. The 1816 Tariff Act of Upper Canada was the kind of evidence cited to prove Canadian intransigence. James Monroe complained to John Quincy Adams that this measure,

> is calculated to excite such Sensibility in the United States. The palpable unfairness of the measure, as well as its injurious tendency, will strike everyone, and the more forcibly as we get little or nothing from Canada. . . . The minuteness of the gain to Great Britain in this case makes the proof stronger of her rigid adherence to her monopolising policy.[68]

Martin Van Buren, as Secretary of State in Andrew Jackson's first cabinet, argued to Louis McLane, the U.S. Minister in Britain, that a key aspect of American policy was to defeat "the interested views of the northern British colonists [who are] an active agency . . . thwarting your efforts to place matters on their only natural and true footing."[69] This combination of British imperial exclusiveness and British North American self-seeking was designed, according to McLane, to strengthen the British Empire in North America. Britain was attempting "by means of a monopoly to give forced growth to the production of the northern possessions." In 1830, McLane scolded Lord Aberdeen saying that British policy was one "of forcing the trade of the United States with the British West Indies islands through the British northern possessions."[70]

When American observers reviewed this entire period from the vantage point of the 1850s, there was nothing complimentary to say about the behavior of the Canadas and the other British North American colonies. Two reports by Israel D. Andrews, a special agent to the Department of State and the most knowledgeable American official on Canadian matters in the 1840s and 1850s, summed up seventy years of American frustration. "Ever since 1783," Andrews' analysis began, there had been "a great contest between England and the United States with respect to colonial trade related chiefly to the trade between our country and the British West Indies which, prior to 1840, was of great value and importance." The Canadian role in this "protracted and almost useless negotiation produced no other results than a contraction of the trade of the colonies and an estrangement between the people of both countries." The root difficulty, argued Andrews, was that until the 1840s the Canadians had committed themselves to the full-blown maintenance of the imperial system. They had "yielded obedience to the imperial cabinet and cheerfully submitted to its control in all fundamental points of their political, commercial and domestic concerns." Such a posture, observed Andrews, had set Canadians and Americans on an antagonistic course that might have adverse, long-term consequences.[71] As Louis McLane put the same point back in 1830, such policies produced no gains for Canada but rather fostered "a spirit of jealousy between two neighboring nations [and] the sowing in the population of those Northern possessions of the seeds of commercial hostility which may produce roots of bitterness difficult to be eradicated."[72]

3.

British and Canadian intervention in the Old Northwest, intransigence on the trade issue, and on the navigation of the St. Lawrence combined to put U.S. relations with Canada in an adversarial mode. By the late 1830s and 1840s, American policymakers began to see signs of change inside Canada and in Britain that seemed to offer the chance of improving on this bad start. During these years, as the old imperial trading system broke up and as the Canadian colonies seemed to be on a course that would lead to independence, Americans who paid attention to Canadian matters began to forecast that the tide of imperialism was receding and that Canada would now look to a more cooperative relationship with the United States.

The first of these signs was a political one which suggested that the Canadian colonies were finally going to follow the American pattern and become independent from Britain. In 1837 there were rebellions in Upper and Lower Canada. These armed uprisings were the culmination of over twenty years of political unrest. Reformers in both colonies criticized the narrowly based ruling groups centering around the British governors and their appointed councils.[73] American observers interpreted these developments to mean that the British North American empire (like the Spanish one between 1811 and 1820) was about to disintegrate. As early as 1828, for example, when Canadian affairs were being investigated by a Select Committee of the House of Commons, the American Chargé in

London, W. B. Lawrence, remarked that there was "an increasing belief that Canada will not for many years remain part of the British Empire."[74] The *Niles Weekly Register* in 1834 reported "Canada remains in a very agitated state . . . dissensions have arisen to a great height" to the extent that the whole question of "the future relations of the colony with Great Britain" was now open. The report continued that in the British Parliament Canadian matters excite much attention "and some of the members freely express an apprehension that the people of that important colony may cast off their allegiance and seek admission to the American Union."[75]

Americans could not help seeing developments in Canada as a long-overdue repetition of their revolution in 1776. As he witnessed the debates in the Commons, Aaron Vail told Secretary of State John Forsyth that the occasion recalled "the parliamentary scenes of the American Revolution" and referred to "the republican bias of the public mind in Canada." Americans described the 1837 uprisings as "revolutionary movements."[76] For three years there were tensions along the border—dramatic enough at times to threaten war between the United States and Britain. There was a wave of Anglophobia in the United States, one manifestation of which was the forming of the secret Hunters Lodges to facilitate the overthrow of the British regime in Canada. Tensions between Britain and the United States reached a peak in 1840 when Alexander McLeod, who had participated in the *Caroline* raid, was arrested and tried for murder in Lockport, New York. The Canadian authorities responded to these pro-rebel activities in the United States by mobilizing the militia and putting the colony on a war footing against a possible American invasion.[77]

Prior to all this drama, the rebellions themselves had quickly fizzled out, but Americans continued to view the entire affair as evidence that revolution and independence were now inevitable. Even in 1841 Governor William Seward of New York, a future Secretary of State, maintained that there were "sufficient indications of popular discontent in Canada to warrant a belief that efforts will be made there to overthrow the Government."[78] As late as 1848, Daniel Webster still retained the terminology of "the revolutionary movements in Canada."[79] These American assessments of the 1837 rebellions were not based on any sound information about conditions in the Canadas. Everything was read through the spectrum of American experience. There was no appreciation of the fact that the debate in Canada was taking place within a British and colonial constitutional setting in which independence was never a popular political option. The American assessment also reflected what was to become a stock element in the American view of Canada—that the people were heading toward American cultural and political values, but the imperial authorities blocked this natural tendency. This misinformed view of 1837 led Americans to see the rebellions as a sign of imperial dissolution.

The second encouraging sign to Americans was the Webster-Ashburton Treaty of 1842 which settled the last outstanding boundary dispute from the 1783 peace treaty.[80] The importance of this issue can be judged by the outbreak of the Aroostook "war" in the winter of 1838-39 when the Maine government broke up camps of Canadian lumbermen in the disputed region. Maine and New Brunswick called out their militias, the Nova Scotia legislature made war appropriations, and the U.S. Congress authorized the raising of a force of 50,000 men and appropriated $10 million in emergency funds. While there was bitterness in Maine about the "loss" of territory, a bitterness that was used by Democrats against the Tyler administration, the more measured American response was that the treaty revealed a new responsiveness on the British side to American views. Indeed, on the Canadian side the treaty was castigated on the grounds that it sacrificed Canadian territory on the altar of Anglo-American rapprochement.

The appointment by the British of Lord Ashburton to lead their side in the negotiations was taken as an earnest of British good intentions. Ashburton had visited the United States in 1795 and had many connections through his family's banking business (he was a Baring); he had also married the daughter of William Bingham, a U.S. Senator for Pennsylvania from 1795 to 1801. During and after the negotiations, Ashburton encouraged the view that Britain had now dropped her efforts to maintain the imperial trading system and to aggrandize Canada. He informed George Bancroft, the U.S. Minister to London, "the Canadas were to Great Britain an inconvenient possession."[81] Along with American assumptions about the significance of the 1837 rebellions, the accommodating attitude of Ashburton in 1842 seemed to confirm the judgment that the British colonies were on the road to separation.

For those who cared to pay attention to them, the underlying trade patterns were additional evidence that the colonial relationship was changing. Figures for exports to Canada in the years 1840 and 1849 show American gains over the British. In 1840, Canada received $15,385,166 worth of goods from Britain and $6,100,501 from the United States. By 1849, the British total had declined to $11,346,334 while the American figure had improved to $8,342,854.[82]

The most dramatic development suggesting the end of Canada's relationship with the empire was the abandonment by Britain of the old colonial trading system. Following the repeal of the Corn Laws in 1846 (which had protected British agriculture and allowed colonial grains into Britain at preferred rates), Britain shifted toward free trade. Now that she was the most powerful industrial nation in the world, Britain saw the imperial trading system as too restrictive. Britain needed cheap foodstuffs and raw materials, while she also looked to the markets of the world to sell her manufactured products. It made no economic sense to confine herself to colonial sources and markets. The victory of the Whig-Liberal party, following the abrogation of the Corn Laws, confirmed that the old protectionist days were over.[83] In November 1847, George Bancroft, the U.S. Minister in London, reported excitedly to Secretary of State Buchanan, "no sooner were the elections over than it seemed to me what alone Pitt and Fox had wanted, namely a House of Commons free from prejudices in favor of the Navigation Laws, had, after sixty-five years of waiting, come about."Lord Palmerston, the new Foreign Secretary, assured the American Minister of "his preference for the most liberal commercial system."[84]

The United States responded expectantly to these long-sought-after changes in British policy and, among more general considerations, hoped that Canadian trade could now be directed into more natural American channels. In 1847, Secretary of State Buchanan expressed his conviction that Britain would now "consent to abandon her entire colonial system. . . . This is equally required by the enlightened spirit of the age, the avowed policy of both nations and the mutual interest of their people."[85] The advantages to the United States of the dismantling of the imperial trade restrictions were as obvious as they had been since 1783. "Such a system [free trade]," Bancroft explained to Secretary of State John Clayton, "would give us much of the trade of Canada and pretty nearly the whole of that of the British West Indies while it would leave Great Britain the whole cost of their defence." Bancroft summarized in March 1849 that the tendency of these developments was "to connect their [the British colonies] interests with those of the United States."[86]

The break-up of the old imperial system encouraged the State Department to take stock of the relationship with Canada. All previous assessments had been intertwined with Anglo-American issues, but now there was an attempt to identify a likely future relationship between the United States and the Canadas. A sign of the new seriousness of purpose with respect to Canada was that for the first time since 1783 the Department of State appointed an expert on Canada. Israel D. Andrews began his career as the U.S. Consul at St. Johns, New Brunswick, in 1843. In 1849, this appointment was elevated to

U.S. Consul for Canada and New Brunswick. While holding these posts, Andrews' responsibilities were enlarged by ad hoc assignments from the Department. In July 1847, he was appointed as a special agent to visit Canada and gather statistical information on trade and economic matters. He was again a special agent to Canada in 1851 and 1852 and for all the British North American colonies from 1852-1854. On 5 March 1855, he was made U.S. Consul-General for the British North American Provinces. Andrews was also employed on two occasions by the U.S. Treasury Department to prepare material on commercial conditions in Canada. Based on his work for the State and Treasury departments, Andrews wrote two lengthy reports—of 775 pages and 906 pages—for the Senate. In addition to his regular, written communications to the State Department, Andrews had "full and frequent conversations" with Secretary of State William Marcy. For the first time since 1783, the United States had an official whose full-time assignment was to become an expert on Canada. He was to collect information and advise the administration and Congress about British North America as a separate entity rather than simply as an aspect of Anglo-American problems.[87]

The first response to Britain's abandonment of her old colonial system was a predictable one. It had always been assumed by American leaders that Canada's ties to Britain were the artificial result of imperial trade and military policies. Once these were removed, Canada and the other British North American colonies would place themselves naturally in the continental economic patterns centering on the United States. Writing to Secretary of State Buchanan from New Brunswick in 1846, Israel Andrews reported, "this Province is gradually yielding to powerful American influences and . . . they are daily becoming Americanised." Andrews continued that the trade patterns showed U.S. exports to British North America increasing at a greater rate than British exports. He also added that if trade between Canada and the United States were made completely free, "the consumption of American manufactures would greatly increase."[88] Buchanan was assured that the colonists were fully aware of the long-term consequences of these shifts in British policy and were prepared for a fundamental change in their relationship with the United States. "The North American colonist," Andrews reported in 1848, "is now on the look out for a market for his products finding he has no protection in the markets of Britain. . . . A great revolution in public sentiment relative to the United States had taken place in these colonies." If the United States responded boldly to these changes in British policy by allowing Canadian products free entry into the United States, Canada would turn her back on Britain.

Andrews predicted that this measure "will produce such grand results to our country and surely lead to the termination of foreign rule on this continent."[89]

Andrews, in his numerous despatches to the State Department and reports to Congress, made a case for economic integration of the United States and Canada based on geographical factors and the relative stages of development of the two economies. Much of the difficulty he encountered in persuading administration officials and politicians to accept his views stemmed from the widespread American ignorance of conditions in Canada. The need to educate opinion was reflected in the character of Andrews' writings which were largely repetitions of elementary geographic and economic facts about British North America. Andrews emphasized the theme that geography made the American and Canadian economies complementary. "There is," he proposed in his 1851 report, "a physical adaptation of the surface of the northern continent to a commercial union of the people inhabiting it." To substantiate his case, Andrews again drew attention to the flow of trade, pointing out that American trade with Canada "has increased to a remarkable extent since 1839, and particularly since 1846, while that of the colonies and Great Britain has proportionately declined since discriminating duties in favor of British manufactures have been abolished." Andrews' advice was that the United States should seize the opportunity presented by the reversal of British imperial policy and arrange a liberal system of trade that would draw Canada decisively into the American economic sphere.[90]

In spite of his massive accumulation of data, frequent writings, discussions with significant politicians on both sides of the border, and the weight of expertise he achieved, Andrews made little impact on U.S. policy. The explanation for his ineffectiveness is obvious enough. There was no considered policy formulation because at the very time when radical economic changes were taking place in Canada, the great domestic issue of slavery occupied attention and affected all aspects of American thinking about the western hemisphere, including the Caribbean, Mexico, and Canada. The changes in colonial policy, which Andrews reasonably argued were pregnant with benefits for the United States, came in the period after the Mexican War when the issue of annexation and expansion in any direction became part of the controversy over slavery. The slavery issue complicated American responses to change in Canada. Andrews' single-minded view became somewhat academic as it took no account of these domestic complications. In the southern states where support for low tariffs was strongest (and which might be expected to support a liberal trade arrangement with Canada), the prospect of freer trade, leading to annexation, was anathema. The addition of such a large "free state" area to the Union could not be accepted.

In the northern states there were many politicians who shared Andrews' confidence about Canada's break from Britain but feared freer trade would allow British manufacturers to slip in by the back door. The problem of dealing with a solidly Catholic Quebec was also a matter of concern. It was by no means clear that the addition of Canada to the Union would be a benefit to the free states. Besides these cross-currents caused by domestic issues, the U.S. was not certain that closer trade ties would lead to integration and eventually annexation as Andrews forecast so confidently in his analysis. It could be argued that if freer trade were allowed this would enable Canada to recover from the loss of the imperial market, become prosperous, and so avoid having to sue for annexation. If annexation were the ultimate goal, it might be better to let Canada struggle economically and so force her to request annexation as a solution to severe economic conditions. In short, the course to take with Canada was obscure to both pro- and anti-slavery forces in the United States.[91]

The situation was cogently summed up by Senator Jacob Collamer of Vermont when he analyzed the reason for the passage of the 1854 treaty. Collamer was "strongly impressed with the idea that the treaty was made for the purpose of persuading Canada not to join the United States lest it might alter the balance of power between North and South." Collamer continued:

> I think that was really bottom of the matter; because if they could have all the advantages of trade with this country and through it, without contributing anything to the support of our Government they would not be very likely to be as anxious to join us as they had been several years before; and they were quieted in that manner. . . . I fancy that in point of fact that consideration entered into the treaty more deeply than anything else.

On top of all this, the attention demanded by the controversy over slavery meant that administration officials in the late 1840s and early 1850s simply did not have the time, energy, or interest in conceiving a systematic response as proposed by Andrews. Late in his career, Andrews dolefully acknowledged that his Herculean efforts had made no impact. In a private note to Secretary of State Marcy, written from

Montreal, Andrews noted regretfully, "the especial attention of the Government and the most anxious solicitude of our Statesmen have been so intently bent on Southern affairs that these British North American colonies, constituting a nation in embryo have not received a fair share of notice."[92]

While acknowledging the limited impact made by Andrews, insofar as there was any thoughtful American response to Canada at this critical juncture in the development of the British Empire, it reflected his assessment of the situation. Andrews' proposals were the only ideas that administration officials and senators had at their disposal in the negotiations and discussions leading up to the 1854 Reciprocity Treaty. The operating premises were that Canada was moving out of the British trade system; that a freer exchange of trade between the United States and Canada would build up a more natural, continental trading system in North America; and that Canada, as the less developed of the two economies, would provide a market for more advanced American manufacturers. The treaty of 1854 could be justified as a step toward these objectives. It would draw the trade bonds tighter in a north-south direction by opening the American market to a range of Canadian natural products. It promised cheap entry into the Canadian market for American manufacturers, especially textiles from New England.[93] It also had the advantage for the Pierce administration of promising prosperity to Canada and thus of putting off the question of annexation, which no Democratic president was willing to face in the 1850s.

In these circumstances there was a sense in the State Department that the United States had been maneuvered into negotiating a treaty which suited Canadian goals in a more immediate and satisfactory manner than American goals. Canada was desperate to gain access to the American market for her agricultural and forest products. In 1849 over one thousand merchants in Montreal signed a petition demanding annexation to the United States as the only solution to their plight. While the annexation fever abated, the Governor General of Canada, Lord Elgin, and his council remained anxious to solve the economic difficulties by negotiating access to the American market. Lord Elgin was sent to Washington by the British government to conduct these negotiations and proved to be a great success. He "wined and dined" senators; he spoke eloquently about the mutual advantages of freer trade; he reassured southerners that the consequent prosperity in Canada would kill off annexation; and he allowed northerners to believe Andrews' line of argument that the treaty would draw the two countries together and prepare the ground for closer union.[94] But while economic conditions made Canadians stake so much on this treaty, the issue was no longer urgent from the American point of view.

In the period between the 1780s and 1820s, Americans keenly felt their exclusion from the British West Indies and consistently complained about the British imperial system which restricted their access to the West Indies and to British North America. However, the growth of the U.S. internal economy and the U.S. penetration of other international markets (including new access to the British grain market) combined with the collapse of the sugar economy in the Caribbean meant that after 1840 or so, the matter was no longer important for Americans. Thus, while the Canadians, through the efforts of Lord Elgin, pushed hard for the treaty, the Americans, for a range of economic and domestic political reasons, were indifferent. An example of this American attitude was the response by Secretary of State Webster in 1850 to a reciprocal trade proposal. "My difficulty," Webster informed the British Minister, H.L. Bulwer, "is that the bill seems much more advantageous to Canada than to us because we give her a large market and she gives us a small one, for articles which are the common products of both."[95]

In this context it was somewhat galling to Secretary of State Marcy and his fellow officials that Canada had been able to force them into negotiations on a matter they found inconvenient to deal with and would have preferred to postpone. In particular, Canada was accused of using the North Atlantic fisheries question to force American concessions on the trade issue. The fisheries question in the nineteenth century was a tangled one that soured Anglo-American-Canadian relations on many occasions—even to the point of threatening war—but the basic causes of the dispute are clear enough. In 1783 the United States gained recognition from Britain of her right to continued fishing on the Grand Banks off Newfoundland and Nova Scotia. The British withdrew this provision after the War of 1812. In the series of negotiations that followed the War of 1812, it was agreed in the Convention of 1818 that the United States would regain access to the fishing grounds but this time as a privilege under specified conditions, the most important of which was that American boats were excluded from the inshore fisheries and could only call at colonial posts to purchase bait and supplies. This arrangement was coming under considerable pressure by the 1840s for two primary reasons. First, the changing nature of fishing conditions and of the market for fish made the inshore fisheries (especially for mackerel and herring) more attractive.[96] Second, the British maritime colonies, as their populations and economies grew, felt the need to protect their local fishing industry from American fleets. The scale of

American presence, off Nova Scotia and New Brunswick, can be discerned from the figures of the U.S. Consul in Pictou, Nova Scotia, on the number of American vessels that foundered during a great storm in the Gulf of St. Lawrence in the 1851 season. The consul reported that there were 900 American ships with 9,000 persons in the area of the storm.[97] As colonial efforts to control the encroachment of the American fleets matured, they concentrated on strict enforcement of the 1818 rules and enactments by local legislatures to apply and sometimes extend those rules. For example, the colonial authorities sought British backing for an interpretation of the 3-mile rule which drew the line from headland to headland, thus excluding American vessels from such large sea areas as the Bay of Fundy and Bay of Chaleurs.

This shift in colonial policy was castigated by Secretary of State John Forsyth in 1841 when he listed American grievances in a despatch to Andrew Stevenson, the U.S. Minister in London. The headland to headland interpretation of the 1818 agreement allowed the colonies "to exclude American vessels from all their bays including even those of Fundy and Chaleurs" and thus directly threatened "a highly important branch of American industry." He continued that the regulations issued by Nova Scotia and the other colonies

> are of the most extraordinary character. . . . Some of these rules and regulations are violations of well-established principles of the common law of England and of the principles of the just laws of all civilized nations; and seem to be expressly designed to enable Her Majesty's authorities with perfect impunity to seize and confiscate American vessels and to embezzle almost indiscriminately the property of our citizens employed in the fisheries on the coasts of the British possessions.[98]

This criticism became even more pointed in the late 1840s and early 1850s when American officials became convinced that the fisheries issue was being exploited to force the United States to negotiate on the trade issue. In August 1851, Abbot Lawrence, the U.S. Chargé in London, reported that the British decision to send nineteen armed vessels to the fishing grounds to enforce colonial regulations "would appear to have been intended . . . to coerce the United States into a system of trade which it is well known the Provinces have long sought for."[99] Americans resented this tactic. Edward Everett, as Secretary of State, informed Jared Ingersoll, the U.S. Minister to Britain, that President Fillmore thought the two subjects of trade with Canada and the fisheries had "no natural or necessary connection."[100]

The way in which the two matters were presented to the Americans can be illustrated by a conversation between Ingersoll and the Duke of Newcastle, Secretary of State for War and Colonies. Newcastle told Ingersoll that the fisheries question might be difficult to settle as Americans wished, but combined with the trade issue, the difference "might more readily be overcome."[101] The Americans thus regarded the heightened tension over the fisheries as an unfair tactic to force them into a trade negotiation. Richard Rush who had been the chief American representative in the 1818 agreement was called upon to confirm the American position that these colonial fishery pretensions were illegitimate. From his retirement in Sydenham near Philadelphia, the venerable diplomat reported to Secretary of State Marcy the standard American view of the fisheries question. The United States had fixed and irrevocable rights to the fishing grounds that went back to the colonial period. Rush's recollection of the 1818 terms, upon which the United States would enjoy continued access to the fishing grounds, was clear. He told Marcy there was no doubt whatsoever that the 3-mile line was to follow the sinuosities of the coast.[102] James Buchanan, U.S. Minister in London, revealed the level of American annoyance when he observed to Marcy in January 1854 that if Andrew Jackson had been President there would have been war over the use of the British Navy to enforce a new and unjustified construction of the 1818 treaty.[103]

These circumstances convinced the Pierce administration that it had been manipulated into the 1854 reciprocal trade treaty. Tangled in the slavery issue at home and hard-pressed by colonial high-handedness on the fisheries question, they conceded free entry to the American market for Canadian natural products, thus giving Canada the opportunity to rebuild her economy. A period which had opened in 1846 with the prospect of Canada detaching herself from the empire ended in 1854 with a treaty which, with British backing, Canada was able to impose upon the United States. American disgruntlement with all this was made evident as James Buchanan reported from London to the State Department. In two letters to Secretary of State Marcy written in August 1854, Buchanan described the British sense of satisfaction with what had been gained by the treaty. "Lord Clarendon [Foreign Secretary]," Buchanan explained,

> is evidently very much gratified with the Treaty and it will probably secure to Lord Elgin a Marquessate or a Dukedom, if not the Governor-Generalship of India to which it is said he aspires. One cause of the favor with which it is regarded in this country, is the belief that Canada, having acquired free trade with the

United States in her most valuable productions, will feel no desire to change her allegiance and annex herself to the American Union.

In another conversation with Buchanan, Lord Clarendon reported how pleased Queen Victoria was with the treaty. "My Lord," Buchanan replied tartly, "the Queen may well be pleased—you have got everything your own way in this Treaty and have secured the allegiance of Canada for a long time to come."[104]

The unfriendly start to United States relations with Canada back in the 1780s and 1790s had not improved much by 1854. The United States, to be sure, no longer felt as threatened by Canada as they had during the early years of independence. The British and Canadian threat to the Old Northwest had ended with the War of 1812; Canada had been kept away from the Mississippi by the Convention of 1818; American territory had been pushed north of the St. John River by the Webster-Ashburton Treaty of 1842; and in 1846 the compromise over Oregon had given the United States the fertile Columbia Valley and port sites on Puget Sound. But the United States had not been successful in responding to Canada's changing role in the Empire. With the British imperial system apparently breaking up in the 1840s, the United States had an opportunity to turn events in a favorable direction by encouraging the Canadian economy to move in an American direction. The slavery controversy and the ability of the British colonies to use the fisheries issue turned the tables, however, and Canada rather than the United States set the agenda in 1854. So much so, in fact, that Secretary of State Marcy and future president Buchanan believed that the Canadians had exploited the predicament in which the administration found itself. In the wake of the 1849 annexation scare in Canada, there was no American policy, as they simply responded to developments in Canada and Britain. As Israel Andrews noted in a confidential letter to Marcy, "the favorable moment for settling this whole matter was allowed to pass away by the United States."[105]

Notes

1. On this theme see William T. Morgan, "English Fear of Encirclement in the Seventeenth Century," *Canadian Historical Review (CHR)* 10(1929):4-22; William J. Eccles, *The Canadian Frontier, 1534-1760* (New York: Holt, Rinehart and Winston, 1969) and *France in America* (New York: Harper and Row, 1972); Max Savelle, *The Diplomatic History of the Canadian Boundary, 1749-1763* (New Haven, CT: Yale University Press, 1940) and *The Origins of American Diplomacy: The*

International History of Angloamerica, 1492-1763 (New York: Macmillan, 1967).

2. The best starting point for understanding North American diplomacy in the period from 1776 to 1814 is still A.L. Burt, *The United States, Great Britain and British North America from the Revolution to the Establishment of Peace after the War of 1812* (Toronto: The Ryerson Press, 1940). J.C.A. Stagg, *Mr. Madison's War: Politics, Diplomacy and Warfare in the Early American Republic, 1783-1830* (Princeton: Princeton University Press, 1983) is excellent for showing how Canada fit into the American view of the world at the time. The best treatment of Anglo-American relations is still Bradford Perkins, *Prologue to War: England and the United States, 1805-1812* (Berkeley: University of California Press, 1961), *Castlereagh and Adams: England and the United States, 1812-1823* (Berkeley: University of California Press, 1964), and *The War of 1812* (New York: Horseman, 1969). Morris Zaslow, ed., *The Defended Border: Upper Canada and the War of 1812* (Toronto: Macmillan Company of Canada, 1964) is a collection of reprinted essays on how the war affected Upper Canada and includes the important piece by C.P. Stacey on "The War of 1812 in Canadian History."

3. Charles R. Ritcheson, *Aftermath of Revolution: British Policy toward the United States, 1783-1795* (Dallas: Southern Methodist University Press, 1969); Charles W. Toth, "Anglo-American Trade and the British West Indies (1783-1789)" *Americas* 32(1967):418-36.

4. Thomas P. Abernethy, *Western Lands and the American Revolution* (New York: DeAppleton-Century Company, 1937); Jack Sosin, *Whitehall and the Wilderness: The Middle West in British Colonial Policy, 1760-1775* (Lincoln, University of Nebraska Press, 1961); Clarence V. Alvord, *The Mississippi Valley in British Politics* (Cleveland: The Arthur H. Clark Company, 1917).

5. The best account of British policy in Quebec during this period is Hilda Neatby, *Quebec: The Revolutionary Age, 1760-1791* (Toronto: McClelland and Stewart, 1966). Neatby has also written a useful overview of the policy issues and the historiography surrounding the Quebec Act of 1774, *The Quebec Act: Protest and Policy* (Scarborough: Prentice Hall of Canada, 1972). Also Charles H. Metzger, *The Quebec Act: A Primary Cause of the American Revolution* (New York: U.S. Catholic Historical Society, 1936).

6. Lyman H. Butterfield, ed., *Diary and Autobiography of John Adams,* 4 vols. (Cambridge: Belknap Press, 1962), 3:275.

7. On the division of Canada in 1791, see Neatby, *Quebec,* 249-63; Vincent Harlow, *The Founding of the Second British Empire, 1763-1793,* ?? vols. (London: Longmans, Green, 1964), 2:714-73; Gerald M. Craig, *Upper Canada: The Formative Years, 1784-1841* (Toronto: McClelland and Stewart, 1972), 1-19.

8. John Jay to John Adams, 6 September 1785, in William R. Manning, *Diplomatic Correspondence of the United States: Canadian Relations, 1784-1860* 4 vols. (Washington: Carnegie Endowment for International Peace, 1940), 1:15.

9. Ibid., John Adams to John Jay, London, 15 December 1785, 1:339-40.
10. Ibid., John Jay to the Continental Congress, 22 March 1786, 1:21.
11. Ibid., Gouvernor Morris to George Washington, London, 17 March 1792, 1:393-94.
12. For Simcoe's career in Upper Canada, see Craig, *Upper Canada*, 20-41.
13. Edmund Randolph to John Jay, Philadelphia, 18 August 1794, in Manning, *Diplomatic Correspondence*, 1:78.
14. Ibid., Rufus King to Timothy Pickering, London, 16 March 1799, 1:514-15.
15. Ibid., Robert Livingston to Viscount Talleyrand, 10 January 1803, 1:548-49.
16. Ibid., Edmund Randolph to John Jay, Philadelphia, 18 August 1794, 1:78.
17. Ibid., George Washington to Gouvernor Morris, Philadelphia, 20 October 1792, 1:53-4.
18. Ibid., James Monroe to the Committee of Public Safety, 25 January 1795, 1:454-55.
19. Ibid., John Jay to Thomas Jefferson, New York, 24 April 1787, 1:38.
20. Ibid., John Jay to Thomas Jefferson, 14 December 1786, vol 1:32.
21. Ibid.
22. Edward Carrington to Edmund Randolph, New York, 8 December 1786, in Edmund C. Burnett, *Letters of the Members of the Continental Congress*, (Washington, DC: The Carnegie Institution of Washington, 1936), 8:516-18.
23. Edmund Randolph to William Short, Philadelphia, 18 August 1794, in Manning, *Diplomatic Correspondence*, 1:79.
24. Ibid., Edmund Randolph to John Jay, Philadelphia, 12 September 1794, 1:81-2.
25. John C. Calhoun to Robert Cresswell, Washington, 10 March 1812, in Robert L. Meriwether, ed., *The Papers of John C. Calhoun*, 8 vols. (Columbia: University of South Carolina Press, 1959), 1:92-3.
26. Jerald A. Combs, *The Jay Treaty: Political Background of the Founding Fathers* (Berkeley: University of California Press, 1970); Samuel Flagg Bemis, *Jay's Treaty. A Study in Commerce and Diplomacy* (New Haven, CT: Yale University Press, 1962).
27. John Quincy Adams, James A. Bayard, Henry Clay, and Jonathan Russell to James Monroe, Ghent, 19 August 1814, in Manning, *Diplomatic Correspondence*, 1:629.
28. Reginald Horsman, *The Causes of the War of 1812* (New York: A.S. Barnes, 1962) provides a useful overview. See also page 52n.2 of this work.
29. Jonathan Russell to James Monroe, London, 3 February 1812, in Manning, *Diplomatic Correspondence*, 1:609-10.
30. Noble Cunningham, Jr., *Circular Letters of Congressmen to their Constituents, 1789-1829*, ?? vols. (Chapel Hill: The University of North Carolina Press, 1978), 2:912.
31. R.C. Brown and S.F. Wise, *Canada Views the United States: Nineteenth Century Political Attitudes* (Seattle: University of Washington Press, 1967), 109.
32. John Quincy Adams to James Monroe, London, 8 February 1816, in

Manning, *Diplomatic Correspondence*, 1:783-84.

33. Ibid., John Quincy Adams to James Monroe, Ghent, 5 September 1814, 1:647-48, 652.

34. Ibid., James Monroe to John Quincy Adams, 21 July 1815, 1:231.

35. Ibid., Richard Rush to John Quincy Adams, 25 February 1820, 1:296; John Quincy Adams to Richard Rush, Washington, 19 November 1819, 1:916-17.

36. Lewis Cass to John C. Calhoun, Detroit, 3 August 1819, in Meriwether, *Calhoun Papers*, 4:200-4.

37. Lewis Cass to John C. Calhoun, Washington, 24 October 1821, in Meriwether, *Calhoun Papers*, 6:460-71. Cass estimated 6,000 Native Indians made the visit to Fort Malden in 1820. See also Thomas Forsyth to John C. Calhoun, Fort Armstrong, 23 September 1823, in Meriwether, *Calhoun Papers*, 8:282.

38. Lewis Cass to John C. Calhoun, Detroit, 4 December 1823, in Meriwether, *Calhoun Papers*, 8:393.

39. Stagg, 519-24.

40. Rufus King to James Madison, London, 1 June 1801, in Manning, *Diplomatic Correspondence*, 1:525.

41. Ibid., James Madison to James Monroe and Robert L. Livingston, Washington, 20 July 1802, 1:159.

42. Ibid., Thomas Jefferson to Gouvernor Morris, New York, 12 August 1790, 1:44.

43. Ibid., Albert Gallatin to James Monroe, Ghent, 20 August 1814, 1:634-35.

44. Ibid., Richard Rush to Henry Clay, 26 March 1825, 2:488-89.

45. Kenneth Bourne, *Britain and the Balance of Power in North America, 1815-1908* (London: Longmans, 1967), 33-52.

46. Brigadier General Simon Bernard to John C. Calhoun, New York, 8 March 1823, in Meriwether, *Calhoun Papers*, 7:505-9.

47. Bourne, 12-71; James Monroe to John Quincy Adams, 16 November 1815, in Manning, *Diplomatic Correspondence*, 1:234-35.

48. Ibid., Gouvernor Morris to George Washington, London, 29 May 1790, 1:375-76. At the 1814 peace negotiations in Ghent, Lord Gambier described the Great Lakes as "the natural military frontier of the British possessions in North America." Ibid., Lord Gambier to U.S. Ministers, Ghent, 14 August 1814, 1:633. In 1802, when discussing the differences between the French in Louisiana and the British in Canada, Robert Livingston drew attention to the "natural boundary" which separated British from U.S. territory. Ibid., Robert Livingston to James Madison, Paris, 10 August 1802, 1:539.

49. David R. Deener, *Canada-United States Treaty Relations* (Durham, NC: Duke University Press, 1963) lists all the treaties and agreements with respect to the Canadian-American boundary. See also John B. Brebner, *North Atlantic Triangle: The Interplay of Canada, the United States and Great Britain* (New Haven, CT: Yale University Press, 1945), 95-7. The best analysis of the diplomacy surrounding these issues is Perkins, *Castlereagh and Adams*.

50. William A. Slocum to John Forsyth, American Brig Loriot off San Blas, 26 March 1837, in Manning, *Diplomatic Correspondence*, 1:387-91; John S.

Galbraith, *The Hudson's Bay Company as an Imperial Factor, 1821-1869* (Berkeley: University of California Press, 1957).

51. John Quincy Adams to Albert Gallatin and Richard Rush, Washington, 28 July 1818, in Manning, *Diplomatic Correspondence*, 1:279.

52. Ibid., Albert Gallatin to Henry Clay, 25 November 1826, 2:539. The despatch is on the subject of the Columbia River and its navigation.

53. Ibid., John Quincy Adams to Richard Rush, Washington, 20 May 1818, 1:268-69.

54. Bourne, 75-169.

55. Louis McLane to James Buchanan, London, 1 December 1845, in Manning, *Diplomatic Correspondence*, 3:986.

56. Frederick Merk, *The Oregon Question: Essays in Anglo-American Diplomacy and Politics* (Cambridge: Belknap Press, 1967); David M. Pletcher, *The Diplomacy of Annexation: Texas, Oregon and the Mexican War* (Columbia: University of Missouri Press, 1973); Galbraith, *The Hudson Bay Co.*; Thomas R. Hietala, Manifest Design, *Anxious Aggrandizement in Late Jacksonian America* (Ithaca: Cornell University Press, 1985).

57. See pages 133-38.

58. John Quincy Adams to Richard Rush, Washington, 23 June 1823, *American State Papers. Foreign Relations (ASPFR)* (Washington, DC: Government Printing Office, 1859).

59. Ibid., Richard Rush to John Quincy Adams, London, 12 August 1824, 7:761.

60. Ibid., 7:759.

61. Protocol between Richard Rush, William Huskisson, and Viscount Canning, 19 June 1824, in Manning, *Diplomatic Correspondence*, 2:413.

62. Ibid., Henry Clay to Albert Gallatin, Washington, 19 June 1826, 2:81.

63. British Paper on the St. Lawrence, 24th Protocol "N", ASPFR, 7:772.

64. Ibid., Henry Clay to Albert Gallatin, Washington, 19 June 1826, 6:762.

65. Richard Rush to John Quincy Adams, 12 August 1824, in Manning, *Diplomatic Correspondence*, 2:433-35.

66. Ibid., Martin Van Buren to Louis McLane, Washington, 26 December 1829, 2:216-17, gives a summary of the trade issue since 1815.

67. Ibid., James Madison to James Monroe and William Pinckney, Washington, 17 December 1806, 1:172-73.

68. Ibid., James Monroe to John Quincy Adams, 21 May 1816, 1:244; Ibid., Henry Clay to Charles Vaughan, 11 October 1826, 2:111.

69. Ibid., Martin Van Buren to Louis McLane, Washington, 26 December 1829, 2:216-17.

70. Ibid., Louis McLane to Lord Aberdeen, 6 March 1830, 2:823.

71. Report on the Trade, Commerce, and Resources of the British North American Colonies made in pursuance of instructions from the Hon. Thomas Corwin, Secretary of the Treasury, *Sen. Ex. Doc.* 23, 31st Cong., 2d sess. diplomatic correspondence 1851 [hereafter Andrews/1851], 9-10.

72. Louis McLane to Lord Aberdeen, 6 March 1830, in Manning, *Diplomatic Correspondence*, 2:832.

73. The two standard accounts are Helen Taft Manning, *The Revolt of French Canada, 1800-1835* (New York: St. Martin's Press, 1962) and Aileen

Dunham, *Political Unrest in Upper Canada, 1815-1836* (Toronto: McClelland and Stewart, 1963), but there is an extensive literature on the rebellions. See Craig, *Upper Canada*, 188-251, 310 and Fernand Ouellet, *Lower Canada, 1792-1841* (Toronto: McClelland and Stewart, 1980), 291-516.

74. W.B. Lawrence to Henry Clay, London, 21 June 1828, in Manning, *Diplomatic Correspondence*, 2:734.

75. *Niles Weekly Register*, 46(7 June 1834):244-45 and 46(5 April 1834):85.

76. Aaron Vail to John Forsyth, London, 21 March 1835, in Manning, *Diplomatic Correspondence*, 2:972-73.

77. A.B. Corey, *The Crisis of 1830-1842 in Canadian-American Relations* (New Haven, CT: Yale University Press, 1941), while still useful, has been superseded by the work of Howard Jones culminating in *To the Webster-Ashburton Treaty: A Study in Anglo-American Relations* (Chapel Hill: The University of North Carolina Press, 1977). See also O.A. Kinchen, *The Rise and Fall of the Patriot Hunters* (New York: Bookman Associates, 1956).

78. William H. Seward to Daniel Webster, Albany, 22 September 1841, in Manning, *Diplomatic Correspondence*, 3:153-54.

79. Ibid., Daniel Webster to Caleb Cushing and other members of Congress, Washington, 27 August 1848, 3:191.

80. Jones, *To the Webster-Ashburton Treaty*, passim., Albert Gallatin's case for the U.S. has been reprinted, *The Right of the United States of America to the North-Eastern Boundary Claimed by Them* (Freeport, ME: Books for Libraries Press, 1970).

81. George Bancroft to James Buchanan, London, 16 May 1848, in Manning, *Diplomatic Correspondence*, 3:1150.

82. Andrews/1851, 27.

83. There is a useful summary of imperial issues in Britain and the historiographical debate over them until the 1970s, in C.C. Eldridge, *Victorian Imperialism* (Atlantic Highlands, NJ: Humanties Press, 1978), 1-41.

84. George Bancroft to James Buchanan, London, 3 November 1847, in Manning, *Diplomatic Correspondence*, 3:114-15.

85. Ibid., James Buchanan to George Bancroft, Washington, 29 September 1847, 3:349.

86. Ibid., George Bancroft to John M. Clayton, 9 March 1849 and 23 February 1849, 4:247-48, 251-52.

87. Andrews' career is summarized in Manning, *Diplomatic Correspondence*, 3:202 and 4:693. His appointment and instructions are in John Clayton to Israel Andrews, 6 July 1849, 4:13-14. His two reports are: *Sen. Ex. Doc.* 23, 31 Cong, 2d sess., 6:(1851) and *Sen. Ex. Doc.* 112, 32d Cong., 1 sess., 1:(1852).

88. Israel Andrews to James Buchanan, 15 August 1846, in Manning, *Diplomatic Correspondence*, 3:1007.

89. Ibid., 15 January 1848, 3:1135.

90. Andrews/1851, 44-50.

91. Lester B. Shippee, *Canadian-American Relations 1849-1874* (New Haven, CT: Yale University Press, 1941), 1-62; *Congressional Globe*, 33d Cong., 1st sess., 2212.

92. Shippee, 88; Israel Andrews to William Marcy, Montreal, 13 May 1854, in Manning, *Diplomatic Correspondence*, 4:576.
93. The standard work is Donald C. Masters, *The Reciprocity Treaty of 1854* (Toronto: McClelland and Stewart, 1963). See also Charles C. Tansill, *The Canadian Reciprocity Treaty* (Baltimore: The Johns Hopkins University Press, 1922). The best analysis of the economic impact of the treaty is Lawrence H. Officer and Lawrence B. Smith, "The Canadian-American Reciprocity Treaty of 1855 to 1866," *Journal of Economic History* 28(1968):598-623.
94. Shippee, 82-4.
95. Daniel Webster to H.L. Baliver, 14 September 1850, Department of State, Notes to Foreign Legations, M99, Reel 36, National Archives.
96. For general background on the fisheries question see Shippee, 262-87. Shippee referred to it as "The Everlasting Fisheries Question." Charles S. Campbell, "American Tariff Interests and the Northeastern Fisheries 1883-1888," *CHR* 45(1964):212-28 is excellent for showing the relationship between the fisheries and the tariff questions. Charles C. Tansill, *Canadian-American Relations 1875-1911* (New Haven, CT: Yale University Press), 1-120.
97. B. Hammond Norton to Daniel Webster, Pictou, 27 November 1851, in Manning, *Diplomatic Correspondence*, 4:4039.
98. Ibid., John Forsyth to Andrew Stevenson, Washington, 20 February 1841, 3:130-32.
99. Ibid., Abbott Lawrence to Daniel Webster, London, 10 August 1851, 4:456-58.
100. Ibid., Edward Everett to Jared Ingersoll, 4 December 1852, 4:47.
101. Ibid., Jared Ingersoll to William Marcy, 10 June 1853, 4:510.
102. Ibid., Richard Rush to William Marcy, Sydenham, 18 July 1853, 4:514-23.
103. Ibid., James Buchanan to William Marcy, 14 April 1854, 4:563-65.
104. Ibid., James Buchanan to William Marcy, London, 18 August 1854 and 25 August 1854, 4:592-94.
105. Ibid., Israel Andrews to William Marcy, St. John's, New Brunswick, 3 April 1854, 4:555.

III
"A Second Empire"
1854-1892

In the 1840s, Americans had anticipated the disintegration of the British Empire in North America. The end of the old colonial trading system, the advent of responsible government, and the reduction of the garrisons appeared as steps toward independence for the British North American colonies. Yet the next fifty years thoroughly undermined these American hopes. In 1867 the Canadas, Nova Scotia, and New Brunswick joined to form the Dominion of Canada. By 1871 this strengthened British colony extended its reach across the continent as it took over the vast territories of the Hudson's Bay Company and secured the entry of British Columbia. The United States was now faced with a single, greater Canada of continental dimensions instead of a group of loosely connected colonies left over from the eighteenth-century empire. Moreover, in the 1880s and 1890s, the British Empire took on a new lease of life during Europe's last great burst of imperialism. Among other manifestations of this reinvigorated imperialism was the emergence of an Imperial Federation movement dedicated to the strengthening of economic and military links between Britain and the white settlement colonies. As the oldest, most populated and wealthiest of these white settlement colonies, Canada played a leading part in this imperial resurgence.[1]

In an 1857 letter to Secretary of State Lewis Cass, Israel Andrews warned about such a growth of Canadian power. "The colonies," he reasoned,

> cannot now be conquered; at present they are disjointed and weak; united with their collateral strength, they would be an increasing power. The strength of Canada in your front controlling one half of the Great Lakes or the Hydrographic Basin, and the Maritime or lower Colonies on your flank or rear supported by the strategic positions of Quebec, Bermuda and Halifax

would be, if united and supported by any European power, a formidable antagonist. Such is the desire of England and is advocated by her officials in the colonies.[2]

These warnings appeared to be turning into reality by the 1880s. As *The American Economist*, which represented Republican protectionist circles, phrased it in 1889, "the purpose of the Canadas, supported by Great Britain, is to establish on this continent a second empire to confront and rival our own."[3]

1.

Notwithstanding the American resentment that they had been outfoxed by Canada in 1854, the Reciprocity Treaty could still be viewed as a promising new start to the realization of long-term American expectations with respect to Canada. The fisheries question, which had grown to a dangerous stage, seemed settled. The trade patterns encouraged by the treaty would weaken Canadian links with Britain and multiply those with the United States. Once the resentment brought on by the circumstances of the treaty negotiated subsided, it could be seen as a further stage in the reduction of the British imperial factor in North America. Such was the optimistic outlook that ran through Secretary of State Marcy's instructions to the ubiquitous Israel Andrews when he was appointed Consul-General for the British North American Provinces. This appointment was made "in view of the new relations between the United States and the British North American Provinces under the treaty." Marcy forecast that now "all these disturbing questions are . . . set at rest for ever," the future would be characterized by "rapidly growing intercourse between them [the British colonies] and this country." In Marcy's view, a new era was about to open up in which Canada would become more and more integrated into the United States economy and culture. "Many of the impediments have been removed," he explained, "which short-sighted legislation too long fostered to prevent the unrestrained flow of commerce and social intercommunication. . . ."[4]

In expressing these hopes, Marcy was simply reiterating to Andrews the argument the latter had been pressing on the State Department since 1846, namely that Canada was becoming Americanized and that closer commercial ties would accelerate that development. In a note to Marcy, the new Consul-General wrote of the beneficial effects of the treaty "throughout the Northern Sections of America from Lake Superior to Newfoundland." Andrews announced that there was "a steady active intercourse maintained [by the United States] with all the Provinces which will continuously increase and every day partake more of the character of the trade between Massachusetts and New York."[5]

Canfield Dorwin, the U.S. Consul in Montreal, shared this view of the likely assimilative effects of the 1854 treaty. In even more explicit terms than Marcy or Andrews, he forecast that reciprocity would stimulate trade between the two countries and "knit together in an indissoluble tie of amity and greatly assimilate these colonies to one of the great Western States; in short, commercially annexing them."[6] In Nova Scotia, the U.S. Consul at Pictou expected to see an increase in the market for American manufactured items. This new current of trade suggested that "the day is not far distant when Nova Scotia will take rank among the States of the Union."[7] The theme that Canada would become simply an extension of interstate commerce was taken up by Consul Dorwin when he advised Marcy on the impact of the treaty on transportation routes. "Commercially speaking," he informed Marcy,

> [it is] tantamount to annexation . . . by conveying the products of this Province over the railroads and canals of the Union, thereby placing Canada and the Lower Provinces so far as their trade is concerned, in the position of one of the states of the union.[8]

This American optimism concerning the impact of the treaty was undermined by Canadian actions and policies. The problem was that Americans were not properly informed (in spite of Andrews' effusions) of the view from the Canadian side. For example, while Consul Dorwin thought the treaty would make Canada another state of the Union in terms of transportation, the Canadian administrations of the 1850s expected the opposite outcome—that the St. Lawrence would once again become the great route from the continental interior to the markets of Europe. With this goal in mind, colonial governments since the 1820s had sunk millions of dollars into canals and railroads in order to improve the St. Lawrence corridor route. Moreover, the Canadians, partly as a revenue measure and partly as their response to the new economic relationship with Britain, began in 1858 to impose tariffs on manufactured imports.[9] Thus, at the very time when Americans—from Secretary of State Marcy to the Consul General in Montreal and the humble consul in Pictou—were expecting the colonies to realign themselves to American patterns of trade and transportation, the Canadians were working to build a rival transportation system as part of a plan to nurture their own autonomous economic growth.

This divergence between American and Canadian expectations in the 1850s led to an American critique of Canada in which the Canadians were portrayed as deliberately misusing the Reciprocity Treaty. In the phrase that was repeated by American politicians and policy-makers for the next fifty years, the treaty had been a "jug-handled" one in favor of the Canadians who managed the treaty in a one-sided manner.[10] It is important to understand that this line of criticism was developing even before the severe tensions between the United States, Britain, and Canada during the Civil War.

In 1857, the U.S. Consul-General in Montreal, Wyman Moor, took stock of the operation of the treaty and concluded that all of the advantages were being won by the Canadians. In a dispatch to Secretary of State Cass (who needed little encouragement to think of Canadians as perfidious), Moor pointed out that the United States received from Canada goods, with free entry under the terms of the treaty, to the value of $17,810,684; whereas, Canada took in goods valued at only $7,899,554. According to Moor's calculations, of the total Canadian exports to the United States, only 4 percent paid duty in contrast to the 50 percent of American exports to Canada which still had to face customs payments. Moor emphasized the unfairness of the Canadian policy which put all articles listed free in the Reciprocity agreement on the general free list "thereby extending the privileges which the United States secured by the most liberal concessions to the rest of the world."

Even more confirmatory of Canadian bad faith was the imposition in 1858 of large tariff increases on manufactured items imported into Canada "amounting almost to a prohibition... on American manufactures." Moor demanded rhetorically of Secretary Cass "whether any measures injurious to our commerce are left for Canada to adopt." The indictment of Canada was extended by Moor to include the growth of the milling business and the expansion of railroads within Canada. Three Canadian roads (the Great Western, the Buffalo and Huron, and the Grand Trunk) competed with the New York and Pennsylvania roads by bringing grain from the American midwest to Hamilton, Toronto, and Montreal where it was milled into flour and sold free of duty on the American market. The income of the Canadian railroads was derived from transporting goods from one section of the United States to another. "These lines," insisted Moor, "are all built as competing lines to our Railways and Lake Navigation in transporting the produce and the Commerce of the West."[11]

Throughout his tenure at Montreal, Moor stuck to this theme that Canada, backed by British capital, was building railroads and canals not to meet the domestic needs of Canada but to siphon off the trade of the American west. In January 1860, he reported as an example of this policy the opening of the Victoria Bridge across the St. Lawrence at a cost of $7,000,000. "I have seen within the past weeks," Moor reported, "large quantities of cotton raised in Tennessee passing by this route to the factories in New England." If the extent of the Canadian canal system was borne in mind, continued Moor, then the State Department would get some sense of "the magnitude of the internal improvements of Canada." He ended his dispatch to Cass by concluding that "the Government of this Province and the Capitalists of Great Britain are united in their efforts to make their Canals and Railroads the thoroughfare of Western commerce to the Atlantic."[12]

These observations from the Consul-General's watchpost in Montreal were elaborated upon and developed into a comprehensive critique of Canada's abuse of the treaty. The culmination (before the Civil War) of this attack on Canada was the 1860 report on the workings of the treaty prepared by Israel T. Hatch for the Treasury Department. The report opened by asserting that while the United States was fully committed to a liberal trade policy with respect to Canada, as demonstrated in the 1854 treaty, the Canadians had acted "adverse to its spirit." The treaty was "correct in principle" but it had not worked well because of "the perversion of its spirit and the disregard of its substance on the part of Canada." Hatch then filled out the picture sketched by Moor of Canada's aggressive transportation policy. "The railroads and the canals of Canada," he insisted,

> were alike constructed for the express purpose of extending political and commercial power by the diversion of the trade of the great interior of our country through the valley of the St. Lawrence and the Canadian routes of transportation.

This plan by Canada "to control our commerce" had led to a large public debt in Canada which turned to increased tariffs to improve revenue and manage the debt, thus making American manufacturers "pay for public works constructed against us." This policy was contrary to the spirit of the Reciprocity Treaty and was contrary to the natural trade patterns of North America. "To make up the deficiency caused by these speculative expenditures," charged Hatch,

> Canada now seeks to make our merchants and our manufacturers, who have been most damaged by the diversion of western trade to Canadian cities and transportation routes, pay for her unremunerative carrying system. This whole modern movement of Canadian or British policy in transportation is artificial, unnatural

and against the laws of trade, climate and geography—in violation of the spirit of international intercourse as mutually recognized and sanctioned by the reciprocity treaty.

From the American viewpoint, the only economic benefit anticipated from the treaty had been entry to the Canadian market for American manufacturing goods. The United States, while benefiting from some local complementarities along the border, did not need to import agricultural products. Yet because of the Canadian tariff policy, it was not American but Canadian manufacturers who were being helped after 1854. "Under the forcing process of protection," Hatch argued, "Montreal is now rivalling Lowell and Lynn in almost every article of their manufacture and approaching our Atlantic cities in the magnitude of her commerce." This protective course adopted by Canada, Hatch continued, went directly against the purpose of the treaty: "The taxing of the products of American industry almost to their exclusion from the Province must be pronounced to be a violation not only of the letter and spirit of the treaty but of the amity and good faith in which it was conceived."

Hatch took care to make the case that there was nothing haphazard about these developments north of the border but rather that all Canadian policies were deployed with malice aforethought. To prove this contention, he cited Canadian documents which stated that the government-backed canal and railroad development was "for the purpose of drawing the trade of the Western States to the ports of Montreal and Quebec." He also drew attention to Canadian discrimination against American vessels on canals along the St. Lawrence route. Under the terms of the treaty, American vessels were entitled to use the Canadian canals between the Great Lakes and the lower St. Lawrence, subject to the same tolls as Canadian vessels. But the Canadians charged an omnibus toll on all vessels passing through the Welland Canal (between lakes Erie and Ontario) and then gave rebates to those ships that passed through the canals to Montreal. Most American vessels only used the Welland Canal before off-loading at New York ports on Lake Ontario and thus paid the omnibus toll without benefit of rebates. This kind of manipulative toll policy was "another example of the studious and systematic evasion of the spirit and letter of the treaty ratified under the promise of reciprocity."

The scale of publicly supported financing required for transportation projects in Canada led Hatch to conclude that Canada had embarked on a plan of imperial-commercial expansion in North America backed by British capitalists since "neither the population nor the productions of Canada" were sufficient to justify these schemes. British backing for the Grand Trunk Railroad was cited as proof of this imperial game. "These efforts to divert our own traffic from our own territory," fulminated Hatch,

> although important in themselves, are insignificant in comparison with the ambitious schemes developed in the construction of the Grand Trunk Railroad—a work owned by a combination of British capitalists. In our commercial age, British capital is the power behind the throne, and the armies and navies of Great Britain follow and protect the enterprise of her subjects. . . . The managers of this road, in emulation of the ancient influence of the East India Company on an Imperial Government, have subjected the Parliament of Canada to their control.

While placing his evidence in an imperial context that sounded familiar anti-British themes, Hatch gave the Canadians no quarter. "It is equally evident," he charged,

> that a systematic scheme of provincial legislation, affirmatively aggressive upon the great interests of this country, commenced with the ratification of the treaty as the beginning of its opportunity and has progressed in its strength and extent, in its details and its scope, in all its disastrous consequences every day while that opportunity has continued.

Hatch was able to sharpen the tone of resentment in his report by contrasting the disinterested motives of the United States when she agreed to the treaty with the bad treatment she had received by Canada. He repeated the point made by Marcy to Clarendon that the treaty had assured the economic viability of Canada and had therefore postponed any possibility of annexation. Secretary Marcy had

> believed . . . that reciprocal free trade would remove the causes which render any closer union desirable, and would perpetuate alike international good-will and separate nationality, presenting the world a sublime example of two contiguous nations abandoning suspicion of injury from each other and practicing in their intercourse the best principles professed in modern civilization.

These high hopes were dashed by Canada's cavalier abuse of the treaty. "The statesmanlike ideas prevalent at the time when the treaty became law, anticipating the removal of all unnecessary restrictions between two neighboring states," lamented Hatch, "are in strong contrast with the realities of today."[13]

The onslaught by Hatch was a powerful one, obviously constructed to draw on the traditional American suspicion of British imperial designs in North America (the reference to the East India Company cleverly reminding Americans of the Tea Act and the revolutionary struggle against British trade policies), but it did not carry the day in 1860. Hatch's motives were most questionable. He was a banker and a lawyer from Buffalo, a grain merchant and the owner of stock in grain elevators and docks on the lakes. He represented the railroad and storage interests in New York and Pennsylvania that stood to lose if the Canadian routes became successful. A rival report submitted to the Secretary of the Treasury made the explicit charge that "the shipping interests of New York and Philadelphia" were behind the Hatch attack. James W. Taylor, the author of this second report, made the case that while the treaty perhaps favored Canada more than the United States, there were decided benefits for the American side. In particular, Taylor spoke on behalf of the farmers and other shippers of merchandise in the upper-midwest and northwestern states who benefitted from the cheaper transportation costs caused by having a competitive route running against the New York and Pennsylvania railroads.[14] How the balance of American opinion on these matters may have been tipped had the Civil War not broken out is impossible to determine. It is certain however, that the Hatchian version of Canada became more believable in the United States as tensions between Britain and the United States intensified during the war years and as Canada was used as a base by Confederate agents and raiders. In 1864, for example, a group of Confederates raided a bank in St. Albans, Vermont and fled back to Montreal. American resentment over such incidents and American anger with Britain over the Alabama depredations on northern shipping during the war ensured that when the Reciprocity Treaty came up for review in 1864-65 the issues would not be examined calmly.[15]

The tipping of the balance toward abrogation can be seen in the letters of Joshua Giddings, the American Consul in Montreal during the war years. The views expressed by Giddings are particularly telling because Giddings had supported the 1854 treaty. In 1863 he wrote, "I speak the convictions of our most prominent men who favored the reciprocity treaty under the belief that it would promote feelings of kindness and good neighborhood with the Canadians." The pre-war commercial aggressiveness defined by Hatch was linked in Giddings' mind with Canadian support during the war for British "hostility upon our commerce." The British connivance in allowing the USS Alabama to sail was "fully sanctioned and justified by the government and people of Canada." The Canadians were now requesting that the Reciprocity Treaty be extended. "While they support and justify this war upon our commerce," complained Giddings,

> Canadian statesmen and politicians come to induce Congress to continue our kindness and respect for the Provinces by maintaining our reciprocity treaty and continuing the gratuitous privileges of importing and exporting goods through our territory and our ports.

This combination of Canadian hostility during the war with the record of Canadian behavior on tariffs and trade before the war showed that "all our favors to Canada bring no return of goodwill but rather inspire our neighbors with contempt for what they regard as our pusillanimity." Giddings then added a point that became a popular one in Congress for the next fifty years. Canada had been able to misuse the 1854 treaty with impunity because the trade regulations, being the subject of a treaty, could not be changed until the treaty expired. In any future agreement with Canada, trade matters should be dealt with by statutes that could be rescinded or amended to counter Canadian ploys. "If we want to do them the favor of holding open our markets," he urged, "let it be done by statute which can be modified or repealed at pleasure thereby holding them to their good behaviour." [16]

The assault on Canada's misuse of reciprocity was continued by Andrew Potter who was at the Montreal post when Congress debated whether or not to abrogate the treaty. Potter worked actively for abrogation and wrote lengthy dispatches castigating the Canadians to Secretary of State William Seward. He launched his attack on the treaty at the Detroit Commercial Convention in 1865, which he attended at instruction of Secretary Seward. Potter repeated many of the arguments made by Hatch, Moor, and Giddings. He was particularly sharp about the smuggling of British or other empire goods into the United States through Canada. Merchandise that originally entered Canada from Hudson's Bay Company territory was shipped as though it had originated in Canada; wheat was purchased in Chicago and Milwaukee, brought to Canada where it was milled into flour, and then exported to the United States as a Canadian product; and American vessels were forced to pay discriminatory rates as they passed through the Welland Canal.

Potter produced figures showing that the two largest Canadian exports to the United States were tea and flour. He proceeded to describe why that was the case as an illustration of the adverse impact of reciprocity "upon the commercial interest of the United States." Under the treaty, Canadian vessels had access to U.S. lake ports like Chicago where they bought wheat for milling in Canada before sending it free of tariffs into the United States "with the result . . . that the Canadians are fast becoming the manufacturers of our flour." The ships that brought the flour into the United States were then loaded with beef, pork, and other American products and transferred at Montreal into British vessels for transport to the United Kingdom. These ships in turn brought back tea and other East India goods "which are distributed to the West in Canadian vessels [thus] giving them a monopoly of the carrying trade both ways."[17]

In view of this record, it was provoking for Potter to read anti-American statements from members of the Canadian administration. In the summer of 1865, Potter was particularly annoyed by a speech of D'Arcy McGee, Minister of Agriculture, who contrasted the fate of the Irish who emigrated to Canada and the United States. According to McGee, the Irish fared much better in Canada than they did in the eastern cities of the United States. "The speech," expostulated Potter, "was a tissue of libelous misrepresentations in relation to the people and the government of the United States." McGee had referred to the struggle between American democracy and British-Canadian monarchical institutions as "the great fight of the nineteenth century for this continent." It is, Potter continued,

> a remarkable fact that while this minister is using such language at home for the purpose of instilling in the minds of the Canadian people with hostile feelings towards our government, two of his colleagues are on a professedly friendly mission to Washington for the purpose of inducing the Government of the United States to give them free markets for Canadian products.

Alexander Tilloch Galt, Canadian Minister of Finance, also incurred Potter's wrath for a speech made in the Canadian legislature during which "he distinctly threatens that in the event of the refusal of our Government to continue the Treaty, Canada would adopt a policy which would break down the Revenue system of the United States." Such speeches by Canadian ministers, Potter advised Seward, are yet more evidence of "the disingenuous and unscrupulous course . . . to effect a renewal of the treaty."[18]

Potter concluded his long memorandum to the Secretary of State with a pitch that made sense in terms of the original justification of the treaty—that it would strengthen Canada's economy. If termination of the treaty ended such opportunities for Canada, she would be forced to plead for concessions from the United States, perhaps even to the point of requesting annexation. "I have no hesitation in saying," Potter confidently summed up, "that if the Government of the United States regards the future peaceable annexation of the Canadas as desirable, that the Treaty should not be renewed in any form." If the treaty were abogated, Potter forecast, it would be "three years at most" until Canada sued for annexation.[19]

This assessment by Potter was written in the charged atmosphere at the end of the Civil War when many Republicans were bitter about Britain's and Canada's role during the war.[20] But while the bitter tone can be explained in terms of the times, Potter's views were in the same mold as those of Israel Andrews in the 1840s and 1850s. Both argued that natural circumstances would force Canada to break her dependence on Britain and move toward some kind of closer union with the United States. This could happen either (as Andrews suggested) by the United States offering liberal trading terms which would bind the two countries economically or (as Potter proposed) by refusing any trade concessions and thus forcing Canada to beg for closer ties. The approaches were opposite, but the assumption behind both was that Canada was bound to end up dependent upon the United States. However, all American observers from Andrews to Potter made a fundamental error in reading trends in Canada. This misreading was based on the unquestioned assumption that the only conceivable historical development for European colonies in the Americas was to follow the United States' path from colonial status to independence. They were unable to get outside of this mind-set and appreciate that there was another possible line of development for the British North American colonies. As Canadians responded to the momentous changes in British policy in the 1840s, they moved toward a solution (encouraged by the imperial government) which, far from forcing them into dependence on the United States, would enable them to flourish as a separate power in North America. This solution was all the more opaque to Americans because Canada's drive for economic and political autonomy involved no final break from Britain. Canada would remain part of the empire while forging ahead with her own plans for growth in North America.

The American misreading of Canadian development began with the 1837 rebellions and their aftermath. As we have seen, the rebellions were taken as signs that independence was on the way. But the consequences of the rebellions took a quite different direction. While the armed uprisings did not succeed, they did force the British to re-think their colonial policy. This re-thinking was informed by the ideas of moderate reformers in the Canadas like Robert Baldwin and Louis-Hippolyte LaFontaine. The immediate expression of the new thinking was contained in Lord Durham's 1839 report which had been commissioned by the Whig government in London. Beginning with the Durham report, and following a decade of political debate in Canada, a constitutional solution was arrived at that ran completely counter to the American expectations of the course of history. The solution became known as responsible government. As it was worked out in the 1840s, it led to a shift in power from the British governor and appointed officials to the party leaders who controlled a majority in the legislature. The British continued to appoint governors who remained the titular heads of the executive, but governors now chose their council of ministers from the politicians who had a party majority. The new ministry was thus responsible to the elected representatives in the assembly. The Canadians and the British arrived at a new version of colonial government which kept the colonies within the empire while allowing the colonists to control their own affairs (except for foreign relations). Once this new direction in British colonial policy was taken, the already weak case for independence disappeared from the Canadian political landscape. Indeed, the Canadians were able to take pride in their British monarchical institutions, which enabled them to be part of the world's most powerful and prosperous empire while enjoying self-government on the entire range of domestic matters.[21]

The changes in imperial economic policy also led to other consequences unforseen by Americans who watched Canadian affairs. As Britain shifted toward a free trade system and began to reduce her commitments to colonial defense (this latter policy connected to the coming of responsible government and the settlement of the Northeast boundary and the Oregon disputes), Canadians were forced into a re-evaluation of their economic future. The panicked demand by Montreal merchants for annexation in 1849 (so cherished by Andrews as a harbinger of things to come) was not the characteristic response. Canadians turned instead to plans for building up the colonial economy, including the canal and railroad projects to make Canada the entrepot from the American west to the east coast and Europe. The Canadian government in 1858 even placed tariffs on British manufactured imports (the same tariff complained of by Hatch, Moor, and Giddings because of its impact on American trade), a tariff that was allowed to stand by Britain in spite of protests from British manufacturers.[22] Access to the American market for Canadian agricultural products was part of this strategy to strengthen the local economy of Canada now that it was no longer operating within a sheltered imperial system. By the 1860s, this type of outlook led Canadian politicians to think in terms of their own western development as they contemplated the prospect of taking over the huge domain of the Hudson's Bay Company from the Great Lakes to the Rocky Mountains.[23]

These general trends within Canada and the empire combined to lead to the Confederation of Canada in 1867. The prospect of reciprocity coming to an end, with the American announcement that the treaty would be terminated in 1866, focused attention on the solution of an economic union for the British North American colonies. Britain also made it clear that she would only hand over the Hudson's Bay Company territory if Canada was strengthened sufficiently to defend the region. The fear of American invasion during the war and actual incursions into Canada by bands of Irish-American Fenians in 1866 increased the momentum for a strengthened British North America. Within Canada itself political deadlock made the prospect of a federal solution, which would allow French Canadians and English Canadians to control their own provinces, an attractive one. All these factors led to the union of the British colonies of Canada, Nova Scotia, and New Brunswick into the Dominion of Canada in 1867. By 1871, with the inclusion of British Columbia, the new Dominion stretched from the Atlantic to the Pacific.[24] Thus the period which had opened in 1846 with signs that the British Empire in North America was about to disintegrate ended twenty years later with an enlarged and strengthened Canada. American expectations had been disappointed (which perhaps explains the defiant yet despairing tone of Potter's dispatches in 1866-67).

Political, social, and economic factors inside British North America led to Canadian confederation, but it required no jaundiced American interpretation to regard it as a consolidation, and thus, expansion of the British empire in North America. As early as 1858, a Colonial Office memorandum on British North America pointed out,

> the more united, flourishing and powerful are the British provinces in North America, the more durable will be their connection with the mother country. They will be the less likely to desire amalgamation with the great States across their southern frontier and the more capable of resisting annexation.[25]

Leading Canadian politicians like Georges Etienne Cartier and Alexander Tilloch Galt urged Britain to forward the confederation scheme on the grounds that it would not only benefit Canada but enhance the imperial position in North America. "With a population of 3 1/2 million, with a foreign commerce exceeding $25,000,000 and commercial marine inferior only to Great Britain and the United

States," they urged to Sir Edward Lytton in 1858, "it is in the power of the Imperial Government by sanctioning a confederation of these Provinces, to constitute a dependency of the Empire, valuable in time of peace, powerful in the event of war, for ever removing the fear that these colonies may ultimately serve to swell the power of another nation."[26]

In these circumstances the old American view of Canada as a martial colony was easy to maintain. For example, in the same year that Cartier and Galt wrote to the Colonial Office, the young Rutherford B. Hayes, future Republican president, was impressed by the military character of Quebec which he described as "the American Gibralter with its hundreds of cannon." As he traveled between Montreal and Quebec, Hayes noted, "nothing struck me more than the British soldiers."[27] While Americans continued to take note of this military-imperial aspect of Canada, there was none of the sense of vulnerability that had been present in the period before the War of 1812. The population growth, territorial expansion, and economic success of the United States and her ability to raise a massive army, as demonstrated in the Civil War, left no doubt that the United States was the dominant power in North America. As Robin Winks observed in his meticulous study of the Civil War years, the balance of power in North America had tilted decisively in favor of the United States.[28] Nevertheless, while there was no longer any fear of a direct British-Canadian military threat to the United States, there was a troubling awareness that Canada was persisting in her efforts to become a rival power on the continent. As a paper sent to Secretary of State Seward described circumstances in April 1867, "disguise the fact as diplomacy at London may seek to do, it is nevertheless true that an empire is in process of organization along the whole length of the northern border line of the United States under a policy of political antagonism to the American Union."[29]

This imperial orientation of the new Dominion of Canada was evident in the building of the Canadian Pacific Railroad (CPR). The CPR project was part of the arrangement which brought British Columbia into the Canadian confederation in 1871 and after much political and economic travail was completed, with substantial government backing, by 1886. To critical American eyes the building of such an expensive railway through territory still thinly settled and without markets to generate traffic was a continuation of the Canadian strategy of siphoning off American trade. As Theodore Barnett, the U.S. Consul, reported from Ottawa in 1880, the building of the CPR through "the desolate and almost inaccessible region north of Lake Superior" raised suspicions about the actual purpose of the enterprise.

The CPR would be "the shortest and most direct transcontinental route [and] the evident object of such a road would be to divert the traffic of the Northwest from the Atlantic cities of the United States to Montreal and the St. Lawrence."[30] This consular critique worked its way up to the Secretary of State level, complemented by evidence from American railroad lobbyists, to emerge by the late 1880s into a comprehensive American indictment of the CPR. According to this view, the CPR was part of a British-Canadian plan to channel the trade of Japan and China through Vancouver rather than Seattle and San Francisco. Joseph Nimmo, during his appearance before the 1890 Senate Committee, declared that the money spent by Ottawa on railroads like the CPR proved that Canada aimed at "commercial supremacy on this continent."[31]

From its beginning there was British backing for the CPR, making it possible for Americans so disposed to make this charge. The initial British promise of guaranteed loans for the railroad was made in connection with the Treaty of Washington, which had settled Anglo-American tensions after the Civil War. A rider was agreed to by which Canada would drop all claims against the United States on account of the Fenian raids and, in return for removing this obstacle to successful negotiations, the British government "will engage that when the Treaty shall have taken effect . . . we will propose to Parliament a guarantee of 2,500,000 to be expended on canals and railroads through British territory from Canada to the Pacific. . . ."[32] The U.S. Minister in London informed Earl Granville, the Foreign Secretary, that the project to build a railroad "would not be viewed with favor" by the United States.[33]

Once the CPR was completed, British strategic planners regarded it as an important link in their worldwide commercial and military network. Such views were summarized by Major-General Sir Alured Clarke, Inspector-General of Fortifications, when he pointed out, "the strategic importance which attaches to the CPR in providing the British Empire with the possibility of a through route to the East, passing outside the sphere of European complications."[34] A joint committee representing the Admiralty, the Colonial Office, the Post Office, the Treasury, and the War Office affirmed the importance of this all-British route to Asia which was also considerably shorter than the Suez or San Francisco routes. The committee proposed subsidizing a line of fast steamers from Vancouver to Yokohama, using vessels which could be converted to armed cruisers in the event of war. Such plans, noted the committee, were designed to increase the significance of Canada's role in the empire:

Canada, instead of being to some extent isolated as regards the Imperial relations with European powers, will be brought into intimate contact. . . and will realize that the military importance of her position extends far beyond the defence of her southern frontier. Regular steamer service with the East via the Pacific once established, the whole empire will be firmly knit together and the chain of communications between British stations will literally girdle the world.[35]

The Colonial Secretary, Frederick Stanley, urged the cabinet to view support for the CPR in broad terms. "It is difficult," he warned the cabinet, "to overrate the importance of being able in time of war or emergency to send troops, munitions of war etc. to the Pacific, China and the Straits Settlements without passing through, or even by, other than British territory." At one end of the CPR (linked by the Intercolonial Railroad) was the British naval base at Halifax; at the other end a similar base would help British influence in the Pacific. "Our possession of Halifax," argued Viscount Wolseley,

helps to secure to us a dominion over the Atlantic Ocean that no other nation can at present aspire to. From the other side of the Atlantic for over 3,000 miles our troops, means of war naval and military, and our commerce, would be conveyed by railway through territory exclusively British [and] . . . Vancouver would be the great coaling station of our fleet in that ocean.[36]

It was this imperial dimension to the confederation of Canada that some Americans had foreseen and feared. While the strategic planning of the British policy-makers did not always get implemented, this view of Canada's place in the empire was common enough knowledge. As early as 1861, for example, Ernest Watkin of the Grand Trunk Railroad (one of Israel Hatch's favorite targets) argued in an editorial in *The Illustrated London News*, "our augmenting interests in the East, demand for reasons both of Empire and of trade, access to Asia less dangerous than by Cape Horn, less circuitous even than by Panama, less dependent than Suez and the Red Sea."[37] It was within this large geo-political context that Secretary of State Seward considered the purchase of Alaska from Russia in the same year as Canadian confederation. In an article that was part of the evidence to convince senators to ratify the purchase, the issues were laid out. The British Empire was strengthening itself in Canada; the United States was now pushing into the Pacific; it was essential to counter the growing British-Canadian influence by acquiring Russian Alaska to outflank the Canadians on the Pacific rim. "As the acquisition of Russian America," ran the argument, "will vastly strengthen the United States on the Pacific Ocean frontier, giving the Union harbors and strongholds on both flanks of the early colossus which meditates the building of Montreal into rivalry with New York, and Victoria into competition with San Francisco," it would help check Canadian designs.

> On the one part . . . the new British American Confederation will have for its neighbor henceforth on its northwestern frontier instead of an overloaded and overengaged monarchical Power, a free and independently striving Republic—and on the other part British America will be almost entirely cut off from the Pacific Ocean having left for herself only a distance of some 100 miles of free coast.

Inspired by such ambitious thinking, Seward wrote in grandiloquent terms to President Johnson, "the theatre of our greatest business is to be the Pacific, where we will soon have no formidable European rival—the consequences are ultimately the political and commercial control of the world." The Alaska purchase, assessed in this global context, would be, Seward assured Johnson, "the greatest act of your administration."[38]

While Secretary of State Seward viewed the acquisition of Alaska as part of a policy to check British-Canadian imperial expansion, the U.S. Consul in Montreal tried to do his part by intervening in the first election in the new Confederation. In January 1867, Consul Averill recommended "the strengthening of our naval force on the Pacific Coast" in response to Canada's dramatic expansion. He identified the Tory-Conservative party, or, as he called it, "the Confederation party," as the Canadian party that was energetically cooperating with Britain in plans for imperial consolidation in North America. This turn of events in 1867 was an obstacle to "the establishment and maintainance of a homogeneous civilisation under one government on this continent." Consul Averill had a remedy. He proposed to Secretary Seward that secret funds be used to support the Liberal party in the first post-confederation Canada elections on the grounds that the Liberals were continentalist rather than imperialist in outlook. The Liberals were at a disadvantage because they did not have "the Government patronage or the benefits of its subsidies." Averill then listed the candidates in the election, putting a mark against the names of the Tories who could "be replaced by the use of the amount set opposite their names." This plan had been concocted when "some leaders of the Liberal Party . . . represented to me that they would be very glad to receive some assistance from the friends of the United States." Averill reckoned the Liberals would require about $25,000 in direct subventions to individual campaigns, "and for the Press, a list of which I enclose, about as much more." He cautioned Seward, "these estimates are made at a low figure and I should say that $100,000 will be required to make certain of the defeat of the Tory party."[39]

Averill's plan was not supported by the State Department, although some money did flow to opposition candidates and newspapers as it had during Israel Andrews' tenure at the Montreal post in the 1850s. The scheme reflected the American view that the Liberals, who were more committed to free trade ideals, would steer Canada away from British imperial collaboration to a closer orientation with the United States. It was a harebrained scheme and should not be seen as part of any carefully planned American policy to change the course of Canadian politics. Still, Averill's line of thinking at the bottom of the State Department hierarchy had parallels with Seward's geo-political thinking at the top of the State Department. The evidence of contemplated intervention in Canada to stall the imperial cause reveals the persistence of old American fears about Canadian aggrandizement. In 1870, even President Grant was stirred to declare that the continued British presence in Canada was "unnatural and inexpedient." This remark was viewed by the British Foreign Office as an invocation of the Monroe Doctrine against the new Dominion of Canada. It came "three years after—and in protest against—the formation of a Canadian Federation."[40]

2.

The shenanigans of the U.S. Consul in Montreal, Seward's purchase of Alaska, and Grant's ritualistic inveighing about the unnatural presence of European powers in the Americas, were not elements in a formulated policy toward Canada. They were simply scattered signs of the ongoing American concern about Canada's stubborn adherence to imperial ways when Americans kept expecting her to develop a North American view of the world. Such critical attitudes toward the new confederation made it even less likely that the United States would be receptive to another reciprocal trade treaty with Canada. Three factors made it difficult for Canadian ministers, even Liberal ones, to persuade the United States to sign a new treaty. The first was the impact on American policy of Republican ascendancy and the popularity of protection in Congress. The second was the revenue question after the war. The need to pay off war debts, to support the pension plans for veterans, and to repair the nation's finances in general made it difficult for administrations to give up revenue from Canadian imports. Thirdly, there was the now conventional view that Canada had deviously manipulated the 1854 treaty to her own advantage.

Americans were also determined that whatever arrangement was agreed to, it should include terms that forced Canada to reduce her ties with Britain. In a note to President Johnson, Secretary of State Seward summed up the position. As soon as Congress had determined the least oppressive method of raising the revenue needed to meet post-war expenses, it should turn to "this important question" of freer trade with Canada. Seward argued that the most "satisfactory arrangement would be the adoption of a Zollverein or Customs Union similar to that which has secured great reciprocal benefits to the states of Germany."[41] This would force Canada to raise tariffs against non-North American countries, including Britain, prevent her from readjusting tariff schedules at will, and lead to Canada becoming an integral part of the United States economy. The Americans believed they had been too generous in 1854; now they would only discuss a more binding agreement—such as a Customs Union—that would force Canada in the desired direction.

The American view of things was noted by the British Minister in Washington when negotiations were underway for the renewal of the 1854 treaty. "The exclusion of the Southern Representatives," he explained to Foreign Secretary Clarendon, "throws an exceptional power in such matters into the hands of the Protectionists of the North and Central parts of the country and their ranks are swelled by the agriculturalists of the Northwestern states who dread the competition of the wheat and barley growers of Canada."[42] The accuracy of this general assessment was confirmed by the treatment meted out to George Brown when he came to Washington in 1874 to discuss the possibility of a new treaty. The American reaction was all the more telling because Brown was a leading member in the Liberal party, which was in power from 1874 to 1878 in Canada (the only Liberal regime between 1867 and 1896). The Liberals, as we have seen in the Averill correspondence, were regarded as the party friendliest toward the United States. But Brown's hopes that he would be able to change American thinking—after some initial encouragement by Secretary of State Hamilton Fish and Senator Charles Sumner—were dashed against the protectionist rock. Brown's initial conversations with senators and representatives appeared to go well, but Secretary Fish pointed out to the British Minister, Sir Edward Thornton, that members of Congress had only been polite to Brown and "had spoken in a very different sense to him and had even declared their intention to oppose any such measure." Fish's tone, added the British minister in March 1874, was "most discouraging."[43]

This led Thornton to ruminate on the general nature of American policymaking with respect to Canada. Fish had told Thornton and Brown in private that he had "opposed the cessation of the treaty of 1854," but this view of Fish's meant little in the face of Congressional feelings about protection. "I have always found that he, like most statesmen in this country," observed Thornton, "endeavours to find out the opinions of influential members of Congress before he commits himself on any question. . . ."[44] This way of doing things had a particularly deadening impact on any formulation of State Department policy toward Canada because tariff reduction was the most important issue for Canadians. But even Fish's own views were decidedly cool toward a new treaty that did not guarantee access to the Canadian market for U.S. manufacturers. When Thornton presented the Canadian proposals in 1874, Fish had replied "is that all?" Upon being asked what he did want, the Secretary of State put, "the free admission of American manufacturers into Canada" as his top priority.[45]

Administration views were simply pulled along in the wake of majority opinion in Congress which was set against reciprocity with Canada. Speaker of House and future Secretary of State, James G. Blaine, told H.C. Rothery from the British Legation that he was "not prepared to accept the principles of the Reciprocity treaty, holding . . . that Canada ought to belong to the United States."[46] William Kelley, Republican Senator from Pennsylvania between 1861 and 1890, denounced the 1874 discussions as part of the familiar old British imperial plotting. "The story of the British army and navy," he began,

> is a continuous page of glory but in no sense has England made her most remunerative conquests by her army and navy. Diplomacy is the instrumentality by which these have been achieved and should the treaty now pending be submitted to by the American People, it would be the greatest of her diplomatic conquests.

Kelley then pointed to British commercial advances into the markets of Turkey, Portugal, and China and asserted that if reciprocity with Canada was now renewed, the "maritime frontier of the British provinces will be extended to the wharves of New York. . . ." To add drama to his picture of British-Canadian commercial penetration, Kelley could not resist adding a warning that "an ample channel would be provided for the approach of English war ships of light draught to our commercial metropolis." Kelley concluded with a reminder of Canada's role during the Civil War (besides getting in a twist on the revenue question) as he urged that "trade between the Dominion and us can be reciprocal only when the same flag shall wave over both countries and the people of each shall bear their share of the burdens imposed upon us by the recent war which the Canadians did so much to prolong."[47]

Senator Justin Morrill, author of the 1861 Tariff Act and one of the stalwart defenders of protectionism over the following forty years, also made a major speech against reciprocity with Canada. It is worth quoting at some length because the arguments deployed by Morrill reflected common American assumptions about Canada and revealed the basis of the American response to Canada for the remainder of the nineteenth century. Morrill began by proposing annexation as the best and simplest solution for Canada and the United States. Annexation would stimulate the Canadian economy out of its doldrums and, once Canada was part of the United States, she would no longer have to "fear becoming the American cock-pit in case of a war with Great Britain" (as she had been in 1812). He then made the point which was popular in post-Civil War Congresses that a reciprocity agreement with Canada would cut revenue and force higher taxes inside the United States. Besides, there was a constitutional issue at stake. Since reciprocal trade involved revenue, it was a congressional rather than an executive responsibility. Morrill proceeded to counter the argument that reciprocity would encourage Canada to improve its canals and railroads by reminding the Senate that Canada would continue with her transportation programs no matter what the United States did. As for the trade benefits to be derived, Morrill could see no advantages for the United States who had no need for the Canadian market and no need for foreign agricultural produce. "Our own territory," declared Morrill, "is sufficiently large to hold all the population of a first-rate power among nations, including the accretions of future centuries and we have a soil and climate so broad and various as to furnish all the chief products required by the most advanced civilization."

Morrill rounded on the Canadians for their continuing attachment to monarchy and empire and for their propensity for making sharp deals with the United States. "The Canadians are not yet republicans and very feebly yearn for their own national independence. Their devotion to royalty—of which we do not complain—is strong because it is afar off and is only less than their loyalty to the pursuit of gain." Ever since Britain had become a free trade country, Canada had been seeking desperately to gain access to the American market. "What more do they desire," Morrill demanded rhetorically, "now having a cheap market [Britain] from which to buy, than a dear market in which to sell, or such relations with the United States as will serve greater commercial prosperity without any of the incidences and responsibilities of annexation." It is "clearly the greed of trade which now prompts our neighbors who evidently are not inspired by the ambition which makes men dare to be masters of their own fate."

Morrill then turned to the argument made by some American proponents of reciprocity—that it would prepare the ground for annexation. The behavior of Canadians after the 1854 treaty and during the Civil War disproved this contention. Canadians had shown they were duplicitous. "There was," fulminated Morrill,

> hardly any greater malevolence exhibited towards the United States than that so offensively displayed by the ruling spirits of the Canadian Dominion. They coldly calculated the profit and loss of planting thorns in our bleeding sides . . . they hated the Union and would love us better in smaller and broken parcels. . . . This bait [of annexation] is growing stale and has strongly scented the trap.

Canada's ties to Britain ensured that no movement toward annexation would follow another trade agreement. "So long as the Canadians are bound to consult the interest and supremacy of the Imperial Government," Morrill summed up,

> it is, and will be impossible for them to offer any terms of reciprocity which can be to the advantage of the United States to accept. Our manufacturers do not want to meet Great Britain when they are nominally invited to meet the Canadians. . . . Our national patrimony should not be shared with the Canadas so long as they cling to greater expectations from other foreign relations.[48]

Morrill spoke for the protectionist, Republican constituency that was well represented by the National Association of Woollen Manufacturers. Back in the 1850s, when the imperial system had seemed about to disappear, Andrews had forecast that Canada would be a useful market for American textile manufacturers. But twenty years of Canadian tariffs and imperial expansion had shown how much Andrews had misjudged the future. By the 1870s American manufacturers wanted nothing to do with freer trade with Canada because they feared they would be in competition with cheaper British goods. The Association, in a memorandum to Secretary of

State Fish, denounced the reciprocity negotiations of 1874 and resolved at its annual meeting "that those who desire true free trade with Canada such as is enjoyed by the different states of a common country will find their hopes frustrated by a treaty which shall permit the Canadians to sell their natural products in the dearest market in the world while buying their chief manufactures in the cheapest." Like Seward and Morrill, the woollen manufacturers only saw the possibility of real movement if Canada agreed to cut her ties to the Empire. "We will welcome the Canadians to a free participation in the advantages of our markets," the memorandum concluded, "when they are prepared to be partakers of our burdens and defenders of our common nationality as thereby we may extend the line of our protective defenses and close the postern gate through which British goods now surreptitiously enter our country."[49]

One of the consequences of the American rejection of reciprocity in 1874 was that Canada turned to her own comprehensive policy of protective tariffs. When he came back to power in 1878, the Conservative leader John A. Macdonald began implementing his "national policy" to promote Canadian growth.[50] Under this policy the Canadian government continued to support the transportation project of the CPR; immigration was vigorously pursued in Britain and Europe to boost settlement of the Canadian west; and a tariff policy was put in place to nourish Canadian industry. Over the next several years the U.S. consuls in Ottawa reported on the impact of this new Canadian policy, but none of them saw it as threatening to the United States. Consul Barnett in 1880 pointed out that "the fiscal policy of Canada is [now] formed on the same principles as that of the United States," but he reckoned Canada could not duplicate the dynamic growth of the American economy. "Canada," he assured Assistant Under Secretary of State John Hay, "is not so well situated politically or geographically as the United States are for the development of native manufacturers." To support this contention, Barnett drew attention to the emigration of thousands of French Canadians since the 1830s to mill towns in New England which suggested that American conditions were more conducive to industrial success. The tide of emigration from Canada to the United States was proof enough of the "superior advantages and better opportunities" south of the border. It would be many years before this relative position of the two countries would change. "Not until the United States was much more densely populated and the struggle for existence consequently intensified will Canada begin to rise to that measure of prosperity of which its vast resources undoubtedly contain both the promise and the potency."[51]

Consul Barnett came down from these speculative heights to include in his report an assessment of the practical impact of the national policy. He acknowledged that American manufactured exports in Canada in 1880 "had fallen below any preceding year in a long period" but, on the other hand, the "principal article" in American exports (anthracite coal) had actually increased its share in the Canadian market by 25 percent. The consul concluded that "the duty of $.60 a ton has therefore failed to affect the trade; it having been found impossible to force Nova Scotia coal as far west as this point." Such arguments were always important for American observers to make because they supported the view that there were natural, North American trade patterns dictated by geography that Canada's policies cut across in an artificial manner.

If there seemed little likelihood of a Canadian, industrial take-off, to Consul Barnett's mind, there was great potential for growth in the natural resources business in Canada. Far from seeing this as threatening, Barnett argued that such growth presented opportunities for American businessmen and American capital. He pointed to the major American presence in the Ottawa Valley lumber industry as an example of American participation in such Canadian enterprises. "The mineral resources of this region have begun to attract the attention of American capitalists," he reported, "and as Americans have been mainly instrumental in developing the former [lumber resources] so do they seem destined to develop the latter." Americans would be able to take a leading role because, according to Barnett, there was a lack of economic energy in Canada attributable to the mixed nature of the Canadian population and to the artificial nature of the Canadian state. "Ottawa has all the characteristics of a capital created by Act of Parliament," he asserted.

> The same lack of homogeneity which distinguishes the people of the Dominion is to be found here in many ways; and though a similar admixture of races may be seen in some U.S. cities, even to a greater extent, here a prevalent feeling of uncertainty in regard to the future of the country deprives the political and social state of the most desirable elements of stability. French Canadians comprise nearly half the population and are much less enterprising than their English speaking fellow subjects.[52]

This consular report of 1880 assessed the national policy as an annoyance rather than a danger and suggested that natural trade patterns and energetic American businessmen would ensure that plenty of opportunities remained open in Canada. That Barnett's views were conventional enough can be seen from an exchange between Wharton Barker and James A. Garfield in the same year. The occasion was the consideration by the House Ways and Means Committee of commercial relations with Canada. The Dominion of Canada, Garfield was assured, "as we all know, is a purely artificial union of the English colonies which possesses no internal coherence." Canada persisted in maintaining close relations with Britain and the policy of Britain "looks toward the commercial isolation of the Dominion from the continent to which it belongs." Canada was deeply in debt and she looked to reciprocity to lift her out of difficult economic circumstances. In Barker's view however, the United States should be suspicious of Canadian overtures, for the Canadian definition of reciprocity as shown in her working of the 1854 treaty and in her 1874 proposals, was "one-sided and unfair."

Canada's "great object" was to gain access to the U.S. market for her agricultural products which of course would hurt the interests of "the farmers of our great West." Barker concluded that the long-term goals of the United States would be best served by refusing to enter into any more reciprocity arrangements. Reciprocity

> would leave Canada in her present position of commercial dependence upon England and would encourage her to continue that position by our removal of the disadvantages which would naturally accompany it. . . . It would leave her free to follow a policy hostile to the interest of the continent at large and European rather than American in its character."

The United States surely has the right, Barker insisted, to refuse closer ties until Canada "feels herself part of the great American continent and is not ready to lend herself to such glittering imperial schemes as recently found favor in the ministerial councils of the United Kingdom.[53]

3.

Canada's national policy had thus merely hardened the American unwillingness to enter into any new reciprocity agreement. This unwillingness was further intensified in the late 1880s and early 1890s when a series of incidents reinforced the critical view of Canada. The beginning of this renewed American criticism was the fisheries question once again. As part of the 1871 Treaty of Washington, this perennial issue in nineteenth-century Anglo-American relations had been settled by allowing American fishermen access to Canadian grounds while compensating Canada for the losses its fishing industry was likely to sustain (in addition, Canadian fish were given free entry to the U.S. market). The amount of compensation to be paid to Canada was to be determined by an arbitration commission on which Belgium was to serve as the neutral third party. In 1885, the commission finally awarded $5,500,000 to Canada. American officials and politicians were outraged by the size of the award. So outraged in fact, that the United States cancelled the fishery articles of the Washington Treaty.

From the outset, the fisheries question, as it had developed after the Washington Treaty, vexed Americans. Secretary of State Fish in 1873 objected to the naming of the Belgian King as the third commissioner. "Belgium was so completely under the control and protection of Great Britain," Fish told the British minister, "that the American people would never be persuaded that her representative could be anything but partial towards England."[54] When the award to Canada was made public, The *New York Herald* expostulated against the entire arrangement that was agreed to in 1871. "Under this compact and by means of sharp diplomatic practice, the United States has been mulcted out of $5,500,000 by an unjust Award. . . . This one-sided arrangement ought to be brought to a speedy end."[55] James G. Blaine, Speaker of the House, detected Canadian influence behind the decision by supplying biased arguments and slanted figures to the Commission. This was particularly galling to Blaine because he thought Canada should have had no role in the case. "The Dominion of Canada," he asserted, "had no more right to interpose in the matter than had the states of Massachusetts and Maine."[56] William Frye, Senator from Maine, denounced the award as "a most munificent gift to the Dominion of Canada because every single cent of it is a gift."[57]

The Canadian response to the U.S. abrogation of the fisheries articles of the Washington Treaty was to return to a strict interpretation of the 1818 Convention. Under the Canadian reading of the regulations it was well nigh impossible for American fishing vessels to legally enter Canadian ports. Secretary of State Thomas Bayard (as a member of the first Democratic administration since the Civil War) was anxious to improve relations with Britain and Canada, but even Bayard became exasperated with Canada over the fisheries question. Bayard asserted that there was no reason to deny American ships the right to buy supplies and to land their catches. Canadian actions were creating "exasperation and unneighborly feeling [leading] to collision between the inhabitants of the two countries." Bayard suggested pointedly that Canada was at the root of the trouble. Britain and the United States could settle the fisheries problem but normal diplomatic obligations had "become obscured by partisan advocacy or distorted by the heat of local interests." In June 1886 Bayard informed Lionel West, the British Minister, that there was "no possible justification . . . of such harsh and harassing action on the part of the provincial authorities against peaceful commerce."[58] In September the American Minister in London complained that "interference with American vessels by Canadian authorities is becoming more and more frequent and more and more flagrant in its disregard of treaty obligations and of the principles of comity and friendly intercourse."[59]

If the Democratic administration was insistent but correct in its condemnation of Canadian behavior over the fisheries, the Republicans in Congress and the press were much less restrained. The *New York Tribune* in August 1886 charged the Canadian authorities with committing "a series of outrages upon American fishing vessels and fishing crews." These harsh measures were "adopted by the Canadian government with the deliberate intention of forcing concessions from this Government." The *Tribune* berated the Cleveland administration for not responding more firmly to "the humiliation of our situation."[60] In face of this Republican criticism and Congressional pressure, Bayard began to lose patience, and by November 1886, his criticism of Canada was much sharper. The Secretary of State referred to one incident involving the schooner *Laura Sayward* out of Gloucester as "inhospitable and inhuman" as Canadian customs officials "refused to allow Captain Rose to buy sufficient food for himself and his crew to take them home." Such conduct was "wholly unworthy of any one entrusted with the execution of a public duty."[61] Secretary of the Treasury Manning joined in the chorus of complaints against Canada. He denounced her "reactionary fishery policy" and accused Canadian officials of having a "passionate spite" against Americans.[62] *The New York Times* applauded Secretary Manning's vigorous language which would "make Ottawa and London sit up." As for Canada's claim that she was simply enforcing the 1818 agreement, *The Times* responded that "the truth is that Canada's notion of forbidding certain of our vessels to visit her ports except when driven in by distress for the bare rights of hospitality, even though founded on the treaty language employed nearly seventy years ago, is contrary to the spirit of this progressive age."[63]

In Congress, a House Report in January 1887 spoke of "Canadian inhumanity" over the fisheries and criticized Canada for making an unjustified use of the 1818 agreement. Once again, the report asserted, Canada was abusing her ambiguous position in international affairs. She was part of the Empire and Britain conducted diplomacy on her behalf; and yet she undertook strong, independent action over the fisheries. The Report insisted that Canada had no right to interpret the treaty which was between the United States and Great Britain. The treaties of 1783 and 1818 "were made with the British Crown not with the Dominion of Canada. The Government at Washington is not called or required, or to be expected, either to deliberate or debate with Canada any more than is the British Crown with a separate member of our Union." Canada's aggressiveness over the fisheries was linked to her ambitious transportation policies, and the committee warned Canada she would face retaliatory action if such behavior continued. "It is difficult to believe," the report concluded,

> that Canada having within the last twenty years or so severely burdened herself with taxation by the construction of railways and bridges to bring about easy communication with Detroit, Chicago, St. Paul, and the whole west of our country, as well as with New York and Boston, will now deliberately and offensively enter upon and pursue a policy towards our fishermen which, if persisted in, can but end either in a suspension of commercial intercourse by land or sea between her and ourselves, or in consequences even more grave.[64]

The crisis over the fisheries was defused by the *modus vivendi* agreed to in 1888 by the joint Anglo-American commission meeting in Washington.[65] But the whole course of the fisheries dispute, from the Halifax award to the harassment of American vessels, kept alive the American mistrust of Canada. There was always the suspicion that Canada heated up the fishery issue to force the United States into trade negotiations (as had happened in 1854). In 1874, for example, George Brown complained to H.C. Rothery at the British Legation that "the United States always desired access to our fisheries and we ought to have made it a lever to compel the United States to accord us a more liberal tariff."[66] Again, in the Spring of 1884, Charles Tupper, Minister of Finance in Macdonald's cabinet, suggested to Secretary of State Freylinghuysen "that the fisheries question might perhaps be satisfactorily solved by a renewal of the Reciprocity Treaty of 1854 on the basis of the free exchange of the natural products of the two countries."[67] Also, the renewed Canadian pressure on the fisheries came at a time when there was a powerful public campaign for unrestricted reciprocity between Canada and the United States.[68] Thus, American policymakers never accepted that Canada was simply trying to protect her own fisheries but suspected Canada of manipulating the fishery question to force tariff concessions.

This image of Canada was sustained by other Canadian actions in the late 1880s and early 1890s, most notably by Canadian interference in a related matter, U.S. negotiations with Newfoundland. At this time Newfoundland was still a separate colony (she did not become a province in Canada until 1949) and the United States was interested in negotiating an agreement which would allow Newfoundland fish into the United States duty-free, in return for concessions to the U.S. over local fishing regulations off the coasts of Newfoundland. In 1890, an agreement between the United States and Newfoundland was almost in place. The Canadian government acted energetically to stop this proposed convention by urging the imperial government to disallow Newfoundland's attempt to reach a separate accord with the United States. Lord Stanley of Preston, the Canadian Governor General, informed the Colonial office in 1890 that his ministers reacted "with alarm at the proposed convention between Newfoundland and the United States."[69] Sir Terence O'Brien, the Governor of Newfoundland, complained frequently about the blocking role being played by Canada. "My responsible advisors," he informed the Marquis of Ripon, "strongly protest against the interests of Newfoundland being sacrificed to those of the Canadian Dominion."[70] In July 1890, Secretary of State Blaine, in a note to Julian Pauncefote, the British Minister, complained about Canada's role. Blaine stated it was clear that negotiations between the United States and Newfoundland "abruptly closed because the Canadian government objected." This Canadian intervention "against the conclusion of a Convention which had been virtually agreed upon except as to details was in the President's belief a grave injustice to the Government of the United States."[71]

Canada's trouble-making over the fisheries question and her interference in the negotiations with Newfoundland came at a time when Canada began to play a central role in the reinvigorated imperialism of the late nineteenth century. To be in the vanguard of the movement for imperial consolidation gave Canada a sense of power and a sense of purpose in North America which otherwise would have been difficult to create, in view of the disparity between Canadian and American power. In the 1891 election in Canada, John A. Macdonald ran on a platform that emphasized the success of the national policy in keeping Canada in the British Empire. In 1897, the new Liberal government of Wilfrid Laurier introduced an imperial preference tariff which allowed British goods to enter Canada at a lower rate than American and foreign merchandise. Throughout these years, the Imperial Federation League, dedicated to strengthening the military and economic links between Britain and her colonies, had two English Canadian leaders, George Parker and George Dennison. When the Boer War broke out in South Africa in 1899, English Canadians were enthusiastic in wishing to respond to the jingoistic call to arms from Joseph Chamberlain.[72] This imperial activism in Canada helped keep alive—in official and Congressional circles in Washington—the old critique about Canada's role in British commercial imperialism. In the late 1880s and early 1890s the most energetic and articulate spokesman for this critique of Canada was Joseph Nimmo. Speaking before the Senate Committee on relations with Canada in 1890, he emphasized the plan of the Canadian government in "controlling for political purposes a railroad across the continent."[73] The same committee was told by Josiah J. White, President of the New York City Chamber of Commerce, that the United States was menaced

> by the realisation of that ancient policy of Great Britain which has successfully wrested from us the ocean-carrying business of even our own products and now seeks to secure what naturally belongs to American transportation lines, viz. the overland carrying trade by which the most rapid transit is offered to commerce between the continents of Asia and Europe.[74]

The Senate Committee was then presented with a historical assessment of the CPR which placed it squarely within the pattern of British commercial imperialism. The CPR project, in William C. Coffin's account, was conceived back in 1858 as a key link between Britain and Asia. The creation of the Dominion of Canada in 1867 was part of this grand plan. "The object from that time to the completion of the road . . . [was] to become the great thoroughfare between England on the one hand, and China, Japan, Australia and the islands of the Pacific on the other—the shortest and quickest possible line of communication between these countries." Coffin added some drama to his case by describing his investigative travels. He reminded the senators that Vancouver was 500 miles closer to Yokohama than was San Francisco. When in India, Coffin noted that the railroad ties in the Ganges Valley had been cut in British Columbia. In Victoria he saw ships from Canton and Shanghai bringing in tea consigned to Chicago, St. Paul, St. Louis, Cincinnati, Detroit, New York, and Boston via the CPR. "In the commercial history of the world," Coffin asserted, "no nation has ever approached Great Britain in completeness, thoroughness and far reaching policy."[75]

Anthony Higgins, Republican Senator from Delaware, summed up this critical view of Canadian railroad policies during an 1892 debate.

The CPR is a "Canadian Government railway" and plans were afoot to add to its reach by subsidizing steamer routes at either end of it on the Atlantic and the Pacific. The CPR and the Dominion Government "are now making strenuous efforts to establish a line of British steamers between Vancouver, British Columbia, and Australia and New Zealand . . . at once driving from the seas the American steamer line now employed on the route between San Francisco and Australia, touching at Honolulu, Apia, Auckland and Sydney." Higgins, like Coffin and Nimmo, saw a long history to this Canadian policy and linked it to anti-American actions during the Civil War. "The entire scheme of Canadian commercial aggression," he thundered, "was conceived and inaugurated during the late war of rebellion in this country, largely upon military considerations and is now accompanied by a formidable naval and military establishment on the island of Vancouver."[76]

All these tirades of Higgins, Nimmo, and Coffin were partisan, reflecting the special interests for which they spoke. They represented the Pennsylvania and New York railways which thought their profits were suffering from CPR competition; they spoke for the shipping and railway companies which hoped to secure subsidies and favors from the U.S. Government similar to those granted to British lines. Nevertheless, the public airing of this condemnation of Canada and the way in which Canadian policies were put into a historical context (which dredged up memories of her actions during the Civil War) show how easy it was in this age of imperialism to mount effective public criticism of Canada.

That critical view, while dramatically depicted by interested parties inside and outside of Congress, was also shared by American cabinet members. An example of this mode of thinking with respect to Canada can be seen from correspondence between Secretary of State Blaine and President Harrison in 1891 on the subject of Hawaii. Blaine warned the President of Canadian designs on Hawaii as part of an ambitious plan to supplant the United States in the trade of the Pacific basin. The Secretary of State endorsed the case made in *The Reviw of Reviews,*

> while England is comparatively indifferent to American domination in Hawaii, it is quite otherwise with Canada, who is habitually sensitive about her great neighbor's ascendance. Especially are the commercial interests of British Columbia, and peculiarly so those of the CPR, concerned to supplant San Francisco in the trade with Australia. . . . Yankee influence in Hawaii is hence obnoxious to Canada as interposing a barrier to the Australia trade as well as being a general obstacle to Canadian influence in the Pacific.

Blaine concluded with a warning that these Canadian designs meant "there is a good deal of trouble brewing in those islands."[77]

Within Canada, the U.S. Consul in Ottawa added to the refrain of condemnation. In 1889 Consul Hotchkiss, angered by an export tax placed on raw timber, penned a diatribe to the State Department. "Canada," he fumed, [was] apparently bent upon a system of hostile legislation." The U.S. Consul traced this sharp anti-American policy to the revitalized imperial sentiment or "the British Confederation fact" as he described the Imperial Federation movement.[78] Canada's canal toll policy, which had raised the ire of Americans during the 1854 treaty years, also resurfaced at this time to expand the range of American annoyance. Once again the Canadians instituted a rebate system for vessels that passed all the way through the canal system from the upper lakes to Montreal. American ships off-loading at New York ports did not qualify for the rebate and so found themselves paying higher tolls than Canadian ships. The Lake Carriers Association based in Cleveland made a vigorous protest to the State Department and to Congress. "All efforts to secure a just interpretation of the treaty rights of American citizens," the complaint ran, "have been met in a spirit of evasion, avoidance and delay. Such conduct is not only dishonest in purpose and deceitful in method but almost reaches the point of contumely and insult."[79] The solicitor to the State Department, Frank L. Rutledge, advised Secretary of State Blaine that the Canadian practice was discriminatory and violated the treaty. The second Assistant Secretary of State, Alvin Adee, endorsed this view and added that it was yet another example of Canada arranging matters to divert exports from American ports to Montreal. The Canadian explanation for their policy, Adee informed Blaine, "fails to meet the just complaints of the United States."[80]

Blaine was angry with the Canadians for their failure to alter their system which, he said, they had promised to do during a meeting in Washington. "The more serious phase of the situation," he explained to President Harrison, "is that instead of rescinding the discriminatory canal tolls of which this Government complains, the Canadian ministry, after the return of their commissioners from their visit to Washington . . . re-issued without any communication with this government, the order to continue discrimination." Canadian intransigence on this matter led to a presidential rebuke. In a message to Congress preparing the way for retaliatory measures, President Harrison declared in July 1892 there was "no doubt that a serious discrimination against our citizens and our commerce exists and quite as little doubt that this discrimination is not the incident but the purpose of the Canadian regulations."[81]

This accumulating annoyance with Canada paved the way for an American rejection of Canadian overtures for reciprocity in 1891-92. The McKinley tariff increases of 1890 led to these Canadian advances, but the Republican administration was in no frame of mind to listen sympathetically. In an exchange between the President and Secretary of State in the fall of 1891, even before discussions got under way, Blaine set out their mutual understanding. "I see you are equally anxious and equally determined," Blaine wrote to Harrison,

> that there shall be no treaty made. We can make a good point on them by reciting that every Reciprocity Treaty made was one giving our own articles in exchange for different articles produced in other countries and not the same for the same. Canada can offer nothing that we cannot duplicate and that we do not actually duplicate; so our answer when the efforts for a treaty are rejected will be easy and logical.[82]

President Harrison elaborated on this theme that reciprocity with Canada was impossible and placed the matter in the context of Republican protectionist policy as it had developed since the Civil War. He reminded his Secretary of State that "it was absolutely essential that we should confine our reciprocity regulations within such limits as not to attack the protective system—in other words, to the admission to our markets of non-competing goods as much as possible." Harrison was convinced that Canada could never fit into such a scheme. "I have never seen," Harrison wrote to Blaine,

> how we could arrange a basis of reciprocity with Canada short of a complete customs union, by which they should adapt our tariff and everything should be free between the two countries. This would be an absolute commercial union and is probably not practicable unless it is accompanied by political union.[83]

This statement of the U.S. position by Harrison in 1892 was exactly the line taken by Seward in the tense years after the Civil War.

The Canadian approach to the United States in 1892 did nothing to soften American views. The British minister in Washington informed the State Department that Canada wished to set up a conference to discuss the canal toll issue and the question of reciprocal trade.[84] Canada appeared to be using the canal tolls as a lever to press the United States into negotiations for lower tariffs, in much the same way she had used the fisheries problem back in 1854. This simply intensified the American negative response. In their various replies to the Canadian proposals, Harrison and Blaine took pains to draw attention to the obstacles posed by Canada's role in the Empire. Reporting on the failure of discussions, the President informed the Senate that

> a reciprocity treaty limited to the exchange of natural products would have been such in form only. The benefits of such a treaty would have accrued almost wholly to Canada. . . . A treaty that should be reciprocal in fact and of mutual advantage must necessarily have embraced an important list of manufactured articles and have secured to the United States a free and favored introduction of those articles into Canada against the world.[85]

This, of course, would have required Canada to give preferential entry to American over British merchandise and the administration knew that Canada could not do this because of her commitment to the Empire. "As Canada was part of the British Empire," Blaine explained, the Dominion government could not "enter into any commercial arrangement with the United States from the benefits of which Great Britain and its colonies should be excluded."[86]

Blaine rubbed in this point about the problems caused by Canada's imperial orientation. During the discussions, he told the Canadians that Canada could expect better access to the American market only if she was prepared to cut her imperial ties with Britain. Blaine seemed to take pleasure in spelling out the consequences. Canada, Blaine intimated, "would then be in the same position in trade and industrial matters as a state of the union." He also expected that, in such an eventuality, Canada would be only a supplier of agricultural products and raw materials to the rest of the union. She would be a "non-manufacturing and mainly an agricultural state."[87]

The American rejection of reciprocity in 1892 was sharper than it had been in 1874. To some extent this reflected Blaine's more blustery manner compared to Hamilton Fish and Blaine's penchant for parading an anglophobic image for the benefit of the Republican party, but it also reflected the development of American attitudes toward Canada since the signing of the first reciprocity treaty in 1854. All American observers in the 1850s had shared the assumption that the North American colonies were disengaging themselves from Britain. Even those like Secretary of State Marcy, who understood that the 1854 treaty would ensure Canada's allegiance to the empire by removing the economic argument for annexation, believed that Canada would gradually become Americanized in terms of culture.

Yet events of the next forty years had contradicted those assumptions of the 1850s. Canada had increased tariffs against U.S. manufactures; the colonies had joined together in a transcontinental Dominion which undertook ambitious transportation schemes to divert trade from U.S. routes; she was (with British backing) apparently bent on extending such policies into the Pacific basin with an eye to channeling the China and Japan trade through Canada to the markets of the United States and Europe; English Canadians joined enthusiastically in the imperial movement in the 1880s and 1890s; and major British naval bases at Halifax on the Atlantic coast and Esquimault on the Pacific provided tangible physical confirmation of her role in the Empire. As well as participating in this commercial imperialism, Canada, taking advantage of her ambiguous position in the diplomatic world, had proved to be an untrustworthy and occasionally deceitful agent in dealings with the United States. She had treated American fishermen "inhumanely." She had tried to use the fisheries issue and the canal tolls issue to pressure the United States into tariff concessions. She had broken up a treaty between the United States and Newfoundland. Secretary of State Blaine's hard words and dismissive attitude in 1892 encapsulated four decades of American frustration over the course being pursued by Canada.

This frustration with Canada was not a fundamental molding force in American policy, for by this time, the United States was such a power on the continent that it had nothing to fear from Canada. The nature of the American response by the end of the nineteenth century was nicely summed up by Samuel E. Moffatt, chief editorial writer of the *New York Journal* who prided himself on his knowledge of American views of Canada. "The American policy is simple," Moffatt began, "It is based upon the fact that the United States is, and intends to remain, the paramount power in the western hemisphere." The one force working against this American hegemony was Canada, that now strengthening remnant of the British Empire in North America. Other European powers had demonstrated their acceptance of American hemispheric power by withdrawing from the continent, as Russia had done with Alaska in 1867, but Britain had remained and augmented her presence through the Canadian confederation. From the American viewpoint, this had created an "unfortunate situation in Canada." The economic development in the Great Lakes basin, characterized by the emergence of great cities such as Buffalo, Cleveland, Detroit, and Chicago, was a prominent feature of America's growth as an industrial power. "But for the position of Canada," argued Moffatt, they would rest in perfect security. No enemy could ever get at them. . . . Nowhere in the world is the key of one country's treasury thus left in the hands of another. The nearest position to such a situation is the position of Russia, with the Dardanelles in possession of Turkey. But Russia's interests in the Black Sea do not compare with those of the United States in the Great Lakes. Odessa, Batum and Sebastapol are a small stake beside Chicago, Cleveland, Buffalo, Detroit, Milwaukee, Toledo and Duluth.

To be sure, Canada was not strong enough to be an actual threat to the United States but, warned Moffatt, "it is evident that this position of Canada is one that needs to be treated with the utmost circumspection." Moffatt concluded by turning to a metaphor that aptly summed up the attitude of Blaine, Harrison, and Bayard, those Republican and Democratic cabinet officers who had dealt with Canada on the fisheries and canal tolls and of lobbyists like Nimmo who had castigated Canada's imperial transport schemes. "A cinder in the eye," declared Moffatt, "may be bearable so long as it rests quietly but if it begins to wriggle around and attract attention to itself the victim is likely to express annoyance."[88]

Notes

1. Carl Berger, *The Sense of Power: Studies in the Ideas of Canadian Imperialism, 1867-1914* (Toronto: University of Toronto Press, 1970).
2. Israel D. Andrews to Lewis Cass, 15 April 1857, in William R. Manning, *Diplomatic Correspondence of the United States: Canadian Relations, 1784-1860* 4 vols. (Washington, DC: Carnegie Endowment for International Peace, 1940), 4:688-89.
3. *The American Economist* 6(8 November 1889):299-300.
4. William Marcy to Israel D. Andrews, 24 March 1855, in Manning, *Diplomatic Correspondence*, 4:108-9.
5. Ibid., Israel D. Andrews to William Marcy, Boston, 2 July 1855, 4:626- 27.
6. Ibid., Canfield Dorwin to William Marcy, Montreal, 1 November 1854, 3:606.
7. Ibid., B. Hammett Norton to William March, Pictou, 20 March 1854, 3:539.
8. Ibid., Canfield Dorwin to William Marcy, 9 October 1855, 3:646.
9. J.M.S. Careless, *The Union of the Canadas: The Growth of Canadian Institutions, 1841-1867* (Toronto: McClelland and Stewart, 1967), 145-46. Careless points out that tariff policies in the Union laid the foundation for the post-Confederation national policy.
10. Senator Morrill in 1855 declared, "Our Reciprocity Treaty with the Canadas was so obviously unequal and jug-handled." Congressional Debates on Reciprocity, U.S. Congress, *Sen. Doc.* No. 80, 62d Cong., 1st sess., 1911, 2893; Charles Pepper to Secretary of State Knox, 24 May 1910, SDDF 1910-1929, Box 5795, RG 59, National Archives.

11. Wyman B.S. Moor to Lewis Cass, Montreal, 31 December 1857, in Manning, *Diplomatic Correspondence,* 4:711-12; Ibid., Moor to Assistant Secretary of State John Appleton, Montreal, 11 December 1858, 4:749-50.
12. Ibid., Wyman B. S. Moor to Lewis Cass, Montreal, 23 January 1860, 4:834-36.
13. Israel T. Hatch to Howell Cobb, Secretary of the Treasury, 28 March 1860, *Sen. Doc.* No. 80, 62d. Cong., 1st sess. [hereafter cited as Hatch Report 1860].
14. Report of J.W. Taylor, *House Misc. Doc.* 96, 36th Cong., 1st sess.
15. Paper on Canadian Affairs 1863, Joshua Giddings to George W. Julien, Montreal, 12 April 1864, Giddings-Julian Correspondence, Reel 3, Michigan State University Libraries.
16. Ibid.
17. Andrew Potter to William Seward, Montreal, 31 July 1865, 23 August 1865, 2 November 1865, Despatches from U.S. Consuls in Montreal, Reel 7, National Archives.
18. Ibid., 5 August 1865, 13 August 1865.
19. Ibid., 26 June 1865.
20. Consul Potter explained to President Johnson that when he arrived as Consul-General in 1864 he "found a very large party in these Provinces, led by rebel emissaries from the South and encouraged by the political organs of the Canadian Government animated by a bitter hostility to the Government of the United States and loud in the expression of their desire that the Union of the States should be severed and our national power forever destroyed." Ibid., Potter to President Johnson, Montreal, 26 September 1866.
21. There is an extensive literature on responsible government and Canada's place in the Empire in the middle and late decades of the nineteenth century. The best starting point for the 1840s and 1850s is Careless, *The Union of the Canadas.* Berger, *The Sense of Power* and *Imperial Nationalism; A Conflict in Canadian Thought* (Toronto: Copp Clark, 1969) are the authoritative treatments of the late nineteenth century.
22. Careless, 145-46.
23. W.L. Morton, *The Critical Years: Canada 1857-1873* (Toronto: McClelland and Stewart, 1964).
24. Ibid., 21-40, 245-62.
25. Memorandum on the Federation of the British North American Provinces, 4 November 1858, Public Record Office (PRO), London, CO 880 21/x1.
26. George E. Cartier, Jonathan Ross, and Alexander T. Galt to Sir Edward Lytton, London, 25 October 1858, PRO, CO 880/2/xxxviii.
27. C.R. Williams, ed., *Diary and Letters of Rutherford B. Hayes, Nineteenth President of the United States* vols.1-?? (Columbus: The Columbus Archaeological and Historical Society, 1922), 3:529.
28. Robin Winks, *Canada and the United States: The Civil War Years* (Baltimore: The Johns Hopkins University Press, 1960), 375.
29. *U.S. Railroad & Mining Register,* Philadelphia, 6 April 1867.
30. Theodore Barnett to John Hay, Ottawa, 6 December 1880, Despatches from U.S. Consuls in Ottawa, M643, Reel 1, National Archives.

31. Select Committee on Relations with Canada submitted by Mr. Hoar, 21 July 1890, Senate Report 1530, Part 2, 51st Cong., 1st sess.
32. Lord Kimberley to Lord Lisgar, Downing Street, 16 March 1872, PRO, CO 880/6/67.
33. Earl Granville to Sir Edward Thornton, London, 14 July 1870, PRO, CO 880/6/67.
34. Ibid., Earl Granville to Sir Alured Clarke, Inspection General of Fortifications, June 1886, PRO, CO, 880/9/116.
35. Ibid., Committee Appointed on Behalf of the Admiralty, Colonial Office, Post Office, Treasury and War Office, PRO, CO, 880/9/116.
36. Ibid., Frederick Stanley Memorandum to the Cabinet, 14 January 1886, PRO CO 880/9/115. Report of Committee on Subsidizing a Line of Steamers to Vancouver, PRO CO 880/10/124.
37. Edward W. Watkin, *Canada and the States: Recollections, 1851 to 1886* (London: Ward Lock and Company, 1887), 58.
38. William H. Seward to Andrew Johnson, 2 July 1868, Andrew Johnson Papers, Ser. 1, Reel 33, Michigan State University Libraries.
39. Consul Averill to William H. Seward, Montreal, 15 March 1867, Despatches from U.S. Consuls in Montreal 1850-1906, Reel 8, vol. 8, National Archives.
40. Memorandum on Relations between Great Britain and the United States, January 1908, PRO, FO 414/210.
41. William H. Seward to Andrew Johnson, 2 February 1867, Andrew Johnson Papers, Ser. 18, Reel 55, Michigan State University Libraries.
42. Frederick Bruce to Earl of Clarendon, Washington, 11 February 1866, PRO, CO 880/6/47a.
43. Edward Thornton to Earl of Derby, Washington, 30 March 1874, PRO, FO 414/33; Lester B. Shippee, *Canadian-American Relations, 1849-1874* (New Haven, CT: Yale University Press, 1939), 463-71.
44. Edward Thornton to Earl Granville, Washington, 26 January 1874, PRO, CO 880/7 72.
45. Edward Thornton to Earl of Derby, 2 March 1874, PRO, FO 414/33.
46. H.C. Rothery to Earl Granville, Washington, 9 February 1874, PRO, FO 414/33.
47. Edward Thornton to Earl of Derby, Washington, 2 November 1874, PRO, FO 414/33; on this general topic of American anglophobia in commercial matters, see Edward Crapol, *America for Americans: Economic Nationalism and Anglophobia in the Late Nineteenth Century* (Westport, CT: Greenwood Press, 1973).
48. Congressional Record, 4 February 1875; Edward Thornton to Earl of Derby, Washington, 8 February 1875, PRO, FO 414/34.
49. *New York Tribune*, 4 July 1874; R.G. Watson to Earl of Derby, Washington, 13 July 1874, PRO, FO 414/33.
50. R.C. Brown, *Canada's National Policy 1883-1900: A Study in Canadian American Relations* (Princeton, NJ: Princeton University Press, 1964).
51. Theodore Barnett to John Hay, Ottawa, 6 December 1880, Despatches from U.S. Consuls in Ottawa, Reel 1, National Archives.
52. Ibid.

53. Wharton Barker to James A. Garfield, 27 April 1880, *Hse. Doc.* 1417, 61st Cong., 3rd sess., 1911.
54. Edward Thornton to Earl Granville, 11 August 1873, PRO, FO 414/33.
55. *New York Herald*, 10 February 1883.
56. James G. Blaine, *Political Discussions, Legislative, Diplomatic and Popular, 1856-1886* (Norwich: The Henry Bill Publishing Company, 1887), 179.
57. Lionel West to Earl Granville, Washington, 11 January 1883, PRO, FO 414/54.
58. Thomas F. Bayard to Lionel West, 10 May 1886 and 1 June 1886, PRO, CO 880/9/118.
59. Minister Phelps to Earl of Iddlesleigh, London, 11 September 1886, PRO, CO 880/9/118.
60. *New York Tribune*, August 1886; Lionel West to Earl of Iddlesleigh, Washington, 26 August 1886, PRO, CO 880/9/118.
61. Thomas F. Bayard to Lionel West, Washington, 11 November 1886, PRO, CO 880/10/121.
62. Lionel West to Marquis of Salesburg, Washington, 15 January 1887, PRO, CO 880/10/121.
63. *The New York Times*, 13 January 1887.
64. *House Report*, No. 3648, 49th Cong., 2d sess., 112, 117, 118.
65. Brown, 63-90; Charles C. Tansill, *Canadian-American Relations, 1875-1911* (New Haven, CT: Yale University Press, 1943), 1-120.
66. H.C. Rothery to Earl Granville, New York, 24 November 1873, PRO, FO 414/33.
67. Lionel West to Earl Granville, Washington, 28 April 1884, PRO, FO 414/54.
68. Brown, 125-60.
69. Lord Stanley of Preston to Lord Knutsford, 19 November 1890, PRO, CO 880/12/143.
70. Sir Terence O'Brien to Marquis of Ripon, 3 January 1894, PRO, CO 880/14/168.
71. James G. Blaine to Julian Pauncefote, Bar Harbor, 19 July 1890, Benjamin Harrison Papers, Ser. 1, Reel 28, Michigan State University Libraries.
72. Berger, *The Sense of Power.*
73. Senate Select Committee, *Sen. Doc.* 1530, 51st Cong., 1st sess., 1890, 885-935.
74. *Senate Report*, No. 847, 51st Cong., 1st sess., 1889-1890, 301-302.
75. Ibid., 465-70.
76. *Sen. Misc. Doc.*, No. 217, 52d. Cong., 1st. sess., 1892.
77. James G. Blaine to Benjamin Harrison, 16 September 1891 and Benjamin Harrison to James G. Blaine, 18 September 1891, Benjamin Harrison Papers, Ser. 1, Reel 33, Michigan State University Libraries.
78. James Hotchkiss to William Wharton, Ottawa, 19 January 1889, Despatches from U.S. Consuls in Ottawa, Reel 4. In a phrase recalling American reaction to the 1854 treaty, Hotchkiss told Wharton, "the import is repulsive through its jug-handle feature." Idem, 4 May 1889.
79. U.S. Congress, *Hse. of Rep. Rpt.* 1957, 52d Cong., 1st sess., 1891-92.

80. U.S. Congress, *Sen. Ex. Doc.* No. 114, 52d Cong., 1st sess., 1892.
81. Ibid.
82. James G. Blaine to Benjamin Harrison, Augusta, Maine., 29 September 1891, Benjamin Harrison Papers, Sec. 1, Reel 33, Michigan State Univesity Libraries.
83. Ibid., Benjamin Harrison to James G. Blaine, 1 October 1891.
84. U.S. Congress, *Sen. Ex. Doc.*, No. 114, 52d Cong., 1st sess. 1892.
85. Ibid.
86. Ibid.
87. Minutes and Proceedings of Washington Conference in 1892 for the Discussion of a Commercial Arrangement and Adjustment of Questions Pending between the United States and the Dominion of Canada, enclosed in Charles Turner to Assistant Secretary of State David Hill, Ottawa, 2 December 1902, Despatches from U.S. Consuls in Ottawa, Reel 10, National Archives.
88. Samuel E. Moffatt, "How America Really Feels Towards England," *The Living Age: A Weekly Magazine of Contemporary Life and Thought* (14 September 1901):666-74 in Theodore Roosevelt Papers, Series 1, Reel 18, Michigan State University Libraries.

IV
"Broad Questions of National Policy"
1892-1911

In 1892, the Republican administration led by Harrison and Blaine refused to consider the possibility of reciprocity with Canada; in 1911, a Republican administration led by President Howard Taft and Secretary of State Philander C. Knox worked energetically to promote a reciprocal trade agreement with Canada. In 1892, Harrison and Blaine concluded that Canada could never fit into American economic needs because she duplicated American agricultural production; in 1911, Taft and Knox argued that Canada's agricultural and natural resources were urgently needed by the United States. What caused this complete turnaround in American thinking?

It is tempting to explain the reversal as a consequence of the diplomatic rapprochement that took place between the United States and Britain during this period. One aspect of this rapprochement was the settling of a number of vexing issues, such as the fisheries question and the dispute over the Bering Sea seal harvest, which had bedeviled Canadian-American relations. From the settlement of the Alaska boundary dispute in 1903 to the Passamoquody Bay agreement in 1910, all outstanding issues were cleared from the diplomatic deck. The success of this diplomacy had a great deal to do with the energy and intelligence of James Bryce, the British ambassador in Washington, and the effective relationship he established with Secretary of State Elihu Root. The Canadian Prime Minister, Wilfrid Laurier, wrote to Bryce in 1910, "You have so efficiently cleared the slate that really there is nothing of much importance to be addressed. . . . Our relations now are closer and more friendly than they ever were at any time and for this happy condition the largest share must be allowed you."[1]

There is no doubt that the Anglo-American rapprochement created a favorable context for the rethinking of the American response to

Canada. Following Canada's acceptance of the Boundary Waters Agreement in 1910, Root complimented Bryce and observed that their combined work had inaugurated a new order in relations with Canada. Root wrote of "a new departure of the greatest importance."[2] But the rapprochement, it must be remembered, had not been all plain sailing. In the Alaska boundary matter, for example, President Roosevelt had been angered by the Canadian claim which he viewed as "an outrage pure and simple." Roosevelt reluctantly went along with the solution of an Arbitration Commission but remained convinced that the Canadian position was "outrageous and indefensible" which made Canadian claims for compensation "dangerously near to blackmail."[3] On the Canadian side, there was resentment that Britain was once again sacrificing Canadian claims for the sake of better relations with the United States. The rapprochement was first and foremost a British agenda rather than a Canadian one. But even if these crosscurrents of tension are ignored, the improved diplomatic climate still does not explain why a Republican administration would turn so wholeheartedly to reciprocity in 1911. James Bryce, the central figure in Anglo-American-Canadian relations at this time, saw no prospect for such a shift in American policy. Writing to Foreign Secretary Grey as late as 1908 Bryce reported, "there does not seem to be the smallest chance that Congress will look at such a policy. . . . Protection is far too strong to permit even the policy of reciprocity with Canada to have a fair chance."[4]

That Bryce saw no connection between rapprochement and reciprocity is telling evidence that other factors were at work reshaping American thinking on this hoary issue. One of these factors actually cut against the grain of rapprochement. By the first decade of the new century, with Canada's economy booming and with the tariff reform movement led by Joseph Chamberlain making an impact in Britain, it seemed that Canada might be heading decisively and permanently into an imperial pattern of development. Since 1867, the refusal of the United States to change her high tariff stance toward Canada had backfired. Instead of bringing Canada to plead for annexation it had contributed to the emergence of a separate power on the continent. Goldwin Smith, the former Regius Professor of Modern History at Oxford, who was convinced that the United States and Canada formed a natural, unified market and that the two countries should work toward closer union, attributed American failure to the blindness of U.S. tariff policy. All expectations about the end of the British Empire in North America were now exposed as false because of the narrowness of the Republican approach to tariffs.

"The emergence on the north of this continent," Smith observed, "of a power antagonistic to the American Republic and its institutions would be such a monument to the weakness of American statesmanship as I believe would have few parallels in the annals of political misadventure."[5]

This view that since the Civil War American policy toward Canada had failed and had contributed to the emergence of Canada as a power in her own right, was also held by British policymakers at the turn of the century. A secret report prepared for the Foreign Office in 1908 concluded that American intransigence on tariff matters had indeed turned Canada decisively on to an imperial course. The report outlined the establishment of U.S. dominance on the continent by mid-century and noted the next stage of expansion during the 1890s as the United States acquired Hawaii, the Philippines, and intervened in Central America. But this steady enlargement of American influence (which the Foreign Office by 1908 accepted as natural and beneficial for British interests) encountered its only check by the counter-growth of Canada. With the benefit of hindsight, and with a perspective provided by the new imperial spirit which had emerged since the late 1880s, the British officials now viewed the development of Canada since 1867 as part of a plan to provide an imperial counterweight to American power. The British North America Act of 1867, according to the Foreign Office report, "was not only a great act of policy but also . . . the sharpest check which the extreme pretensions advanced in pursuance of the Monroe doctrine had yet received." Since 1867, a hostile American attitude had stimulated a spirit of nationalism in Canada. To be sure, Canada had gone through a difficult economic patch from the 1870s to the 1890s; but by 1900, instead of losing population to the United States, Canada was now receiving thousands of American immigrants to the booming Prairie provinces. This economic success story in Canada, as she consolidated her hold on the northern part of the continent, was now tied into plans for strengthening economic cooperation throughout the Empire. The imperial preference tariff introduced by the Laurier government in 1897 had increased British exports to Canada from £ 7 million in 1899 to £ 17 million in 1906.[6] As they took stock of events in the past fifty years, the Foreign Office agreed with Goldwin Smith that British policy with respect to Canada had turned out to be a success in contrast to the failure of American policy to bring Canada within the American sphere of influence.

This reading of the situation in North America was one of the basic influences at work in 1911. On numerous occasions (both private and public) President Taft set out the case for reciprocity on the grounds that it would stop Canada's unnatural gravitation back toward Britain and the Empire. Speaking to a press banquet in New York, Taft urged that the time had come to turn Canada back into an American path of development. He explained that the United States must act quickly

> because no such opportunity will ever come again. . . . The forces that are at work in England and Canada to separate her by a Chinese wall from the United States and to make her part of an imperial commercial bond reaching from England around the world to England again by a system of preferential tariffs will derive an impetus from the rejection of this treaty.[7]

In Taft's mind the reversal in Republican policy between 1892 and 1911 was impelled by the need to prevent Canada from growing into an autonomous and imperial power. Thus, far from being a byproduct of rapprochement, the reciprocity policy was, in part, a fearful reaction to Canada's revitalization within the Empire.

1.

This perceived need to try a new tack with Canada could not in itself have led to a policy of reciprocity because reciprocity was above all a question of tariffs and there would have been no movement on tariffs unless some fundamental changes in domestic American politics were underway. The American tariff stance had been at the heart of the American response to Canada since 1866 and any new initiative would necessarily involve significant change in tariff rates. These changes could not be induced by developments in Canada alone (as was evident in 1866, 1874, and 1892). But by 1911 there were fractures within the Republican position which opened up the possibility of a reciprocal trade treaty with Canada.[8] By 1908, the protectionist policy of successive Republican administrations was under renewed attack from the Democrats who took up the cost-of-living issue on behalf of workers and consumers in northeastern and midwestern industrial cities. Within the Republican party those who preferred a stand-pat policy of no tariff changes were under some pressure from tariff-revision advocates who argued that the stand-patters would bring electoral disaster to the party. The tariff issue was linked to a fear that the population pressure on available food supplies in the United States would further drive up the cost of living in the cities. All these internal factors intersected with growing American worries that since the 1890s Canada had been pulling away from her natural destiny (which would keep her in a secondary and dependent status to the U.S.) and was heading on an imperial course of development that would be harmful to American hegemony on the continent. Another tendency in domestic politics that influenced American thinking on Canada was the concern over declining natural resources in the United States, an issue that was given publicity by Theodore Roosevelt. In 1908, the former president organized a national conference on the topic, on the grounds that, as he told Secretary of State Root, "there is an urgent need for taking stock of our resources." With characteristic gusto, Roosevelt added that his conference "ought to rank among the more important meetings in the history of the country."[9] Roosevelt viewed this issue in a continental context and invited Prime Minister Laurier to send Canadian delegates to Washington. "The progress of the people of the United States obviously depends on the availability of natural resources," he explained to Laurier, "and it is evident that natural resources are not limited by the boundary lines which separate nations. . . ."[10]

That these trends were working to change the circumstances of the American-Canadian relationship did not mean that a new policy would emerge. The trends and connections between them had to be identified and an appropriate plan of action thought through. President Taft and Secretary of State Knox relied on officials within the State Department who appreciated how this conjunction of trends might lead to policy formulation with long-term goals in mind. The key figure was Charles H. Pepper of the Bureau of Trade Relations who, as the great intellectual driving force behind the policy, undertook the mammoth task of researching past trade relations to see how American-Canadian trade related to hemispheric and world trade patterns. He made the case that Canada's grain supplies and natural resources would benefit the cost-of-living question and enable some tariff reduction that would be beneficial for the American economy. Along with John Osborne, Chief of the Bureau of Trade Relations, he negotiated the terms of the agreement with the Canadians. From the beginning to the end of the reciprocity process he was the energizing force. He briefed the president, cabinet members, senators, and congressmen; he drafted the major speeches by Taft and his cabinet. Whenever Secretary of State Knox or Secretary of Agriculture James Wilson spoke on reciprocity with Canada, they spoke along the lines set out by Pepper. He originated modern American policy toward Canada.[11]

Pepper began where all intelligent policy formulation begins—he looked at the facts. American leaders and politicians had spoken about Canada often enough, as we have seen, on such matters as transportation competition, obstructionism over the fisheries, and canal toll controversies. Blaine, and then Roosevelt, had continued the old tradition begun during the Civil War years of blustering about Canada's untrustworthiness, but no influential American official or politician had made a serious study of Canada. Israel Andrews had done a lot of work in the 1840s and 1850s, but the political circumstances of the time ensured that no one paid attention. Pepper made the first serious, professional evaluation of the relationship to result in an actual policy outcome.

Pepper educated opinion in the administration by placing the Canadian case in a broad context of long-term, economic strategy in the western hemisphere. In a memorandum on "Trade Relations with Canada, Newfoundland and Mexico," Pepper set out American goals with respect to Canada. He began by defining an elementary concept that was to reappear frequently in American policy-statements thereafter: U.S. policy toward Canada should be made "on the basis of geography, that is, the special relation resulting from contiguous territory." Pepper also based his argument on another standard American view that the east-west economy of Canada produced by her national policy and backed by British capital was unnatural. Freer trade between the two countries would undermine this east-west economic axis in Canada and open up easier channels of trade between the geographic regions of North America. A reciprocity arrangement with Canada should aim at "wiping out as fully as possible the long boundary line and obtaining closer commercial intercourse for the different sections of both countries."[12]

Within this general context, the immediate priority of the United States was to gain access to Canada's natural resources, particularly her grain production "with a view to cheaper food products for consumers in the United States." In Pepper's evaluation, "the prime consideration from the standpoint of the United States should be to open freely the sources of food supply." He argued that it was essential for the Taft administration to overcome opposition from regional agricultural protectionist interests who preferred to shelter behind the tariff acts. If a reciprocity agreement could be made with Canada "a guarantee would be given that the nearest and most abundant source of food supply was opened to consumers in the United States." While negotiations should proceed on a range of items including cattle, other livestock, and fish, Pepper's case concentrated on wheat. He emphasized that this was "the dominating factor in closer trade relations" with Canada.[13]

Pepper used the wheat issue to link his two main themes that reciprocity would encourage economic integration of the two countries and provide cheaper food in the United States. "Aside from the possibility of cheapening the food supply, or at least preventing it from becoming higher in the future," he explained, "wheat would be a very important means of diverting the trade currents of the Canadian Northwest into north and south channels instead of leaving them to follow east and west channels which is not a natural one." To counter the fears of American farmers about this inflow of Canadian grain, Pepper advised that the farming lobby should be told that the flow of grain into Minneapolis and Chicago from Canada would weaken the influence of the Liverpool market for the setting of world grain prices. The United States would thus be in a better position to "maintain market prices."[14]

Pepper next turned to the issue of manufactured goods. The United States should insist on some reduction of duties placed on American manufactured exports to Canada, but this should not have the same priority as agricultural produce and natural resources. Pepper reasoned, "a general readjustment of schedules on manufactured articles would go outside the geographical or neighborhood relation which should be the basis of the reciprocity treaty."[15]

Through this rather obscure statement, Pepper was reasoning that it would be politic not to disturb the U.S. protected manufacturing companies, since reductions in the Canadian tariff would necessarily require reductions on the American side. But, Pepper then added a sound and perceptive argument for not pressing on manufactured articles which showed he had a good knowledge of conditions in Canada. The Canadian national policy had led to the emergence in Canada of a politically powerful manufacturing class that had flourished (like its U.S. counterpart) behind protective barriers. If the U.S. pushed too hard, this nationalist and pro-imperial lobby would fight hard against reciprocity. Pepper, then proposed soft-pedalling the tariff on manufactured articles to satisfy Republican businessmen in the U.S. and (it was hoped) to prevent alarm from spreading among Canadian manufacturers.

It would be possible to negotiate with Canada simply on the basis of agricultural and natural products, a possibility that would have been extremely attractive to Canadians, but Pepper rejected that option on the grounds that it would give too much ammunition to U.S. opponents. A treaty covering natural products alone would mean, "the advantage would be very largely with the dominion." A treaty that did not force some reduction in Canadian tariffs would lead to charges in the United States that the agreement was lopsided in Canada's favor. American opponents would be able to mount an:

agitation against such a treaty as a jug-handled one. The Elgin treaty which was negotiated in 1854 and was denounced in the United States in 1866 was limited to natural products. Usually the feeling growing out of the attitude of Canada during the [Civil] war has been given for the cause of the denouncement of the treaty. The very great preponderance of the exports from Canada was a much stronger reason.[16]

Various explanations have been advanced by historians to explain the abrogation of the first reciprocity treaty by the United States in 1866. Whatever the merits of these explanations, Pepper's memorandum shows that, at this stage of new policy formulation for Canada, a highly placed and well-informed American official believed the 1854 treaty had been abrogated because Canada had worked it in a one-sided manner. She had exported her agricultural and natural products to the United States but had put tariff barriers against a return flow of American manufactured articles. Even at this late date, the old suspicions about Canada still had an impact on American thinking.

In addition to helping the administration deal with the argument that they were negotiating another jug-handled treaty, the insistence on some tariff reduction from Canada would be a significant move in the struggle against the further consolidation of the British imperial trade system. While Pepper was convinced on the basis of the trade figures that imperial preference had not been working well, he feared the tariff reform movement led by Joseph Chamberlain might be on the verge of political success in Britain. So far, the prospect of a closer imperial trading system had been weakened because Britain remained a free trade country. Should Britain adopt a protectionist tariff like Canada then the possibility of a closed imperial trading bloc would become much more likely. He began this phase of his argument by pointing out that while the protectionist national policy had led to "new industrial conditions" in Canada, the Liberal party (which had been in power since 1896) was still very much attracted by "closer trade intercourse with the United States." The Liberals in Canada had traditionally been the home of nineteenth-century, free trade philosophy in Canada; and, while they had accepted the protectionist national policy when they achieved office in 1896, they were still likely to be swayed by freer trade arguments, especially when pushed by their farming support in the Prairie provinces. The United States should encourage this strain in the Liberal party to prevent Canada from being drawn into more solid and elaborate schemes of imperial trade such as those being proposed by Chamberlain. "British Imperial politics," warned Pepper, now add to the importance of finding practical expressions for this sentiment [an imperial trading system]. The possibility of a so-called Tariff Reform or protectionist government within the next few years, if not within a few months, is taken into account. The reflex of this movement is felt in Canada in the demand for closer commercial bonds between the Dominion and the United Kingdom as a means of strengthening the political connection. An indirect and covert movement against reciprocity with the United States has already been inaugurated both in Canada and in England.

Pepper knew that there would be opposition in Canada to closer ties with the United States, but he insisted on the need to move quickly to open negotiations and present Canada with the prospect of "the market of 100,000,000 prosperous people across the boundary line in the United States for the surplus natural products of the Dominion." This would be more valuable, obviously, than "the overseas market of 40,000,000 consumers in the British Empire." In short, Pepper presented reciprocity as a means of stopping the trend towards closer economic and political cooperation within the British Empire.[17]

Another sign of the times which Pepper's case took into account was the commercial treaty of 1908 between Canada and France. W.H. Hoyt of the State Department had informed the U.S. Consul in Ottawa that the treaty discriminated against the United States and that under the recently passed Payne-Aldrich Act, unless the United States received the same treatment as France, Canadian exports to the U.S. would face the maximum tariff rates. Consul-General Foster warned in his reply that if the American maximum tariff were applied this would simply force Canada into more extensive commercial relations with Britain and other countries like France. If this trend of Canada building up trade outside of North America took hold then "the United States might never regain as good a relative position in the Canadian market as it now holds."[18] The State Department received numerous complaints about the Franco-Canadian treaty. One typical letter from James Spencer, president of a New York export company, declared, "our treatment of Canada is positively impartial but Canada in her dealings as to imports from the U.S. is contemptibly unfair. The tariff commission should give Canada no quarter but should tell them that if they do not treat us with fairness we will build a wall around them so high that it will take them a long time to get over it."[19] This reaction was based on fears that Canada would take the lion's share of the agricultural implement trade from North America to France. As Governor-General Grey explained to James Bryce, the Canadians expected "the French treaty will probably give the

Canadian manufacturers the agricultural implement trade now existing between France and the United States."[20] These Canadian hopes were a mirage, but the fact that Canada was thinking along these lines was another piece of evidence that she was embarked on a course that sought to make her more independent of the North American market. As Pepper argued, the goal of the United States was to turn Canada's trade into north-south directions. The system of imperial preference, and now the trade treaty with France, suggested Canada was moving away from the American gravitational pull.

President Taft conducted an energetic political campaign in Congress and across the country on behalf of the reciprocity agreement. His response to Canada was formed by Pepper's analysis and general view of the times. This can be seen most tellingly in a confidential note he sent in January 1911 to former President Roosevelt in which he explained why he was pressing so hard for reciprocity. Besides meeting the political necessity of some downward movement in tariffs, a reciprocity agreement with Canada would have a beneficial impact on food prices in American cities. In private he was not as certain as he was in public that Canadian grain would lower prices, but he still thought reciprocity would help on the consumer price front by at least stabilizing food prices. He outlined to Roosevelt that the treaty "might at first have a tendency to reduce the cost of food products somewhat; it would certainly make the reservoir much greater and prevent fluctuations." Taft then continued, in a more enthusiastic tone, to explain that

> the amount of Canadian products we would take would produce a current of business between western Canada and the United States that would make Canada only an adjunct of the United States. It would transfer all of their important business to Chicago and New York, with all their bank credits and everything else and it would increase greatly the demand in Canada for our manufacturers. I see this as an argument against reciprocity in Canada and I think it is a good one.[21]

2.

Taft was able to present such a clear-headed view of reciprocity because of the thorough preparation of the administration's case by Pepper. Pepper was aware of his key role—the leading expert in the State Department who had thought through a new Canadian policy. In January 1911, he thanked Charles Norton for his support and remarked that it was, "a great privilege for me to see the subject in which I have been for many years interested brought to a head under President Taft's administration. The full significance of his action will grow on the whole world although at the start there seems to be a pretty general appreciation of what his Canadian policy means."[22] Pepper drafted Taft's Special Message to Congress; and during the ensuing public debate, he supplied speeches and position papers for Taft and other cabinet members. When complaints flooded in from affected interests—above all from American farmers—Pepper took the principal role in answering the criticism and reminding individuals and groups of the long-term view they ought to be taking.[23]

One of the more difficult criticisms to counter was that it made little sense for such a prolific agricultural producer as the United States to negotiate for the cheaper inflow of even more farm products. Moreover, the fact that wheat was the main item in the agreement seemed most unfair to farmers who complained that their incomes were being threatened by this first step away from stand-pat protectionism while the great manufacturing companies remained shielded from foreign imports. Pepper responded by setting the reciprocity agreement in a broader context. He reminded C.E. Bibbee, who had demanded to know whether the United States could not produce enough wheat to supply bread for its citizens, that the question was more complex. Pepper noted, "the surplus for export in the form either of wheat or flour has been steadily decreasing and some believe that within a very few years we will not produce enough wheat for our own people." But beyond this concern about the future, Pepper argued that American farmers would derive some immediate benefits from reciprocity. The entry of Canadian wheat would help the American farmer in terms of prices and marketing. "The admission of free wheat from Canada," he argued,

> in addition to helping prevent corners and speculative rises in prices, which are no good for the farmer, will be useful in enabling our people to control the Canadian surplus much of which will be made into flour for export by our millers. In this way the price of wheat will not be entirely controlled by the surplus that is dumped in Liverpool. In short, it will be to the advantage of our farmers to have control of the Canadian surplus wheat and have it milled into flour in this country rather than let it be controlled in Europe.[24]

In his defense of the trade agreement, Secretary of Agriculture James Wilson also urged farmers to think in these terms and pointed out that the United States gained access to the Canadian market for fruits and vegetables and to Canadian natural resources. Fifty years ago, Wilson reminded the National Grange, American farmers shipped their surplus to foreign markets; but since the Civil War, protection had provided a domestic market. The theory behind the protective policy which guarded this market was that the tariff equalized the cost of production for American and foreign products. In the case of Canada, the cost of production was "more nearly identical than it is between the United States and any other country." Moreover, inside the United States the urban population had grown so fast that the cost of food in American cities had become a major cause for concern. In 1908, the lower tariff cry "carried the election by default." Thus, there were political and economic justifications for the reciprocity agreement with Canada. "This treaty," the Secretary of Agriculture summed up, "is not one-sided giving our markets for meats and grains to the Canadians for nothing in return. We get into the Canadian woods, ninety million or more of us for timber products, things very much needed as our home supplies are so much reduced that prices have gone up markedly in the last few years and our development in the future will draw heavily on what remains."[25]

Pepper replied to the criticism that farmers were being left without protection by making the argument that the reciprocity treaty created a larger, protected productive area in North America. "The view of the President and the Secretary of State," explained Pepper, "is that the Reciprocity Agreement is not a free trade measure but is in fact a measure of protection because it simply extends the area of protection on this continent." In a similar vein, Pepper patiently explained to John Atkinson in California that it was not just a question of immediate commercial benefit but that there "were broad questions of national policy involved in making our trade relations with Canada even closer than at present. The Canadian Reciprocity Agreement in substance amounts to extending the area of protection on this continent."[26] In these letters, written as part of the ratification campaign, Pepper always circled back to this long-term view which looked to the integration of Canada into the American economy. When, for example, one critic who was obviously familiar with the case for reciprocity, demanded to know why, if cheaper food prices for the urban consumer were a goal, the consumer was not entitled to cheap meat from Argentina, wool from Australia, and silk from China, Pepper retorted that such an approach "ignores the whole point of the Presidential message which is that the reciprocity agreement is desirable for geographical and other reasons which do not apply to Argentina, Australia, China etc."[27]

112

Even the method of negotiation was designed by the State Department to encourage this goal. The regular channel of communication between the United States and Canada was through the British Ambassador in Washington; but as J.B. Osborne pointed out, the British government was an interested party and might try to prevent any agreement. "It is obvious," he warned Hoyt, "that precisely to that extent which the United States will secure tariff concessions in Canada, the United Kingdom will suffer an impairment of the value of the tariff privileges now extended to British products in Canadian markets. Hence it is desirable that our negotiations with Canada not be conducted through and controlled by the British government." Direct negotiations with Canada would also appeal to Canadian pride which had been hurt by previous American refusals to enter into a new reciprocity agreement. Because of this history of rebuttals "the temper of the Canadian government and perhaps the Canadian people is distinctly opposed to opening negotiations."[28] Thus, the decision of the Taft administration to open direct negotiations in Ottawa was taken to mollify hurt Canadian pride and to place a wedge between Canada and Britain.

Indeed, it was the openness with which Taft and his cabinet expressed the goal of separating Canadian and British interests (so that Canada would be more fully drawn into a continental orientation) that led to difficulties on the Canadian side and in the end doomed reciprocity. In the course of a speech at Decatur, Illinois, Taft hammered away on the theme of gaining access to Canada's natural resources. He emphasized that the agreement "will bring to us the almost inexhaustible resources of the great northwest of Canada when we ourselves are beginning to find that our resources have been wasted and are rapidly reaching their limit."[29] In his special message to Congress announcing the agreement, President Taft declared, "we have reached the stage in our own development that calls for a statesmanlike and broad view of our future economic status and its requirements. We have drawn upon our material resources in such a way as to invite attention to their necessary limit." Reciprocity with Canada was designed to "enlarge our supply of natural resources [by gaining] direct access to her great supply of natural products without an obstructive, prohibiting tariff." Taft crowned his message with a phrase that was seized upon by anti-reciprocity forces in Canada: "They are coming to a parting of the ways," the President announced, "they must soon decide whether they are to regard themselves as isolated permanently from our markets by a perpetual wall or whether we are to be commercial friends."[30] For Canadians "the parting of the ways" phrase meant that through reciprocity they were expected to abandon their ties with Britain and become an economic extension of the United States. Taft was even more uninhibited on this point at another rally in support of reciprocity. During a speech in Champaign-Urbana, Illinois, he declared that he was "advocating commercial union between Canada and the United States."[31]

This theme—that reciprocity was a prelude to the incorporation of Canada into the United States—was also given life by Secretary of Agriculture Wilson when he compared the reciprocity agreement to the Louisiana Purchase which had brought half a continent into the United States. Wilson reminded Americans that since the abrogation of the first reciprocity treaty in 1866, "the Canadians have been rapidly building up their country." If the agreement were to go into operation, Canada would become part of the American economy. "We will become more and more one people," Wilson continued, "developing along similar lines and supplementing each other in many respects; the raw material that comes from the Canadian farm will be manufactured in the United States and what is not needed will be sent to foreign countries." To those American farmers who worried about the inflow of Canadian products, Wilson urged that they take a long historical view which placed expansion into Canada in the same context as westward expansion inside the United States. Farmers in the east had certainly had to make adjustments to the consequences of western expansion since 1803, but there was no doubt that the expansion had benefited all sections of the economy. All stages of westward expansion had been opposed by groups who feared their interests would suffer but without that expansion "and especially the Louisiana Purchase, the United States would be a much less important country than it is." There were no new lands available for agriculture in the United States except in semi-arid regions. "These considerations," the Secretary of Agriculture summed up, "lead me to the conclusion that the adoption of the pending reciprocity treaty would, from the national standpoint, be as much an act of wisdom as was the adoption of treaties in the past that have added to our common country more than half its present area."[32] President Taft developed this same theme at the National Corn Exposition at Columbus, Ohio, when he proclaimed, "the result [of reciprocity with Canada] will be like the change in trade effected by the settlement and opening up of our far western States upon the business of the older States, except that it will come more quickly."[33]

While this justification for reciprocity made sense to American audiences and the American view of history, it had the opposite impact in Canada where such justifications were seen as further masked references to annexation. The situation was made worse by the utterances of Champ Clark, the Democratic leader in the House and the prospective Speaker in the next Congress. In a speech that more than any other helped the annexation charge stick, Clark declared that he "looked forward to the time when the American flag will fly over every square foot of British North America up to the North Pole. The people of Canada are of our blood and our language." This was unmistakable, old-fashioned, annexation bluster and opponents of the treaty in Canada had a field day with it.[34] The question is, did it reflect American policy? Did Pepper, Taft, and Knox think like Clark but do a better job of being more careful in their speeches and writings on the subject? Taft immediately tried to distance himself from Clark's views and told Ambassador Bryce that he was "greatly angered." He also instructed Representative McCall who introduced the enabling Bill into the House, "this agreement if it becomes law has no political significance. No thought of future annexation or union was in the mind of negotiators on either side." Secretary of State Knox told the Chicago Association of Commerce, "there is not the slightest probability that this racial and moral union will involve any political change or annexation or absorption."[35]

There is no evidence to suggest that Taft and Knox were being disingenuous in making these statements. Before the negotiations in Ottawa had opened, internal State Department memoranda drew attention to the necessity of avoiding any implication that reciprocity had annexation as an ultimate goal.[36] The problem was that Taft's own phrasing of the issues, above all "the parting of the ways" remark, seemed to Canadian minds to be rather close to Clark's cruder statement of the case. Clark's remark and the observations by Taft, Knox, and Wilson about the benefits to be derived from closer economic integration fed the ancient Canadian fear of the United States that went right back to the War of 1812 and the invasion scares during the Civil War years. Thus the annexation cry had a political impact in Canada. In the United States, however, no responsible official or cabinet member could see how it could be taken seriously. As James Bryce pointed out, "the annexation tale was from the first felt to be silly and has quite died out. If the United States were keen on using fiscal methods to promote annexation, all they had to do was to offer free trade without an agreement at all."[37]

Taft's policy was not based on old American attitudes as expressed in Clark's speech but was the result of the careful analysis made by Pepper of the United States' long-term national interests. This view certainly envisaged a weakening of Canada's ties with Britain and anticipated the emergence of a continental economy. As the formal instructions to the American negotiators noted, the agreement was to "fully recognise . . . the natural channels of commerce."[38] The new policymakers made a careful distinction between this economic planning for the future needs of the United States and the issue of annexation which simply led to mutual suspicions and recriminations without beneficial policy outcomes. James Bryce noted this change in Washington, "I have been struck in finding during these four years," he wrote to Governor-General Grey in Ottawa, "that nearly all sensible and educated Americans have come to understand the position and have dropped all notions of political union..."[39] To take Champ Clark as evidence of underlying American intentions was simply to be ill-informed. "Champ Clark," explained Bryce,

> tho' selected as the Speaker of the next Democratic House has none of the qualities of a statesman. He is rather a crude Western man of the Chautauqua lecturer type with a sort of rough humour and picturesqueness of phrase which catches a popular audience, and he has no knowledge of international relations, much less of international courtesies. He didn't mean to be offensive but in the heat of debate blurted out what he thought would sound fine and patriotic and is now surprised to find that his language has been resented.[40]

Ambassador Bryce had a wide range of social and political contacts in Washington, and he knew of no informed Americans who shared Clark's simplistic views. Even more positively, Bryce thought that there had been a marked shift in American thinking on Canada since the middle and later decades of the nineteenth century. "There are, of course, many half-educated Americans," he acknowledged, "who still think that 'manifest destiny' will bring about a union with Canada but most sensible men are aware that this is more unlikely now than it ever was before." Bryce also reminded Grey that in contrast to Britain, where the speech of a party leader in the Commons might be significant in terms of policy, Clark "talked to the House just as he would have talked to a party gathering in Missouri. . . . It was said thoughtlessly and was a mere unconsidered outburst of that stupid and arrogant 'spread-eaglism' which still lingers among the less educated sort of politicians though it is happily much less frequent and more reprobated now than in former days." "To treat it as policy," summed up Bryce, "would be to give it and its author far more significance than they possess."[41]

Inside the State Department, Pepper was distressed to see the disastrous impact of the ill-informed annexation talk on his carefully conceived policy. When Charles Hilles, the President's private secretary, assured Pepper that Taft understood the use made of the annexation cry by Canadian opponents of reciprocity and that he (the President) would address the issue on his upcoming trip to the midwest, Pepper imagined the situation slipping even further out of control if Taft failed to make clear the distinction between annexation and "the parting of the ways." He warned Hilles that the President must be careful about how he phrased his speeches because the political situation in Canada was "extremely delicate."[42] In short, prospective annexation was never even considered as part of the new American policy devised by experts Pepper, Osborne, and Hoyt and implemented by Taft and Knox. The policymakers were surprised and dismayed that the discussion degenerated into such crude charges and counter-charges instead of focusing on the broad issues of national interest they had defined in the preparatory memoranda written in the two years leading up to the negotiations.

One of the characteristics of the fresh approach was the gathering of information from the Canadian side. Because the State Department experts knew so well the traditional anti-American fears among Canadians, they took pains to separate economic matters from any hint that political union was on the agenda. A sign of this new approach was the more systematic use of the U.S. Consuls throughout Canada. These officials made occasional contributions to American policies on Canadian issues, above all on tariff matters connected with lumber and fish. The Ottawa Consuls, most of whom were lumbermen, often made policy recommendations in their despatches. In 1897, for example, the Ottawa Consul prepared material on the Canadian militia and the military establishment in the capital for the Adjutant-General's office in Washington.[43] But this information flow was intermittent and usually depended on the individual initiative and energy of the consul. By 1902, the consuls throughout Ontario were meeting annually, but only the Treasury Department sent a representative because the matters discussed were entirely technical. The Ottawa Consul wrote to the State Department suggesting that it might be useful to send its representative.[44]

This situation was transformed by 1910. Consuls were required to send regular reports on public opinion in their districts along with extracts from newspapers and some analysis of the political affiliation of quoted persons. A circular letter from Alvin Adee, the Assistant Secretary of State, briefed all consuls in Canada on the American reciprocity policy and asked them to emphasize in their public presentations that "it is not contemplated to make sweeping reductions which would injuriously affect industries in the Dominion." The State

Department, appreciating the strength of the pro-empire business lobby in Canada, was trying to prepare the ground for the reception of the American offer. As the education campaign inside the United States on reciprocity proceeded, the consuls in Canada were provided with copies of the speeches made by Taft, Knox, and Wilson. For their part, some consuls began giving sustained analyses and advice. For example, Consul-General Foster at Ottawa warned of the danger if Taft kept trying to explain what he meant by "the parting of the ways." Foster explained that the phrase had already taken on an annexationist meaning in Canada and that Taft ought to drop it forthwith.[45]

The general picture presented by the consuls gave a pretty accurate view of the mounting opposition to reciprocity in Canada. They also added some depth and complexity to the facts being gathered by the State Department. In particular they drew attention to the peculiar role of American branch plants which had been set up in Canada to jump over the tariff barrier set up by the national policy. Many of these American companies were opposed to reciprocity because it would hurt their business in Canada and its export markets. In Hamilton there were, according to the U.S. Consul, thirty-four American companies (such as American Steel, Otis Elevator, and Westinghouse) all of which were opposed to the reciprocity agreement. From Montreal, Consul-General Bradley reported, "under present conditions, American manufacturers have established and are still establishing branches here. Nearly every one of these would use all his influence against Reciprocity because it would lower his profits on the large investment made this side of the line. The Canadians seeing them forced to come here bringing capital and labor are quite satisfied."[46] This kind of knowledge and insight into the paradoxes of an already complex economic relationship was symptomatic of how experts in the State Department were developing a more rounded knowledge of Canada during this period.

3.

All this was too little too late. Decades of suspicion about American intentions, resentment over the rejection of previous requests for reciprocity, and the self-confidence derived from a decade of economic prosperity turned Canadian voters against reciprocity in 1911. As W.S. Fielding, the Canadian Minister of Finance, warned Knox, at one time reciprocity had been seen as the ideal solution to Canada's economic difficulties; but with a thriving economy and the popularity of imperial sentiment, there would be "considerable opposition to more intimate trade relations."[47] This general outlook in Canada, combined with the annexation scare roused by Clark's and Taft's speeches, led to the defeat of the Laurier government in the 1911 election and, as a consequence, the defeat of the new American policy toward Canada.

While the reciprocity policy of the Taft administration failed because of Canadian opposition, it did win approval in the United States and reflected the rethinking of the American response to Canada. The approach which viewed Canada as an unnatural remnant of the empire that would someday become part of the United States now appeared definitely outmoded. It last received some official credence when Secretary of State Blaine bluntly told the Canadians in 1893 that if they wanted tariff concessions they would have to abandon Britain and expect to become an agricultural state in the Union. The old-fashioned thinking could still flare up in political settings, as it did with Champ Clark, but State Department policymakers like Pepper were now working at a more sophisticated level. They accepted Canada's existence as an autonomous and increasingly successful polity in North America, and they analyzed the economic circumstances on the continent to figure out a policy that would meet the long-term economic needs of the United States (as well as helping with some immediate political difficulties connected with the tariff issue).

In his seminal study of the reciprocity policy, Robert Hannigan proposed that this reorientation of American thinking was part of the U.S. open-door foreign policy and that the approach to Canada could fit into the same context as American policy toward China, Latin America, and other parts of the world.[48] This is a refreshing approach which clears away some of the unexamined shibboleths about America's Canadian policies. There is no doubt that strategic thinking about natural resources and the grain market were elements in the general American concern about the patterns of world trade. In that broad sense, the new thinking on Canada was linked to the open-door policies of the period. But the amount of trade that flowed between Canada and the United States—in spite of protective barriers on both sides and the peculiarly intimate business relations— makes open-door terminology ill-fitting for the Canadian case. Osborne remarked that a 3,000 mile common border and interlocking transport systems along with a "marked homogeneity of population have, notwithstanding existing tariff barriers, contributed to bring about extensive and intimate commercial relations between the United States and Canada."[49] Pepper, who was primarily responsible for developing the new policy, did not expect Canada to be a market for a surge of American manufactured exports. As we have seen, the reduction of Canadian tariffs was of secondary importance. Besides, as the report from the U.S. Consuls confirmed, American companies had no trouble setting up branches in Canada and gaining access to the market from the inside. When policymakers and cabinet members wrote about Canada, they always viewed Canada as a special case. Secretary of Agriculture Wilson explained, "reciprocity with Canada must be considered from a viewpoint somewhat different from that of a tariff act affecting our commerce with the entire world."[50] As John Osborne summed up in the January 1911 memorandum that set out the goals for negotiations, the basis for the new policy was "contiguity and identity of interests." He added that the tariff policy of the United States with respect to Canada "should be differentiated, even sharply and radically, from that pursued towards European countries and the world in general."[51]

The Taft administration made extraordinary efforts to secure approval of the agreement in the United States. This was partly because Taft and Knox were genuinely convinced that reciprocity would be beneficial (as we saw in Taft's private note to Roosevelt) and partly because the administration wanted to move away from the stand-pat position on tariffs before the 1912 election. The Laurier government in Ottawa was, by contrast, hesitant because it feared the political repercussions. Thus, it was the Americans who did all the running in 1910-1911. In the spring of 1910, there was some frustration in the State Department because of Canada's slow response to their overtures. In October 1910, Knox was pleading with Fielding to open negotiations and complained to former Secretary of State Root that Canada was "slow in coming to the point where definite propositions can be exchanged."[52] By this time Knox was convinced that the Canadians were deliberately stalling, but so anxious was he to open negotiations (as he explained to Hoyt), "we will not let the matter be hindered or fail through punctiliousness on our part."[53] This sense of the United States doing all the work was strengthened early in 1911 as Taft and his cabinet members lobbied hard in Congress and crisscrossed the country to win support for reciprocity. After the legislation to implement the agreement was passed by the House of Representatives, Knox telegraphed Consul-General Foster in Ottawa instructing him "to point out that the President has done and is doing his utmost in the face of extraordinary difficulties." It would be helpful if the Canadians could be similarly energetic in moving their legislation through Parliament. Knox added pointedly that to do so "would be no more than make equal and mutual the efforts of the two administrations."[54]

It was particularly galling that one of the reasons for Canadian laggardliness was the visit by Prime Minister Laurier to the Imperial

Conference in London in May of 1911. This kept alive the view that Canada's imperial ties were still an obstacle to open and straightforward dealing. During the negotiations themselves, Hoyt told Pepper that the delaying tactics were due to "the coolness on the surface and active opposition underneath of a section of the British Government represented in Canada by Earl Grey, the Governor-General."[55] American suspicion of the imperial factor was deepened when Sir William Van Horne of the Canadian Pacific Railroad emerged from retirement to declare, "I am out to do all I can to bust the damned thing."[56]

There was also resentment on the American side because of a belief that Canada had spurned a genuinely good offer. The United States had not pressed Canada to give up imperial preference or make big reductions in her tariff but offered a market for Canadian natural products. Canada had wanted this since 1849, and it required a considerable risk for a Republican administration to make such an offer. Ambassador Bryce reported that "there is much surprise that Canada should have refused what was thought to be an excellent bargain for her."[57] The anti-American rhetoric in Canada also surprised Americans who knew little or nothing about Canada's long history on this score. American newspapers took the line, "now the people of the United States know what Canadians really think of them . . . it will take a long time to efface the impression of dislike and enmity which Canadian utterances have conveyed." In his academic way, Bryce was intrigued about this mixture of ignorance and prejudice on both sides of the border. "What has happened here and in Canada," he remarked, "illustrates the truth that nations may live close to one another and utterly misunderstand one another. Few persons in the United States had realised how deeply the arrogant superciliousness and almost brutal rudeness of American statesmen 30 or 40 years ago had sunk into the Canadian mind and made it supremely averse to all proposals from that quarter." While appreciating the roots of Canadian stereotyping of the United States, Bryce went on to criticize Canadians for failing to be knowledgeable about changes in the United States. "Few in Canada," he continued, "would seem to have realised that the great majority of sensible men on this side of the border have come to respect Canada, recognising her growing wealth and power, and have ceased to expect the political union with themselves. So little is now said or thought about annexation here that they did not imagine that the fear of it would still be an effective force in Canada."[58]

This mutual resentment in 1911 had an impact on American attitudes toward Canada. Senator P.J. McCumber of South Dakota, noting that the U.S. legislation was still on the books in spite of the Canadian rejection of the agreement, told President Taft in 1912: "This Government has extended the hand of reciprocal fellowship to Canada. The latter has refused the proffered greeting. Is it not a trite humiliating that we should keep that hand extended until Canada may decide whether or not in the future her conduct shall be changed?"[59] The United States, after decades of inattention, had proposed a policy toward Canada that was based on a broad and statesmanlike view of the national interest. Taft, his cabinet, and State Department experts like Pepper and Osborne thought that the new policy, while framed with U.S. national interests in view, would also be attractive to Canada. Instead, Canada delayed, prevaricated, and finally rejected the American offer of reciprocity. As Ambassador Bryce explained to Governor-General Grey, "the Americans have been startled by the disclosure of so much bitterness and suspicion in the Canadian mind against themselves . . . they had not realised til now how the contemptuous attitude and sharp practice of the U.S. statesmen of the last generation had sunk deep into the Canadian heart." Bryce noted that administration officials had taken the rejection "with good temper" but added, "several American newspapers have pointed out that what has been said on your side of the line must leave a painful impression here. The progress that was being made towards good feeling and friendship has been unhappily arrested. . . ."[60] This cinder in the eye could not be washed out even by a generous reciprocity offer. The first constructive American policy initiative toward her northern neighbor had been rebuffed in Canada. American policymakers were in no hurry to try again.

Notes

1. Wilfrid Laurier to James Bryce, Ottawa, 15 June 1910, James Bryce Papers USA/30, Bodleian Library, Oxford.
2. Ibid,. Elihu Root to James Bryce, 30 March 1910, USA/28.
3. Theodore Roosevelt to Secretary of State Hay, Oyster Bay, NY, 10 July 1902, Theodore Roosevelt Papers, Ser. 4B, Reel 416, Michigan State University Libraries.
4. James Bryce to Sir Edward Grey, 21 November 1908, PRO, FO 800/331.
5. Goldwin Smith to Senator Higgins, Toronto, 7 May 1892, Benjamin Harrison Papers, Ser. 2, Reel 81, Michigan State University Libraries.
6. Memorandum on Relations between Great Britain and the United States, January 1908, PRO, FO 414/210.
7. Taft Speech at the Associated Press and American Newspaper Publishers Association, New York, 27 April 1911, William Howard Taft Papers, Reel 399, Case 543, Michigan State University Libraries.
8. L. Ethan Ellis, *Reciprocity 1911: A Study in Canadian-American*

Relations (New Haven: Yale University Press, 1939), 8-10; Sidney Ratner, *The Tariff in American History* (New York: Van Norstrand, 1972), 41-44.

9. Theodore Roosevelt to Elihu Root, 20 April 1908, Roosevelt Papers, Ser. 2, Reel 349, vol. 89

10. Ibid., Theodore Roosevelt to Wilfrid Laurier, 24 December 1908, Ser. 2, Reel 353, vol. 89.

11. Charles H. Pepper wrote two papers that formed the basis for American policy in 1911: "Report on Trade Conditions in Canada by Charles M. Pepper, Special Agent of the Department of Commerce and Labor," Hse. Doc. No. 408, 59th Cong., 1st sess. and "Trade Relations with Canada, Newfoundland and Mexico," Memorandum by Charles M. Pepper and M.H. Davis, Bureau of Trade Relations, 23 May 1910, State Department Decimile File (SDDF) 1910-1929, Box 5795, RG 59, National Archives.

12. Pepper and Davis, 1-2.

13. Ibid., 5-6. They warned of the need to fight "local interests" which would work hard through Congress to prevent an agreement with Canada.

14. Ibid., 6.

15. Ibid., 8-10.

16. Ibid., 10.

17. Ibid., 3-4.

18. Consul-General Foster to Assistant Secretary of State, Ottawa, 23 March 1910, SDDF 1910-1929, Box 5794, RG 59, National Archives.

19. Ibid., James Spencer to Secretary of State Knox, New York, 5 March 1910.

20. Earl Grey to James Bryce, Ottawa, 22 November 1909, PRO, FO 800/332.

21. W.H. Taft to Theodore Roosevelt, 10 January 1911, Roosevelt Papers, Ser. 1, Reel 96.

22. Charles H. Pepper to Charles Norton, 27 January 1911, Taft Papers, Reel 398, Case 543.

23. Charles H. Pepper to W.H. Hoyt, 28 March 1910, SDDF 1910-29, Box 5794, RG 59, National Archives.

24. Charles H. Pepper to C.E. Bibbee, Washington, 10 May 1911, Taft Papers, Reel 399, Case 543.

25. James Wilson to Legislative Committee of National Grange, Washington, 9 February 1911, Taft Papers, Reel 398, Case 543.

26. Ibid., Charles H. Pepper to C.H. Bibbee, 10 May 1911, Reel 399, Case 543; Ibid., Pepper to John Atkinson, 14 June 1911.

27. Ibid., Charles H. Pepper to Charles D. Hilles, 19 June 1911.

28. John B. Osborne to W.H. Hoyt, 30 January 1910, SDDF 1910-1929, Box 5797, RG 59, National Archives.

29. Address of President Taft, Decatur, IL, 11 February 1911, Taft Papers Ser. 9A, Reel 567, vol. 20.

30. President Taft's Special Message to Congress, 26 January 1911, SDDF 1910-1929, Box 5795, RG 59, National Archives.

31. Remarks of President Taft at Champaign-Urbana, IL, 11 February 1911, Taft Papers, Ser. 9A, Reel 567, vol. 20.

32. James Wilson to the Legislative Committee of the National Grange, 9 February 1911, Taft Papers, Reel 398, Case 543.

33. Address of President Taft at the National Corn Exposition, Columbus,

OH, 10 February 1911, Taft Papers, Ser. 9H, Reel 567, vol. 20.

34. R.C. Brown and Ramsay Cook, *Canada 1896-1921: A Nation Transformed* (Toronto: McClland and Stewart, 1974), 121-2; Ellis, 96, 141-196.

35. James Bryce to Earl Grey, Washington, 18 February 1911, PRO, FO 800/314.

36. Minutes of Conference at Ottawa, 4-10 November 1910, SDDF 1910-1929, Box 5795, RG 59, National Archives.

37. James Bryce to Earl Grey, Washington, 25 February 1911, PRO, FO 800/3334.

38. Secretary of State Knox to Charles H. Pepper and W.H. Hoyt, 1 November 1910, SDDF 1910-1929 Box 5798, RG 59, National Archives.

39. James Bryce to Earl Grey, Washington, 4 March 1911, PRO, FO 800/334.

40. Idem., 18 February 1911.

41. Idem., 17 February 1911, PRO, FO 414/225.

42. Charles D. Hilles to Charles H. Pepper, Beverly, MA, 25 August 1911 and Pepper to Hilles, 25 August 1911, Taft Papers, Reel 399, Case 543.

43. For example, in 1895 Consul Riley offered advice on Canadian tariff policy following the 1892 amendments to the Customs Act: "The Canadian Government evidently intend as far as possible to prevent American merchants from selling goods imported into the U.S. in Canada whether dutiable or not." And in 1898, Consul Turner reported on a new rail line from Montreal to Chicago, informing the State Department, "the object of this line seems to be to draw foreign shipments from the United States to Montreal. . . ." Consul Riley to State Department, 19 December 1895, Despatches from U.S. Consuls in Ottawa, Reel 7, National Archives; Charles Turner to State Department, 9 March 1898, and 14 December 1897, Despatches from U.S. Consuls in Ottawa, Reel 8, National Archives.

44. Charles Turner to David Hill, 2 July 1902, Despatches from U.S. Consuls in Ottawa, Reel 10.

45. John Jones to Secretary of State Knox, Hamilton, Ontario, 7 November 1910, SDDF 1910-1929, Box 5795. This box is full of reports from across Canada, November and December 1910 through to June 1911. Consul-General Foster to Secretary of State Knox, Ottawa, 15 September 1911, Taft Papers, Reel 399, Case 543.

46. James Shepherd (Acting Consul) to Secretary of State Knox, Hamilton, Ontario, 16 December 1910, SDDF 1910-1929, Box 5795, RG 59, National Archives; H. Bradley to Secretary of State, Montreal, 9 November 1910, SDDF 1910-1929, Box 5798, RG 59, National Archives.

47. W.S. Fielding to Secretary of State Knox, Ottawa, 19 May 1910, SDDF 1910-1929, Box 5794, RG 59, National Archives.

48. Robert Hannigan "Reciprocity 1911: Continentalism and American Weltpolitik," *Diplomatic History*, 4(1980):1-18.

49. Memorandum for Secretary of State Knox on the Impact of the Reciprocity Agreement with Canada, SDDF 1910-1929, Box 5797, RG 59, National Archives. Huntington Wilson described this as a "splendid memo".

50. James Wilson to Legislative Committee of National Grange, Washington, 9 February 1911, Taft Papers, Reel 398, Case 543.

51. John Osborne Memorandum, 28 January 1911, SDDF 1910-1929, Box 5797, RG 59, National Archives.
52. Secretary of State Knox to Elihu Root, 28 October 1910, SDDF 1910-1929, Box 5794, RG 59 National Archives.
53. Secretary of State Knox to W.H. Hoyt, 5 October 1910, SDDF 1910-1929, Box 5794, RG 59, National Archives.
54. Secretary of State Knox to Consul-General Foster, 28 February 1911; Secretary of State Knox to W.S. Fielding, 28 October 1910, SDDF 1910-1929, Box 5795, RG 59, National Archives.
55. W.H. Hoyt to Charles H. Pepper, Ottawa, 7 November 1910, Taft Papers Reel 398, Case 543.
56. John B. Brebner, *North Atlantic Triangle: The Interplay of Canada, the United States and Great Britain* (New Haven: Yale University Press, 1945), 268.
57. James Bryce to Earl Grey, Washington, 19 October 1911, PRO, FO 414/225.
58. Ibid.
59. Senator P.J. McCumber to William Howard Taft, 15 July 1912, Taft Papers, Reel 399, Case 543.Δ61
60. James Bryce to Earl Grey, 4 October 1911, PRO, F0 800/334.

V

"An Object of American Foreign Policy since the Founding of the Republic" 1911-1988

The Taft administration believed it had offered "an excellent bargain" to Canada in 1911. Even the Canadian Governor-General recognized the generosity of the American position. "The arrangement," Grey wrote to Bryce, "which secures a free entry into a market of 90 million people for the natural produce of Canada while it secures the home market for Canadian manufacturers is a good one."[1] American policymakers attributed the failure of reciprocity, not to the indiscretions of Champ Clark, but to the imperial forces in Canada. In this view they were supported by the assessment of Fielding, the Canadian Minister of Finance. "On the economic side of the question there is absolutely no good ground which any opponent can take against the agreement," Fielding explained, "...the opposition will beat the jingo drum and pretend that the selling of more goods to Americans imperils the British connection, destroys the British Preferences and, above all things, interferes with the sacred cause of tariff reform in England . . . it is all very ridiculous."[2]

With this kind of assessment on the Canadian side it is hardly surprising that Americans resented the rejection of their reciprocity proposal. The rejection kept alive the old suspicions about Canada's relationship with the British Empire, and this remained a noticeable strand in the American response to Canada. During the post-World War I years, there was a swing back to protectionism with the Emergency Tariff Act of 1921, the Fordney-McCumber Tariff in 1922, culminating in the Smoot-Hawley Tariff of 1931. There was a particular concern about U.S. agriculture during this period which made it politically impossible to consider opening American markets to Canadian farm produce. All this ensured that there would be no effort on the American side to keep Charles H. Pepper's policies alive. Special domestic and international circumstances provided a brief window of opportunity for Pepper's case to prevail with the Taft administration. That opportunity was lost because of opposition in Canada.

While the two countries kept their distance in the early 1920s, a fundamental shift had taken place during the Great War. As the slaughter on the Western Front dragged on, Britain faced severe economic and fiscal difficulties which led to important consequences for all of her dominions, especially Canada. By 1915, for the first time in her history, Canada had to turn to New York rather than London to meet her financial needs. By the last two years of the war, the purchase of munitions and other war supplies had also shifted; by 1918, Canada had slid into a huge trade deficit with the U.S. The war toppled Britain from her position of the leading international financial power, and the United States took over the role. Britain's plight and the strengthening of the U.S. had significant long-term consequences for Canada. As J.L. Granatstein observed, "Canada had during the Great War shifted out of the British economic orbit and towards, if not yet completely, into the American."[3] The critical, public recognition of this shift did not begin to appear until the impact of the Depression and World War II forced policy changes on both sides of the border. But in terms of the deep structures of history, the die had been cast in the crisis of the 1914-1918 war.

1.

The "new departure" in U.S. relations with Canada that Secretary of State Root forecast had been stopped at the starting line. Wilfrid Laurier, the Canadian prime minister, captured this sense that the 1911 failure marked the end of a brief period of better relations, rather than the beginning of a new and more constructive relationship. "Our relations with our neighbours," he lamented after the defeat of reciprocity, "had reached a point of friendliness never attained before and perhaps for a long time hereafter, if ever, to be attained."[4] As we have seen, even during this period of warmth in Anglo-American relations, Canadians retained much of their traditional suspicion of the United States and felt that their interests were being sacrificed by Britain to the shrewd Americans. "The idea that Canada has been sacrificed again and again by John Bull in his desire to cultivate the friendship of Uncle Sam is rooted so deep in the conviction of Canada," Grey explained to Bryce, "that nothing I can say, nothing you can say, nothing that any Englishman can say will uproot it."[5] The American consuls in Canada, reporting on the defeat of reciprocity, drew attention to this persistent Canadian attitude.

Consul Slater reported from Sarnia that the Canadian consider Americans to be "shrewd and a little tricky." He added that to this day (referring back to the Webster-Ashburton Treaty), "they think that the state of Maine should have gone to Canada." It was easy in these circumstances for the opposition in Canada to portray the United States as having an ulterior motive behind the apparently generous reciprocity offer. From the outset, Slater reported to Huntington Wilson, the issue was "stormswept by false fears and emotions lest the Yankees had some sinister purpose to make Canada a mere handmaiden of Uncle Sam."[6]

On the American side there was still too much ignorance of Canada for this attitude to be fully appreciated, and the Canadian rejection was put down simply to the British imperial factor. This impression was encouraged by reports from American posts at other places in the Empire. In late 1911, for example, despatches from the Singapore consulate enclosed cuttings from local newspapers lauding the Canadian action as a step in "the onward march of the British Empire."[7] During and after World War I, Canada continued to play a prominent role in the evolution of the Empire. She was the most senior of the dominions and was the key member in the imperial war cabinet in 1917-18. At the Imperial Conference in 1926, Canadian prime minister William Lyon Mackenzie King extolled the close economic ties that had resulted from the modern imperial preference system initiated by Canada. British Colonial Secretary Arthur Balfour asserted at the same conference that the Empire was much stronger than it had been before 1914, and he anticipated further coordination on the economic front.[8]

All this, of course, proved to be a chimera. The Empire could not sustain a program of economic integration because the trade and economic interests of each colony were at odds. Canada and the other dominions, for example, were determined to protect their industries from British imports. But this basic reality, that the Empire was on a declining trajectory, was not self-evident to contemporaries. Imperial territory had actually increased after the war, as Britain gained control of Palestine, Jordan and Mesopotamia, and the former German colonies in Africa. This expansion of the Empire worried American officials. For example, in 1920 Secretary of State Colby pointedly told the British Ambassador in Washington of American fears that "the natural resources of the world should not be allowed to fall into the hands of a monopolistic trust or a monopolistic nation and that . . . there should not be a monopolistic dominion over transportation routes by sea or land."[9] Secretary of Commerce Herbert Hoover reaffirmed this point when he criticized, "the rapid drift in many countries away from these foundations [of equal access and opportunity in foreign trade]. . . . We find today that many nations are restricting development of natural resources within their own boundaries to their own citizens. They do not allow citizens of foreign countries equality of opportunity with their own."[10] Reporting on the American reaction to the 1923 Imperial Conference, Ambassador Geddes explained that the goal of the United States was to keep open access to markets and raw materials. The Imperial Conference was seen as part of the ongoing effort to create "a British protective tariff designed to further trade within the empire." It was clearly in the American interest to "defeat the preferential tariff policy" which had been originated by Canada in 1897.[11]

Americans were puzzled by developments in the Empire in the post-war years. They still expected the settlement colonies like Canada to become independent. For example, when the 1926 Imperial Conference agreed to a declaration confirming the autonomy of the dominions, the American reaction, as reported by Ambassador Chilton, was that the Balfour declaration should be "regarded as a momentous document marking the close of a chapter that began with the Declaration of Independence." But such reactions to the evolution of the Empire revealed a continuing American inability to understand the paradox that recognition of dominion autonomy helped preserve Empire cooperation as the white part of the Empire transformed itself into the British Commonwealth. As Chilton remarked in the course of his report on American reaction to the 1926 conference, relations between Britain and the dominions were "a source of bewilderment to the people of this republic."[12] Apart from the basic inability to understand why Canadians and Australians did not wish for the independence achieved by the United States back in the eighteenth century, American observers in the 1920s were puzzled by the coexistence of greater autonomy within the Empire and the planning for imperial economic consolidation. These plans seemed to come to fruition in 1932, when the Imperial Conference met at Ottawa (the first time it had been held outside London), and agreed on a comprehensive readjustment of tariffs to create a world-wide preferential imperial market. G.H. Ferguson, the Canadian High Commissioner to Britain, writing from London in anticipation of the Ottawa conference, declared, "the imperial spirit has been aroused in a way not witnessed since the war."[13]

A U.S. Department of Commerce report published in 1930 identified these efforts for imperial economic consolidation as the major theme in British economic policy since the 1914-18 war. To make sense of the British world view, the report likened the colonies and dominions to the American West. The United Kingdom was a country of matured industries similar to New England but in contrast to New England "in the British Isles there has been no great underdeveloped West as in the United States." Modern British policy was to use the Empire as the equivalent of the American West to generate new markets and acquire raw materials for aging industries. The Department of Commerce report summarized the history of imperial preference from the abandonment of the old colonial system in the 1840s through the revival of preferences by Canada in 1896 to the new post-war arrangements made in the series of conferences in the 1920s. This policy direction was confirmed by the creation of the Imperial Economic Committee, the Empire Marketing Board, and the support for imperial emigration. In the formation of "Britain's basic scheme," the colonies and dominions were to play a key role as favored markets, fields for investment, sources of raw materials, and as generators of increased transportation and insurance business. The report concluded, "British attention since the war has been concentrated largely on the overseas Empire, with the idea of Canada, Australia, South Africa and other such areas, and especially the less advanced British dependencies, taking a place equivalent to the West in American expansion." As a result of this emphasis in British policy, British goods going to Empire markets paid 9 percent less duty on average than foreign exports and the proportion of total British goods going to the Empire had increased "from 37% before the war to 42% in 1928."[14]

The conclusion of the Ottawa agreements, within two years of publication of this Commerce Department report, seemed to confirm its main point that Britain and her dominions were turning toward Empire markets as a solution to their economic problems. On the other hand, while noting that these imperial policies were of concern to the United States, there was no sense of alarm among U.S. policymakers. All this was taking place within a context in which the United States had replaced Britain as the world's foremost economic power. In 1914, the British produced 15.4 percent of the world's exports and the United States 12.4 percent. By 1927, the roles had reversed, with Britain at 12.8 percent and the United States at 15.4 percent. In the case of Canada, the United States, by 1924, had replaced Britain as the largest foreign investor. The British share of Canadian exports had declined from 48 percent in 1911, to 29 percent in 1931, while the United States, by 1931, took 41 percent of Canadian exports. All of the publicity about Empire trade through the post-war period only led to a minuscule increase of the proportion of British exports going to Canada, from 4.5 percent in 1913, to

4.7 percent in 1928.[15] Still, while there was no sense of alarm in the United States, there was concern at these signs of reinvigorated imperial economic planning, especially at a time when, as the new Secretary of State Frank B. Kellogg was warned in 1926, there was "increasing recognition of the vital part that sources of raw materials play in international relations."[16]

The only way to lever Canada away from the imperial preference system was to offer freer access to the American market, as the Taft administration had been prepared to do in 1911. But that brief period of forward-looking thinking passed; and during the 1920s, the prevailing economic and political circumstances in the United States made reciprocity with Canada an impossible policy. Above all, both parties in the United States committed themselves to high protection for American agriculture. In the course of the 1920 presidential campaign, Warren Harding singled out Canada as a special cause of concern in a generally hostile world climate for American farmers. "There is an increasing menace to our production of a number of farm products in the opening of those countries which can produce under extensive methods with labor cheaper than our own. Manchuria, South Africa, the Argentine, Canada, Siberia, Australia and New Zealand may, in the advancing years, invade our markets and underbid our farmers. In the case of Canadian wheat," Harding warned, "it will be necessary to give full and adequate tariff protection to those industries."[17] An article in the *Quarterly Journal of Economics* by F.W. Taussig drew attention to the upward spiraling of U.S. tariffs in 1883, 1890, 1894, 1897, 1909, 1913, and again with the Fordney-McCumber Act in 1922. The British Ambassador thought there was no hope of a renewal of reciprocity in these circumstances, explaining to the Foreign Office, "the war had produced certain psychological effects one of the most important being an intensification of the feeling of national self-sufficiency. . . . This trend is particularly notable in the agricultural sections of the country whose representatives in Congress, impelled by the severe decline in prices from which the farmers suffered in 1920-21, supported high protection with a vehemence never shown before."[18] The passage of the 1921 and 1922 tariff acts led Taussig to conclude his article with the observation that the agricultural states were committed to "a policy of high even ruthless protection."[19] By July 1923, the price of wheat on the Chicago market had fallen below $1.00 a bushel for the first time since 1914 and the U.S. Department of Agriculture forecast no relief for the bleak conditions. It expected a continued decline in European demand because of the increased production in Russia and the Danube basin. Stocks of grain were piling up in the United

States, and the Department advocated a policy of cutting back on acreage planted. *The New York Times*, on 26 June 1926, included a statement by President Coolidge on a farm relief policy to deal with the "agricultural distress." In the following year, the *Saint Paul Pioneer Press* proclaimed, "for the first time since the Civil War the farmers' problems will force both parties to select a platform and a candidate who will put the agricultural question first."[20] The cornerstone of Pepper's policy in 1910-1911 was the integration of the U.S. and Canadian grain markets. Such a policy would have been political suicide for any administration in the 1920s.

On the Canadian side, there was resentment against the increased American tariffs on agricultural products. Consul Halstead from Montreal explained that Canadians tended to view these tariffs as specifically directed against their agricultural exports. Halstead noted in a despatch on Canadian reaction to the Fordney Act that this was "not unnatural" in view of the volume of Canadian exports to the States. He warned the State Department that such tariff policies would only force Canada to turn more energetically to the Empire market.[21] George Wrong, the Canadian historian who, during the spring of 1921, was giving a series of lectures in the United States on the subject of better relations between the two countries, found himself abused in Canada for his friendly attitudes toward the United States. "Just now," he explained to James Bryce in June 1921, "people here are feeling bitter at the tariff put on our wheat and other products by the U.S. Perhaps this is the Nemesis for our failure to accept reciprocity. The new tariff against us kills any hope of a renewal of the Reciprocity proposals."[22]

This prediction was confirmed when the United States rebuffed Canadian pleas for a reopening of the reciprocity issue. In the last days of 1921, a Liberal government returned to power in Canada (the first since their defeat on reciprocity in 1911). The new Finance Minister was Fielding who, of course, had negotiated the 1911 agreement. Through the U.S. Consul-General in Ottawa, Fielding let the State Department know, "if he assumed the Finance portfolio it would be his purpose at an early date to endeavour to open negotiations with the U.S. for reciprocity."[23] This and other Canadian overtures on the subject over the next decade made no impact on American policymakers. William McClure in the Office of the Foreign Trade Advisor acknowledged that the Canadian approach represented "the most important tariff matter that has come to the Department during my experience," but he could find no reason to proceed. "My predisposition is adverse," he explained as he rejected a basic premise of Pepper's case, ". . . in general I strongly disapprove of special commercial arrangements and I am yet to be persuaded of the soundness of the doctrine of propinquity." Moreover, even if the State Department thought the policy worth pursuing, there was no hope of getting Congressional support. "As a matter of practical politics," he added, "the probable opposition of the powerful groups in Congress representing agricultural interests would seem to make the acceptance of Canadian reciprocity on the Hill exceedingly doubtful."[24] This initial assessment within the State Department remained the standard for the rest of the decade. In 1925, an internal memorandum in the Office of the Economic Advisor recommended against special tariff arrangements with Canada on lumber since this "would open up the whole complicated question of our economic relations with Canada."[25] In 1927, McClure reiterated that the U.S. was not interested in reciprocity but simply sought to receive treatment from Canada that was not less favorable than Canada accorded any other country. Since Canada had an imperial preference tariff as well as an intermediate tariff below the general tariff (which was imposed on U.S. exports to Canada), then clearly the limited American objective should be to get onto that intermediate tariff.[26] Finally in 1929, two memoranda by Harry Hawkins and Henry Carter, in response to the League of Nations' invitation to participate in a tariff truce conference, confirmed that no one in the State Department thought a treaty with Canada was possible. Carter argued that any special tariff arrangement with Canada, "must be regarded as impractical. So long as domestic legislation makes unconditional most favored nation treaties mandatory upon this Department and so long as the temper of the farm bloc is decisively opposed to freer agricultural imports, Canadian reciprocity must be postponed."[27] Hawkins was even more emphatic. It was tempting to think of the Canadian market as a replacement for slack demand in Europe for American produce but that would mean allowing Canadian agricultural products freer access to the U.S. market. There was "no support in Congress for this. Canadian reciprocity . . . seems out of the question at present."[28]

As these internal State Department memos make clear, there was no prospect of movement in the direction of a policy that would allow cheaper Canadian farm products into the American market. Insofar as any hard thinking was being done on the subject of new approaches to Canada, it was to view Canada as a channel through which American agricultural products could reach foreign markets. As T.Y. Wickham, a member of the Chicago Board of Trade, told the *Burlington Gazette* in 1927, "the whole crux of the farm question lies in our foreign trade."[29] To move grain cheaply and efficiently from the Midwest and Upper Plains states required improvement of the shipping route from the Great Lakes down the St. Lawrence. This could only be accomplished through agreement with Canada, and it was a sign of the importance of the agricultural issue that in the late 1920s the St. Lawrence issue became the top priority of the State Department in its Canadian planning.

The planning becomes easier to identify with the opening in 1927 of the U.S. Legation in Ottawa. American policymakers had long wished for this direct diplomatic contact, for they viewed Canada's relationship with Britain through the Colonial Office (which in turn worked through the Foreign Office to deal with U.S.-Canadian affairs) as a complicating factor which gave undue weight to imperial influence. Back in 1887, Secretary of State Bayard had complained about "the wordy triangular duel" that took place whenever Canadian-American relations were discussed; and, as we have noted, the Americans were anxious in 1911 to conduct direct talks on reciprocity with the Canadians in Ottawa.[30] The doubts and hesitations about direct diplomatic ties between Washington and Ottawa were on the Canadian and British sides of the triangle. The Canadian War Mission to Washington in 1917, and the enthusiasm for cooperation which carried over into the immediate post-war period, led to the authorization for the exchange of diplomatic representatives, but this mood cooled in the early 1920s. The post-war evolution of the Empire and, in particular, the declaration of dominion autonomy at the 1926 Imperial Conference helped clear the way for establishing the direct representation of the U.S. in Ottawa and of Canada in Washington during the course of 1927. In January 1927, Secretary of State Frank B. Kellogg wrote to the U.S. Minister in Belgium, William Phillips, asking him to take the new Canadian post. In his letter, Kellogg listed the various issues that were active, including such items as the diversion of lake waters at Chicago and the levels of the Great Lakes. "The questions pending with Canada," Kellogg tried to reassure Phillips, "are of very great importance." At the top of the list was "the negotiation of the St. Lawrence river project." There was no mention of tariff matters and reciprocity.[31]

The question of a cheap water route from the American interior to the Atlantic by way of the St. Lawrence was an old one; Albert Gallatin had waxed eloquent on the American right to navigate the St. Lawrence back in the 1820s. The issue was raised in the 1890s in connection with the creation of the International Joint Commission, but it assumed its modern form in the 1920s as U.S. policymakers began to treat the matter with some urgency as a solution to hard times in U.S. agriculture. Back in July of 1922, Secretary of State

Hughes had asked the new Canadian Prime Minister, William Lyon Mackenzie King, whether Canada would be willing to cooperate on a joint project for deepening the St. Lawrence route to allow passage for ocean-going vessels. He emphasized that it was "a question of considerable importance to the United States who were anxious to see the interior of their country opened to transoceanic traffic."[32] Political pressure on this matter was put on the Republican administrations of the 1920s from the Midwestern and Upper Plains states. The views from that part of the country were set out in a letter from A.H. Comstock, a grain shipper from Duluth, to Secretary of State Hughes. Comstock argued that the Panama Canal had benefited both coasts by providing cheaper water transport for long routes but had been harmful to the Midwest because "we cannot compete with cheap water routes." Comstock estimated that 10 cents a bushel could be saved on grain exports if an ocean-going route could be opened. "The Central West," Comstock concluded, "can be greatly relieved by giving us also the cheap water transportation which would help solve our present troubles."[33] In April 1924, Alfred Crozier of the National Republican Club emphasized to Secretary Hughes the significance of the St. Lawrence as a political issue. In 1920, the Democrats had already put such a plank into their platform, "so too had the LaFollette people and there was no doubt both will do so this year." He warned Hughes that if "our" party ignores the subject, "we would simply be handing the Democrats and LaFollette a ready-made powerful issue with which to take away from President Coolidge many normally Republican States among the 18 Central West States that are officially making attainment of access to the sea their paramount question."[34] This kind of pressure led to the creation of a Presidential Commission to study the St. Lawrence issue. It was led by Secretary of Commerce Herbert Hoover and concluded that an ocean route through the St. Lawrence "would relieve the interior of the continent, especially agriculture, from the economic hardships of adverse transportation costs. . . ." When Hoover made his acceptance speech at the Republican National Convention in 1928, he took care to mention the seaway.[35]

This domestic political and economic background explains why Secretary of State Kellogg gave "the St. Lawrence project" the highest priority when the United States opened its first embassy to Ottawa. The fact that Kellogg himself was from Minnesota gave him a lively appreciation of all the dimensions of the issue. The position on the Canadian side, however, was not promising. The Canadian response was complicated by a jurisdictional dispute between Ontario and Quebec over the existing canals and over the distribution of power from future dams on the river. This dispute was dragging on in the Canadian courts and the King government told the Americans it could not act until all the legal issues were resolved. Moreover, the Canadian government was worried about the impact of a seaway on the two government supported railroads, the Canadian Pacific and the Canadian National. Since railroad rates were in any event cheaper in Canada than the United States, the case for the water route was much less pressing. Finally, the Hoover Commission had mentioned the possible development of power projects in connection with the seaway; but while this aspect became increasingly attractive to the United States (especially in New York) in the 1920s and 1930s, it held no allure for the Canadians whose forecasts suggested that power supplies were adequate for the foreseeable future.

The first assessments from American officials in Canada did not fully describe this complexity but fell back on the old theme of imperial interference. In January 1926, Consul Halstead wrote a strictly confidential letter to Secretary of State Hughes reporting that the CPR was the villain behind Canadian unresponsiveness. Halstead told Hughes that the CPR "whose interests would be affected by the competition, the same railway being largely responsible for opposition to any plan that would increase the trade north and south instead of east and west in Canada" was exerting a "powerful influence" behind the scenes.[36] Even Secretary of State Kellogg in an early despatch to Phillips was inclined to suspect imperial influence behind the Canadian refusal to move forward on the St. Lawrence matter. On 8 August 1927, Kellogg wrote to Phillips that he was "much disappointed by the information you gave me yesterday and the day before on the subject of the St. Lawrence Power project. Evidently there is no prospect of getting such a program through anywhere in the near future." The following day, in the midst of a diatribe against the British position at the Geneva disarmament conference, Kellogg declared to Phillips, "it would not surprise me in the least if the British Government's hand is in the St. Lawrence River project against the United States."[37]

This reading of the Canadian position was far too simplistic—a lingering sign of the stock American reaction since 1867 that Canada was a troublesome imperial appendage of Britain. But with a U.S. Minister in Ottawa, the State Department and Secretary Kellogg began to get an education on Canada. Phillips, as the first U.S. Minister, played a seminal role in this respect. There had been other moments when good information was generated on Canada (for example, in the consular reports in 1911), but this patchy flow of knowledge became sustained after 1927 as regular ministerial reports were sent back to Washington. If Phillips had been lazy or uninterested, many of the old attitudes reflected in Kellogg's impatient remark about a lurking imperial presence might have persisted much longer. But Phillips was a thoughtful, hard working minister who took pains to inform himself about the Canadian political scene and thus provide the basis for an intelligent American response to Canada. Kellogg, to give him credit, was willing to be educated. He told Phillips in November 1927, "I read all your reports in relation to the situation of the St. Lawrence River improvement with the greatest interest."[38] In those reports, Phillips explained a range of factors stalling the project in Canada—the imperial factor was not among them. Phillips summarized the Canadian objections under six headings: 1) such an agreement with the United States would sacrifice Canadian sovereign rights over the St. Lawrence; 2) special interests in the United States wanted cheap power from the St. Lawrence; 3) the Americans must agree to restrictions on the Chicago drainage scheme; 4) Canada's political autonomy would be undermined; 5) the scheme would not be supported in the Conservative-controlled Canadian Senate even if the government were to go ahead; and, finally, 6) the St. Lawrence was Canada's most valuable asset, and she should drive a hard bargain by demanding significant U.S. tariff reductions in return for Canadian cooperation on the seaway project. Phillips also pointed out, as though it would be a novel view for the State Department, that Canadians were suspicious of American proposals in general because Canada had "always suffered in Canadian-U.S. negotiations."[39]

It is doubtful whether anything could have moved the Canadians to act on the St. Lawrence in the 1920s. There were too many domestic cross-currents on the issue and no clear evidence that Canada needed the extra transportation capacity or the power that might be generated by the project. However, as Phillips reported, the Canadian government was ready to use the issue to put some pressure on the United States to lower U.S. tariffs on Canadian agricultural products. Thus, beginning in the Fall of 1927, the King government linked discussion of the St. Lawrence with discussion of the tariff. This exasperated Phillips and Kellogg because the main purpose of the St. Lawrence scheme was to help with the agricultural problem in the U.S. To lower the tariff and allow Canadian agricultural produce in at cheaper rates would nullify the political benefits expected from the project. Some of this exasperation can be seen in a Phillips memo written in November 1928, in which he stated to Kellogg that the tariff issue and the St. Lawrence project "have become so confused in Canadian minds whether intentionally or not that it seems they will inevitably be considered together." The Canadian Prime Minister told Phillips that there would be no hope whatsoever for the St. Lawrence project if U.S. tariffs were raised as promised by Hoover in the 1928 presidential campaign. "This would produce a critical situation," King warned Phillips, "which would affect once and for all the future relations of Canada with the United States. His country would be driven . . . to turn away from the United States and to determine upon a closer economic union with the British Empire and with other parts of the world."[40]

The impasse was set out clearly in a personal note from Phillips to Kellogg on the last day of 1928. Phillips had been holding private discussions with Canadian officials

> to emphasise that the United States cannot wait forever on the decision of the Canadian government. My line of action is that Mr. Hoover is committed to farm relief and so definitely committed that even if he should desire personally not to press the Canadian government, he cannot keep the 22 states interested in the reduction of rates to the sea quiet for very much longer. He must satisfy them either by an assurance that cheap water transportation will soon be open to them or by raising the tariff against agricultural products.[41]

When the new Hoover administration did in fact raise the tariff, Phillips reported that the Canadian press inveighed against the United States for using the tariff "as a club to force Canadian compliance with our desire for the St. Lawrence Seaway development." The U.S. Minister took a gloomy view and concluded that the tariff policy of the U.S. presented "a further and most serious obstacle to progress on the St. Lawrence project."[42]

A last minute effort was made by the new Secretary of State, Henry Stimson, through the Canadian minister in Washington. He wanted to develop a fancy solution by which the new tariff provisions could be delayed (with respect to Canada) in return for forward movement on the St. Lawrence, but this fell through.[43] The two countries remained at this impasse throughout the decade. The United States wished an agreement on the St. Lawrence to obtain a cheap water route to the ocean for American farmers; the Canadians wanted some new version of reciprocity, or at least, a lowering of U.S. tariffs on Canadian agricultural products. The two goals were incompatible. With the Great Crash and the onset of the Depression, the gulf between the two countries seemed to widen further as the U.S. turned to even higher levels of protection and

Canada turned to a more comprehensive system of Empire trade at the 1932 Ottawa Imperial Conference.

2.

By 1932, the relationship appeared to be characterized by mutual incomprehension. The establishment of direct, diplomatic relations in 1927 was obviously a step forward, but no serious reassessment of Canadian policy had taken place since the 1911 debacle. No one in the State Department was giving the careful, long-term consideration to Canada that Pepper had twenty years earlier. In these circumstances, there were two possible lines of development for American policymakers. The first was simply to accept the situation, conclude that each country would stick to its own traditional course, and do nothing. The second option was to follow Pepper's example—examine the underlying facts and propose a new direction. Two documents written by American officials in 1931 represent the arguments for these opposite courses.

The first memo, advocating inaction, was written by Wesley Frost, the U.S. Consul in Montreal.[44] Frost had extensive experience in Canadian affairs. In 1910, as a statistician in the Bureau of Trade Relations at the Department of State, he was asked to make a study of the tariff issue in connection with Taft's reciprocity policy. Throughout the discussions on reciprocity he prepared information for the American negotiators. He was a consul in Canada between 1912 and 1914 and Assistant Trade Advisor between 1918 and 1920. At the Montreal post for three years, the occasion of his memo to the U.S. Legation in Ottawa and the Secretary of State was the Canadian budget announced by the new Conservative Prime Minister R.B. Bennett on 18 June 1931.

Frost placed the higher tariffs proposed by Bennett in the context of a long history of pro-Empire and anti-American tariff policies by Canada. Bennett's tariff increases "appear to the writer as merely one more step in a long succession of measures." Frost assumed that the Department of State had a good institutional memory and that its officers would remember that this Canadian policy had started in the 1860s and 1870s, "when John A. Macdonald formed his so-called National Policy." In 1866, when the United States abrogated the 1854 Reciprocity Treaty, Canadian producers found themselves excluded "from their best and most natural market." There were two schools of thought in Canada as to the best way of responding to these conditions. The Liberal party generally adhered to free trade ideals, was more friendly to the United States, and hoped to earn more favorable treatment from the United States. In contrast, the Conservatives were determined to build Canada's own "national economic system" behind protective barriers. It was "this latter policy which won the day" to the extent that even the Liberal party became committed to protection. "Even when the Liberals have been in power," Frost pointed out, "they have maintained in general the protective rates instituted by the Conservatives although they have endeavored to warp the system somewhat into the direction of free trade by the British Preferential and Intermediate schedules and by the ill-starred Reciprocity Agreement in 1911." Frost concluded, "it may be taken as certain that Canada is wholly committed to a general policy of protectionism against the United States and that no broad plan for economic co-operation between the two countries could be brought forward."

Frost made his assessment even more negative by arguing that the agricultural circumstances of the time made the prospect of dealing with Canada hopeless. The main item on Canada's agenda was to obtain easier access to the American market for her wheat and other agricultural products. "American agriculture," Frost declared, "is in no position to sustain a shock of this kind and would doubtless make very effective political protests against a special agreement with Canada." Even if a tariff reduction was politically possible in the United States, Frost doubted that Canada would respond in a cooperative way given her imperial and protectionist outlook. Canadians distrusted American tariff policy, fearing that Congress might change its mind on short notice. The opposition in Canada would also raise the old cry of annexation if commercial fusion seemed on the agenda. Frost summed up his position with an eloquent and vehement statement that no new policy initiative with respect to Canada should be taken. It would be of

> doubtful utility for the United States to consider seriously either special tariff arrangements with Canada or the general lowering of certain rates in the American Customs Law with a view to favoring Canada. The latter is committed to a policy of building up an entire range of industries within its own borders. The die was cast many years ago and it may be taken as certain that the economic development of the Dominion will be to no small degree separate from that of the United States. For better or for worse Canada will go her own way industrially and nothing which can be done by the United States will have any appreciable effect towards breaking down Canadian economic separatism.[45]

Frost's pessimistic assessment seemed to reflect the course of Canadian-American relations since 1911, but his thinking was outmoded. Inside the State Department there were officials who tried to think their way through to more constructive formulations. Frost's paper was written on 24 June 1931; on 6 December 1931, Benjamin Wallace in the Office of the Economic Advisor drew up a paper which came to the opposite conclusion of Frost and forecast the direction of U.S. policy toward Canada for the next fifty years.[46] Wallace began his case by echoing a point made back in the 1890s by Goldwin Smith, that if the United States permitted Canada to develop into a rival economic power in North America, it would be a great testimony to the blindness of American policymaking. Wallace opened bluntly by asserting, "the greatest error in the commercial policy of the United States has been the treatment of Canada." "Canadians," he continued,

> are of the same language and stock, and have essentially the same standard of living and the same political outlook and ideals as Americans. The boundary between us is largely artificial and Canada is so divided geographically that the natural trade routes are North and South. There is no military, or political, or economic reason for not treating Canada economically as part of the United States.

Wallace was the first State Department official to note in an official document how badly Canada had suffered from U.S. tariff policy. Because of the volume of Canadian trade with the United States, Canada was hurt by U.S. tariff hikes more quickly and more severely than any other country. "Canada's difficulty in reaching other markets," explained Wallace, "makes her peculiarly dependent on the United States, so that our tariff policy has hurt Canada more than it has hurt any other country. We have been in a position to exploit the Canadians and we have done it ruthlessly. In no other country is there so much bitterness against the American tariff and so much reason for bitterness."

Wallace warned that this pattern of American treatment of Canada was driving her into the arms of the Empire. He traced all of Canada's decisive moves toward imperial economic cooperation to Canada's reaction against U.S. tariffs. "Canada initiated the preferential tariff movement in 1897 because of the Dingley tariff," argued Wallace. "After the war, the Liberal party of Canada made several successive reductions in the tariff but the hostile attitude of the United States discredited them, and their opponents made drastic increases during and after the recent revision of the U.S. tariff act and are proposing further large steps toward a union of the British Empire." With Britain now heading toward a comprehensive protectionist system, Wallace reckoned the chances of a successful system of Empire preference were greatly improved, and he recommended that "if anything is ever to be done to initiate closer trade relations between the U.S. and Canada, it should be done well before June 1932 when the next Imperial Conference meets."[47]

Wallace's advice was not followed at the time and as Wallace and Frost (from their differing perspectives) had warned, the 1932 Imperial Conference in Ottawa raised the protective walls around the Empire. But, if Wallace's memorandum did not lead to immediate action, it did point the way to the future direction of the American response to Canada. In 1935, a Reciprocal Trade Treaty between Canada and the United States was signed. Canada began to realize what she had hoped for since 1866—better access to the United States for agricultural and other natural products. The United States, for its part, was finally beginning to implement the policy set out by Pepper in 1910-1911 and occasionally restated in individual position papers like Wallace's in 1931. The treaty enabled easier sales to Canada of U.S. products such as farm implements, automobiles, electrical goods, gasoline, and machinery. Canada had easier access to the American market for her lumber, cattle, dairy products, fish, whiskey, and potatoes.

American policymakers had seen no prospect of a trade treaty with Canada in the 1920s. It was the circumstances created by the Depression that led to changed attitudes. The context for change was set up by the Reciprocal Trade Treaties Act of 1934, which established a general framework for trade treaties. This was a pet project of Secretary of State Cordell Hull, who intended it to be a mechanism for lowering the defensive, protective barriers that had come into being around the world as a result of the Depression. While Hull presented the policy in idealistic terms, it was intended to promote U.S. trade interests. The countries on the initial negotiating list were those that did not threaten to make any major inroads on the American market (the first country on the list was Brazil). Canada was a problem in this respect, as she had been ever since 1866, because she was bound to seek lower tariffs on her agricultural products, and it seemed extremely difficult for the Roosevelt administration to make such concessions to Canada in the midst of the farm crisis of the 1930s. As an internal memorandum of the Division of Western European affairs noted in September 1934, "it was clearly recognized that agreement with the Dominion was basically an agricultural problem."[48]

There was also a problem in proceeding with Canada under Hull's program because of distrust between the two governments. Bennett's Conservative government came into power in Canada in 1930 and embarked on a vigorous imperial solution to the Depression. When the imperial solution failed to improve conditions in Canada, the Bennett administration sought to negotiate a trade treaty with the United States. The Canadian minister to the United States, W.H. Herridge, met with Secretary of State Hull in early February 1934 and made it clear that he was "very desirous" to open trade talks.[49] From Ottawa, Warren Robbins, the U.S. Minister, reported on 10 March 1934, "it is evident that Canada is eager to conclude a treaty at the earliest possible moment."[50] But, by this time a Canadian election was in the offing, and there was some suspicion in the State Department that Canada was trying to set up a situation in which the United States could be portrayed as intransigent. For example, when W.H. Herridge sent a long note to Hull in November 1934 complaining about the impact of U.S. policies on Canada, Robbins sent a cablegram from Ottawa advising Hull that the note was "written with a view to public consumption on Canada for political purposes."[51]

Because of the agricultural problem, and because of this atmosphere of suspicion, the negotiations went slowly. So slowly in fact that Herridge and Bennett believed the Americans were deliberately stalling in the expectation that unsuccessful negotiations would contribute to a Conservative defeat in the 1935 Canadian elections. But all the evidence suggests that the real cause of delay was that increased Canadian agricultural imports threatened too many interests in the United States. Indeed, from the long-range American standpoint, it would have made sense to conclude a trade treaty with the Conservatives rather than with the new Liberal government. The Conservatives were the traditional imperialist and protectionist party. It would have been in the American interest to commit that party to closer trade relations in North America. Pierre de Boal, the American Chargé, recommended this approach in a memorandum on "political considerations" in trade talks. He pointed out that if the United States concluded a provisional agreement with the Conservatives, "it will be difficult for them out of power to criticise extensions."[52]

On 21 January 1935, public notice was issued that Canada was on the list of countries with which a reciprocal trade agreement was to be negotiated; the treaty was in place by November. As was the case in 1911, the papers and memoranda drawn up during the preparations and negotiations for this treaty revealed American thinking about Canada. There is no doubt, of course, that Hull viewed the treaty as part of his general policy to open up world trade and repair the damage done by "the small but powerful Hawley-Smoot wrecking crew."[53] But behind the internationalist and good neighbor rhetoric, there were other items on the agenda.

First, and most obvious, the 1935 treaty with Canada was regarded as a blow to the imperial preference system. As early as July 1933, William C. Bullitt, one of the American delegates to the 1933 London Economic Conference, suggested to Roosevelt that he should be alive to the possibility of negotiating a reciprocal tariff agreement with Canada. Bennett had hinted he was open to this policy option and, as Bullitt put it to Roosevelt, "via Canada we might make a hole in the Ottawa agreements."[54] During the Imperial Conference in 1932, Hanford MacNider of the U.S. Ottawa Legation warned that reinvigorated imperial sentiment would lead to "even more drastic barriers against imports from the United States into Canada."[55] In a strictly confidential note to Hull in February 1933, Pierre de Boal, the U.S. Chargé in Ottawa, reported on some private conversations with Bennett during which the Canadian Prime Minister "assured me of his desire to enter into negotiations." De Boal explained that economic conditions were so bad that Bennett knew he had to turn to the United States to "free himself from the criticism that his economic policy in embracing the Empire has isolated Canada from its natural market, the United States."[56] By the end of September 1934, there was a British Empire committee established in the State Department whose "primary function was to determine the best means of undermining the imperial preference system."[57]

This aspect of American thinking in the early 1930s is not surprising; but inside the State Department, new approaches to Canada were being developed which went beyond this conventional response. This can be seen most clearly in correspondence in early 1933 between John D. Hickerson, Assistant Chief of the Division of Western European Affairs, and Professor W.Y. Elliot of Harvard's Department of Government. During the 1930s and 1940s, Hickerson became the key person in the State Department on Canadian matters. He began to become a Canadian specialist when he was assigned to the U.S. Consulate General in Ottawa in 1925. He developed a close relationship with the top people in Canada's Department of External Affairs, particularly Hugh Keenleyside. Elliot was an important outside expert on international economic matters (he was the Harvard mentor of Henry Kissinger and also taught Pierre Trudeau, to whom he wrote in 1969 complaining about Canada's isolationist policies).[58] He placed the trade relationship with Canada on a more sophisticated level. Elliot opened his case by drawing attention to the issue of American mineral supplies. He argued, "the exploitation of foreign mineral supplies to conserve American resources is a cardinal feature of a wise mineral policy." If this axiom was accepted, then a trade agreement with Canada became an important goal because of

"Canadian mineral and power resources." An arrangement that would secure American access to these resources would have multiple advantages—"it would directly aid in the solution of current economic and political problems such as those of dwindling international and national trade, of exchange transfer and debt payments, falling prices and monetary unsettlement and extravagant economic nationalism and economic imperialism."

Elliot linked this new strategic economic planning to the old American aim of breaking down Canada's imperial orientation. To illustrate the potential danger to the United States if the Empire solution to the Depression became successful, Elliot took the example of U.S. iron and steel exports to Canada. The iron and steel trade was the largest American export to Canada and, warned Elliot, it provided "a most illuminating example of the menace to American industry and to Canadian-American trade of the Ottawa Empire Conference agreements." As a result of those agreements, Canada raised tariffs to provide imperial preference. Elliot forecast that English specifications for iron and steel products would "take over and lead to an even more drastic cut in imports from the United States." Elliot then followed the same line of argument taken by Wallace in his 1931 memorandum—that harsh American tariff policy was drawing Canada into unnatural, imperial economic arrangements. "Canadian participation in this economic imperialism," he told Hickerson, "is based on resentment of American trade policy. Canada's natural economic ties are with the United States and are always quickly recognised when the opportunity is present." The correct American response to Canada was to encourage economic integration; steep protectionist barriers simply encouraged a harmful rival trade bloc to the north. "By allowing natural forces free play, the completely artificial and extremely threatening structure of imperial economic antagonism to the United States would collapse. The economic disadvantages to the United States of the Ottawa Empire Conference are obvious; the damages to friendly relations and international progress are incalculable."[59]

Elliot then urged Hickerson to appreciate the "unique conditions favoring reciprocity with Canada." In doing so Elliot was going down the same path as Andrews back in the 1840s and 1850s and Pepper in 1911; but by the 1930s, the case seemed even more compelling because of all the connections that had been building up between the two countries. Elliot set out four points that made Canada's relationship with the United States unique. First was "geographical proximity, coupled with the bonds of common race and language, common press and radio, common sport and scandal, with close relations in every cultural field, similarity of social legal and political institutions..."   Secondly, Elliot pointed out that in spite of the tariff barriers that had been raised by both countries since 1866, trade with Canada was "by far the largest volume of trade which the United States has with any one country" and constituted "the largest two-way trade in the world." Thirdly, Elliot reminded the State Department that in the past two decades American investment in Canada had increased rapidly. By 1931, the U.S. invested more dollars in Canada than in all of South America, and the amount was now approaching the total U.S. capital invested in Europe. To help Hickerson understand the significance of this development, Elliot related it to another major economic feature of the post-1918 world, the movement of money in connection with the payment of Allied war debts. The interest received by the United States on her Canadian investments "exceeded by 60% the total of similar interest, including all War Debt payments, received from any other country in 1931. In fact, Canada is annually meeting payments in New York far in excess of the total annual sums of both principal and interest due, paid or unpaid, from all the Allied War Debtors."

For his fourth point Elliot returned to the natural resources issue. "From an economic point of view," he explained, "the resources of the northern and southern halves of the North American Continent are in many respects complementary rather than competitive." Canada was rich in non-ferrous metal resources and hydroelectric power but was deficient in iron, coal, and oil. Elliot concluded that the lowering of tariffs on Canadian-American trade would be "an all important step in business and monetary recovery and in dealing with current economic and political problems such as the War Debts and the economic imperialism of the British Empire." A regional agreement with such an important trading partner as Canada might also pave the way for a more general reduction of trade barriers around the world.[60]

Elliot worked hard to make the two governments think in such visionary terms. At the request of Secretary Hull and Ambassador Phillips, he visited Ottawa in June 1935 to examine, first hand, the Canadian situation. On his return he wrote to President Roosevelt urging him to conclude an agreement before the Bennett Conservative government fell from power. Always looking to the long-term outcome, Elliot reasoned that it would be in the United States' interest to "hook the Conservative Party in principle to tariff concessions to the United States." The Conservatives, since the National Policy of John A. Macdonald's era in the 1870s and 1880s, had been the party of Empire and tariffs. If the United States could break this pattern and get the Canadian Conservatives to connect themselves to a policy of reduced tariffs, it would be a significant, strategic victory for American policymakers.[61]

Elliot's vision was not achieved in the 1935 agreement. It was delayed until Bennett fell from power, and it was a very limited arrangement that contained none of the sweeping policy break-throughs he had advocated. The average tariff rate of both countries was still above the level that had obtained before the Hawley-Smoot tariff. There were several reasons for the narrowness of the agreement. The first, as we have already noted, was the distrust between the Bennett and Roosevelt administrations which increased after the opening of talks. Bennett had come into power in 1930 with aggressive rhetoric on tariffs, which he intended to raise to blast Canada's way into world markets.[62] This approach had manifested itself in his pro-Empire rhetoric and in the actual imperial tariff agreement in 1932. Thus, when Bennett told Pierre de Boal of the Ottawa embassy, in private conversation that it was his "desire to enter into negotiations with our government," there was some skepticism in Washington. This skepticism was intensified by the handling of the Canadian case by W.H. Herridge, the Canadian minister to Washington. Herridge composed a long note of complaint against the United States setting out the adverse impact on the Canadian economy of American tariff and fiscal policies which created a huge drain of wealth from Canada.[63] This note, in the American view, was designed for use in the pending Canadian election. In these circumstances American officials treaded warily.

But, much more than the lack of trust engendered by Bennett and Herridge, it was the agricultural issue that delayed the negotiations, lengthened them, and in the end, caused the agreement to be safely limited, both as to the range of items included and as to the volume of trade of those items. The agricultural interests had prevented any American administration in the 1920s from contemplating renewed trade talks with Canada. When Hull formally announced his reciprocal trade policy, Canada was not on the initial list of countries and when negotiations finally began, American officials proceeded with extreme caution. Right to the end, this was the prevailing mood in Washington. In spite of Elliot's vision of the future, in spite of the good neighbor rhetoric that was to surround the announcement of the treaty, when President Roosevelt met in the Oval Office with John Hickerson, Henry Grady, and Francis Sayre (the American negotiators) to go over the terms of the agreement for one last time, the conference was taken up by an explanation of how American agriculture was to be protected from Canadian imports.[64] Apart from

Roosevelt's particular concern about the dairy interests in upper New York state, the condition of American agriculture in general made any dramatic breakthrough unlikely. For example, grain had been the centerpiece of Pepper's strategic plan back in 1911; in 1935 it was not even on the list. To discuss the possibility of allowing Canadian grain into the U.S. would have been politically disastrous. Thus, even those American officials like Hickerson whose outlook was being informed by Elliot's writings, took a tough line throughout the talks and kept U.S. concessions to a minimum. Hickerson understood there was no chance of the strategic leap forward contemplated by Elliot. In 1911, Canadian domestic opinion had been the obstacle; in 1934-35 it was American domestic circumstances that prevented a breakthrough.

But the 1935 trade treaty, in spite of its limited nature, did represent a significant advance for American goals with respect to Canada. To begin with, the concept that Canada represented a special case and that American economic policy ought to recognize this was being established. A sign of this was a new phrasing of the issues, most notably in the memorandum by Pierre de Boal, which referred to the goal of encouraging "a special contiguous country economic regime" to emerge in Canada.[65] Pepper thought in these terms in 1911; Elliot pointed to the future benefits of such an approach in 1933; and now, American officials were translating these think-pieces into phrases that could be included in despatches. Secondly, the 1935 agreement could be viewed as a success in the sense that it contributed to the weakening of the imperial economic system. This was particularly evident since the Conservative government of Bennett, still flushed with the success of the 1932 Ottawa Imperial Conference, had come pleading to the United States for a trade agreement. Even though Elliot's advice was not taken—the treaty was not signed with the Bennett Conservative government but with their Liberal successors—the Canadian pro-Empire party had committed itself to the view that Empire solutions were inadequate and that Canada's future economic fortune required closer economic relations with the United States. Norman Armour, the U.S. Minister in Ottawa, confirmed this reading of the situation in a memorandum to Hull written in October 1935. Armour had just returned from a conversation with O.D. Skelton, the Undersecretary at the Department of External Affairs. Skelton agreed with Armour that the negotiations must succeed and "said that he felt that as far as Canada was concerned they were at the crossroads; they would have to reach an agreement with us . . . or it would mean their being driven into a far narrower Empire agreement which he felt, from their point of view, would be regrettable." Skelton thought it would have been better to have reached an agreement when Bennett was still in power, but he agreed with Armour's reading that the Conservatives had so committed themselves that "their opposition had been pretty effectively spiked."[66]

This impression of American success—turning Canada away from Britain toward an American direction—was amply reinforced by the words and behavior of the new Canadian Prime Minister, Mackenzie King. On 25 October 1935, the Canadian Thanksgiving holiday, the U.S. Minister was surprised by a visit from King, who had only taken office the night before. The new Prime Minister "insisted on coming to my house to see me although I assured him that I felt it was for me to come to see him." King was extremely friendly. He told Armour that he had always been in favor of lower tariffs between the United States and Canada. In 1911 he had gone down to defeat with Wilfrid Laurier on the issue; in 1929 he had talked to U.S. Minister Phillips about reductions, but the U.S. government was not interested; and that failure had been followed by the "disastrous Hawley-Smoot tariff and the defeat of Mr. King's own government." King then criticized the Ottawa agreements as an element in the destructive, economic nationalism that had emerged in the wake of the 1929 crash. It was time to get away from these exclusionist solutions, and the Canadian-American trade agreement would be an important beginning. "'He was himself,' he laughingly remarked, 'accused of being pro-American. In fact they referred to him as "the American" and with a good deal of reason for so much of his life had been spent in the United States.'" Armour continued his account of this extraordinary conversation by noting that King repeated the point already made by Skelton. "He made it plain," reported Armour, "as Dr. Skelton had done that there were two roads open to Canada but that he wanted to choose 'the American road' if we made it possible for him to do so. From every point of view, it was important that our attachment should be strong and our relations brought closer in every way, political as well as economic."[67]

While King's pitch was obviously part of an almost desperate Canadian effort to ensure that the Americans accepted the trade agreement, the dramatic way in which he expressed these views gave Armour and Hickerson a clear sense that an important breakthrough had been achieved. The treaty was certainly narrow; but here was a Canadian Prime Minister who had held office throughout the 1920s and was to remain in power until 1948, declaring in unambiguous terms that the imperial option, in terms of serious economic planning and general policymaking, was being rejected and that Canada was committed to taking "the American road." King's fawning stance in October 1935 was, of course, not a declaration of policy but the signs of the time looked most hopeful to Armour, Hickerson, and other American experts like Elliot who thought about Canadian matters.

3.

Back in 1931, in his bleak assessment of U.S. relations with Canada, Wesley Frost had forecast that there would be no rapprochement between the two countries "unless in the fullness of time a world wide political upheaval should modify national alignments."[68] The next fifteen years proved Frost right. The 1935 trade agreement was the product of the Depression as Secretary of State Hull's reciprocal trade agreement program matched Canada's desperate need for markets. In view of the stalemate that had existed between the two countries since 1911, and in view of Prime Minister King's dramatic emphasis on the agreement as a significant change of direction for Canada, the treaty did mark, as Hickerson noted to Wilgress, "a cornerstone in the economic policy of both our countries in the future."[69] If the impact of the Depression led to this critical change in attitudes, the impact of World War II irrevocably changed the mold of the U.S. response to Canada. Frost's 1931 report had been prescient in this respect. The twin impact of the Depression and World War II created the political upheaval that led to conditions for North American integration.[70]

From the U.S. viewpoint, the 1935 agreement was essential to prevent the imperial solution to the Depression in world trade from working. The buildup of British Empire tariffs in the wake of the Ottawa conference in 1932, led J. Pierrepont Moffatt, the U.S. Consul-General in Australia (and later the U.S. Minister in Ottawa) to expostulate, "in matters of trade London is bitterly hostile. . . . I have reluctantly reached the conclusion that Britain is using her financial pressure to make preferential bargains and that despite lip service to the Secretary's ideals she is fighting his theory . . . to the last ditch."[71] The 1935 reciprocal trade agreement with Canada (the most populous and prosperous of the dominions) appeared to stop this British policy in its tracks. Over the next four years, the U.S. share of Canadian imports increased from 56.4 percent to 62.6 percent, while the share of imports taken by Canada "supplied by the United Kingdom and countries outside the British Empire decreased proportionately."[72] It was this kind of turn in the trade figures that led William Culbertson, the Vice-Chairman of the U.S. Tariff Commission, to declare that, of all the agreements reached in the 1930s, the trade agreement with

Canada "is the most important to this country. . . [and] directly effects a revolution in the commercial relations of the two countries."[73] Culbertson prided himself in having seen long ago the necessity for this readjustment of the American response to Canada. The modern United States' economy required foreign raw materials, foreign markets, and foreign areas for capital investment. He had warned Secretary of State Hughes, back in 1922, of the need for vigorous action by way of tariff agreements to open up markets and sources of raw materials.[74]

The context within which U.S. officials viewed the trade agreements policy of the 1930s was set out at the end of the decade by H.C. MacLean of the Trade Agreements Unit in the Department of Commerce. MacLean explained that the trade agreements program was to "expand foreign markets for U.S. products." He noted that the trade agreements were "accomplishing their purpose of reopening foreign markets for American products" as was confirmed by the "considerably greater increase that has been taking place in our imports to countries with which agreements have been made compared with exports to non-agreement countries."[75] Leo Pasvolsky, the Special Advisor on International Economic Affairs, added his weight to the case for the trade agreements policy. In an 8 January 1941 memo on "Outstanding Economic Events in the Last Twenty Years," Pasvolsky emphasized the importance of the trade agreements policy as a method of destroying the old protective tariff approach (which reached its height in the Hawley-Smoot Act in 1930) and to undermine British attempts, as manifested at the Ottawa conference, to put "the largest single international trading area in the world on a preferential basis."[76]

But while officials in the departments of State and Commerce thought in these global terms about the long-term goals of the trade agreements policy, the need to placate domestic economic interests in Congress made the Canadian agreement, as we have seen, a limited one. And because of the restricted nature of the 1935 agreement, Canada was still actively pursuing the benefits to be derived from British imperial preference. In a memorandum to Secretary of State Hull in October 1937, for example, Hickerson noted that trade discussions with Britain were meeting difficulties because Canada would "not agree to the giving up of any of her preferences." Hickerson had complained in the previous year to the U.S. Minister in Ottawa that Secretary Hull felt he was engaged in "too much of a lone fight against trade barriers" and that "certain policies" of Britain and the dominions were "not on all fours with what we are trying to do."[77] While American officials like MacLean and Hickerson had high hopes of the trade agreement with Canada, they knew that Mackenzie King's honeyed words on Thanksgiving Day 1935 were not enough. Hickerson had told Mackenzie King, in June 1936, that he hoped the 1935 agreement would be "a stepping stone to a broader and more comprehensive trade agreement," but Canada's role in the 1938 discussions with Britain showed the imperial option had not yet been scotched.[78] The future direction of the relationship between the two countries still hung in the balance. World War II tipped the balance decisively in the direction of integration.

In the space of nine months, between August 1940 and April 1941, Canada entered into two agreements with the United States—the Ogdensburg Agreement and the Hyde Park Agreement—which, at both the symbolic and practical levels, marked this decisive shift. The desperate plight of Britain in the war against Germany forced Canada to turn to the United States. Following the fall of France, Britain stood alone against Germany and seemed in imminent danger of invasion by the apparently invincible Nazi armies and the Luftwaffe. Britain's financial resources were stretched beyond their limit, and the British market for Canadian exports collapsed. Canada's traditional source of capital and her traditional market had suffered sudden and severe damage. The only alternative was to open immediate talks with the U.S. to seek out some quick and dramatic solutions to this war-induced crisis.

At Ogdensburg in August 1940, President Roosevelt and Prime Minister King agreed to establish a Permanent Joint Board of Defense. The agreement was a logical extension of Roosevelt's public statement in 1938 that the United States would defend Canada if she were threatened by invasion, but "what was striking about it . . . was that the Board was declared to be permanent." As R.D Cuff and J.L. Granatstein note, "the Agreement marked the shift from Canada as a British dominion, to Canada as an American protectorate."[79] The impact of Ogdensburg emerges with some force if it is placed against the previous fifty years of Canadian defense policy. In spite of the participation of English Canadians in the ideology of imperialism that emerged in the 1880s and 1890s, no Canadian government had committed itself to a common imperial defense policy.[80] During and after the Great War, Canada used her new-found sense of nationalism to distance herself from British military and naval policies and to identify defense and foreign policies that reflected Canada's own interests.[81] Throughout the post-1918 period, Canada and the other dominions became ever more independent of Britain, a process that culminated in the formal recognition of dominion autonomy by the 1931 Statute of Westminster. For fifty years Canada had resisted attempts by

Britain to formalize a common policy of imperial defense; yet at Ogdensburg, she committed herself to a permanent military alliance with the United States for the common defense of North America.

From the American Legation in Ottawa, U.S. Minister Pierrepont Moffatt pointed out to Secretary Hull the radical nature of the Ogdensburg Agreement. "Officials in Ottawa," Moffatt informed Hull, "consider that no more important development in recent times has taken place in Canadian-American relations than arose out of the meeting at Ogdensburg."[82] As in 1935, American views—that a breakthrough had been achieved—were warmly encouraged by the Canadian Prime Minister. On the journey back to Ottawa from Ogdensburg, Prime Minister King had a long conversation with Moffatt during which he expressed his enthusiasm for the agreement. King noted that even the *Montreal Gazette* "which represented a point of view that a few years ago would not have liked any American-Canadian rapprochement, had committed itself in favor of the idea." King continued that the press and radio coverage had been strongly in support of closer ties, though he added, "not enough emphasis had been placed on the word *permanent* to the title of PJBD." The Canadian Prime Minister was so enthused, he declared to the U.S. Minister that he would like to see common citizenship. He promised Moffatt that he would help *Fortune* magazine, as it undertook its survey of U.S. public opinion about Canada because this type of coverage was essential for closer understanding and closer ties. "Tell them," Moffatt reported King as saying, "that the door is wide open. Luce is a help in our cause and we will not let him down."[83] Two weeks later when Edgar Dean of the Council on Foreign Relations visited Ottawa he observed, "the trend towards the United States is growing stronger throughout Canada, particularly in formerly hostile circles such as the Imperialists in Toronto."[84]

Much of this fervor can be attributed to the fact that Canada was at war, but American officials saw beyond the emotion of the moment to a deep and lasting change in the relationship. The manner in which it was viewed is summed up cogently by Adolfe Berle, a Special Assistant at the State Department, who worked as an expert on Canadian matters during the war. In his diary, Berle explained the thinking on the American side which led to the Ogdensburg Agreement. In August of 1939, Roosevelt asked Berle to find "historical precedents tending to show that the object of the Monroe Doctrine is actually to keep war off the American hemisphere." Berle explained that based on this reworking of the Monroe Doctrine, "and on his speech declaring that he would defend Canada, he had in mind undertaking to prevent any hostile action against any European colony in the New World ranging all the way from Canada to Guiana." As Berle noted, this way of thinking which was made urgent by the war, "does really change the status of the New World; a kind of Pax Americana."[85] In Roosevelt's approach then, Ogdensburg was not so much the intimate, bilateral pact that King exulted over, but an element in the completion of American hegemony in the western hemisphere. Berle, as he became involved with his Canadian counterparts, thought this outcome was now inevitable. During March 1941, he was in Ottawa to discuss the coordination of economic policy in the wake of the Agreement. In his talks with Hugh Keenleyside, Berle noted with evident pleasure how far matters had gone in bringing Canada into the American sphere. While they did talk about some immediate issues, Berle explained, "the rest of it goes much farther. Keenleyside realises that this is now one continent and one economy; that we shall have to be integrated as to finance, trade routes and pretty much everything else; and in this I so thoroughly agree with him that it is refreshing."[86]

The Ogdensburg Agreement was followed within a year by the Hyde Park Declaration in April 1941, which provided the basis for comprehensive economic cooperation between the two countries for the duration of the war.[87] Prime Minister King himself appreciated the economic ties being created, which would have a long-term impact. "The Hyde Park declaration," he told the Canadian House of Commons, "will have a permanent significance in the relations between Canada and the United States."[88] The conditions produced by war accelerated and dramatized Canada's economic fate. Canada had run a chronic deficit with the United States (which is what Bennett complained about so sharply in 1934), but she had balanced that deficit by a surplus in her trade with Britain, Western Europe, and the Empire. Most of that market disappeared with the coming of war and Canada faced fiscal and trade disaster unless special arrangements could be worked out with the United States.

These wartime solutions did not carry forward with full force into the post-1945 economy, but as Cuff and Granatstein observe, the Hyde Park Arrangements "foretold the integration of the North American economies that we live with today."[89] After World War II, Canadian governments, while welcoming American trade and investment, attempted to create another economic option for Canada. The Conservative Diefenbaker administration that came to power in 1957 hoped it could revitalize the British and Commonwealth markets. The Liberal governments of the 1960s and 1970s hoped to build up markets in Japan and the Pacific. But all the while, the links with the United States, in terms of trade and finance, tightened further.

Indeed, in the immediate post-war years it seemed as though the final integration might be accomplished sooner rather than later. Canada was facing an economic crisis because of the slow recovery of the British and European markets. The lack of dollars to pay for her U.S. imports led Canadian officials to think they would have to opt for import restrictions which, these officials thought, would lead to damaging economic warfare with the United States.[90] In these critical circumstances, Canadian officials turned to the solution of even more integration of the two economies. The removal of all tariffs between the two countries and the creation of a common market would end the immediate crisis. Canada would no longer have to struggle to pay for her American imports by building up her own trade in other foreign markets. Officials on the American side were taken aback by the sweeping nature of the discussions which took place during the winter of 1947-48. Woodbury Willoughby, Asociate Chief of the Division of Commercial Policy, and Willard Thorp, Assistant Secretary of State for Economic Affairs, were the chief negotiators for the United States. A plan was drawn up to phase out, over a five-year period, all tariff barriers between the United States and Canada. The two principal Canadian negotiators, Hector Mackinnon, Chairman of the Dominion Tariff Board, and John Deutsch, Director of Economic Relations in the Department of Finance, understood the far-reaching consequences of such a plan. They viewed "the proposal, if implemented, to be one of the most momentous decisions in their history." Thorp urged that this golden opportunity be seized and advised Undersecretary Lovett that the administration should begin to prepare Congressional opinion. Thorp underscored "the vital significance of the plan from a strategic as well as an economic standpoint."

Thorp explained that the phasing out of tariffs, "would result in the immediate elimination of all Empire preferences granted by Canada, with important economic and political implications for the United States." He added that it was essential to move quickly because of the imminent retirement of Prime Minister King who had been so warm to the United States—"his successor may not be equally favorable to the plan." Thorp concluded that this was "a unique opportunity of promoting the most efficient utilization of the resources of the North American continent and knitting the two countries together—an objective of U.S. foreign policy since the founding of the republic."[91]

The plan did not proceed beyond this discussion stage. Mackenzie King became worried about the possible political reaction in Canada, and it was clear that in the United States there would have been a tough uphill struggle to overcome special interest opposition in Congress. Moreover, the talks had reached such a radical point because of the post-war exchange crisis and had only proceeded so far because the spirit of cooperation achieved during the war. Sober second thoughts, and the likely solving of the trade and exchange crisis by the Marshall Plan, ended behind-the-scenes talk of drastic bilateral solutions. Still, the discussions revealed clearly the direction of American thinking about the powerful forces that were knitting the countries together.

On all fronts, the dozen years following the 1935 Trade Agreement were a huge success for American policy with respect to Canada. In military and economic terms, Canada was now solidly within the American sphere of influence. The fears that Canada might strengthen her imperial affiliation—fears that had so concerned Taft and Knox in 1911 and had been a matter of concern in the State Department as recently as the 1932 Imperial Conference in Ottawa—now seemed utterly remote. In a long, confidential despatch to the Secretary of State in November 1948, the U.S. Minister to Canada, Lawrence Steinhardt, summed up all the favorable signs. Steinhardt began his assessment by drawing attention to the war and post-war trends which had tended "to strengthen Canadian military integration with the United States." Even as he wrote, the Canadian cabinet was by its pleas for more joint-production programs, "promoting the integration of military resources." Steinhardt emphasized "the major change [in Canada's orientation] since before the war." In economic matters too, the pre-war patterns had "altered fundamentally." No longer could Canada raise sufficient surplus in her trade with Britain to support her adverse balance with the United States. The Hyde Park arrangements had solved this problem and set the stage for "a closer integration of the economies of the two countries."

These trends intensified after the war as the high wartime demand for Canadian goods in the United States fell off and as Britain continued to face severe exchange and trade problems. Canada had nowhere else to turn but to the United States. "One of the results of the changes in Canada's international trade," continued Steinhardt, "is that now three quarters of Canada's total imports are from the United States compared to two-thirds before the war. Similarly, half of her exports are now marketed in the United States compared to two-fifths in the late 1930s." Thus, concluded Steinhardt, "there exists a growing commercial orientation towards the United States." The way in which the Canadian Liberal government had actively explored the policy of further reductions in trade barriers was confirmation that these trends were not temporary war phenomena but had taken hold as a permanent characteristic in

Canadian thinking. The growing influence of the United States on Canadian culture was yet another promising sign of the times. Steinhardt summed up his case:

> economically and militarily, Canada's orientation is shifting from Great Britain to the United States. The Commonwealth tie is still a cherished heritage for many but as Great Britain's economic and military power declines in relation to that of the United States the Canadian government has . . . tended to turn more to the latter as a source of economic welfare and military security. Improved means of transportation and communications have made the full impact of U.S. culture felt in Canada so that in this regard as well a shift in orientation is discernible.[92]

Inside the State Department there was evident satisfaction with Steinhardt's assessment. William Snow, the Assistant Chief at the British Commonwealth desk, told Julian Harrington that he had taken Steinhardt's despatch home and read it over the weekend. "It is a fine piece of work," he told Harrington, "thoughtful, well-written and timely." Snow added that Steinhardt's views were supported by all the other evidence that the Department was reading. "All indications we see at this end, point to the fact that the British tie is not as strong as it was either before or during the war."[93]

4.

The trends of the next forty years proved the basic accuracy of the State Department's 1948 assessment. The defense cooperation that had become so far-reaching during World War II continued to be articulated in various ways. The agreement reached in 1957, to set up a North American Air defense system (NORAD) with its headquarters in Colorado, was a powerful confirmation that the word "permanent" in the Ogdensburg Agreement meant what it said. Trade and investment ties multiplied throughout the post-war years. The signing of the Auto Pact in 1965, which organized a special continental production and marketing arrangement for automobile and parts manufuacturing, was a sign of the unusually intimate and complex economic links that were emerging.

By 1956, there was an annual meeting of the Joint U.S.-Canadian Committee on Trade and Economic Affairs which established quasi-institutional links at the cabinet level. The respective delegations to this annual meeting were led by the Secretary of State and the Canadian Secretary of State for External Affairs. As Steinhardt had forecast, there was also a Canadian nationalist reaction to these intensifying economic and military ties between the two countries. By the 1960s, at the height of the controversy over the war in Vietnam, the New Democratic party (successor to the CCF party which had spearheaded the nationalist critique of American influence in the 1940s) was at the center of Canadian protest against U.S. expansionism in North America and south-east Asia. But as American experts had also forecast in the late 1940s, this rise of Canadian nationalism did not prevent further economic integration. By the mid-1980s the Conservative government of Brian Mulroney recognized this relentless economic reality and entered into negotiations to bring about a complete free trade system in North America.[94]

A useful overview of the modern relationship, from the American perspective, was provided in 1979 when former U.S. Ambassador to Ottawa, Enders, delivered a speech at Stanford University.[95] Enders took stock of the relationship since the 1930s. He opened in a conventional manner by repeating the familiar refrain that the two countries shared a common outlook. The political systems of Canada and the United States were different, to be sure, but Canadian and American political values were "almost the same." While there were many issues that acted as irritants in the relationship and "our individual interests are rarely identical" there was "almost always a substantial overlap." Enders reminded his audience, "we trade more with each other than any other two peoples on earth. We are the only two peoples to have a fully integrated common defense of our territories." Canada and the United States had entered into a special relationship during the war and throughout the late 1940s and 1950s. He singled out the NORAD agreement and once more drew attention to the unique intensity of trade and investment patterns between the two countries. Ambassador Enders reminded Canadians that this special relationship had provided them with access to special treatment not available to other states. Canada was exempted from foreign oil import quotas, from capital export regulations, and from "buy American" clauses in defense procurement rules.

Enders then turned to assess the impact of the Canadian nationalist reaction, which had culminated with the Foreign Investment Review Act of 1974 and the general National Economic Policy designed to monitor and perhaps curtail American influence on the Canadian economy. He reckoned that this reaction had been triggered by the Vietnam war. It had taken various forms, including a broad attack on the invasion of Canada by American culture, but Enders also thought that the "third option" in Canadian trade policy had been inspired by the newly-active nationalism. The "third option," made public in 1972, consisted of an attempt to redirect Canadian foreign trade. The goal was to increase trade flows with Japan and the European Community to counterbalance the Canadian-American trade current, and thus make Canada less dependent on the United States. These political developments in Canada encouraged the United States to take a hard look at Canadian exceptionalism. Enders pointed to the failure of the Nixon administration to provide any exemption for Canada from the 1971 import surcharge as an example of the cooler American treatment of Canada. The fact that Japan, when the surcharge was announced, was wrongly identified as America's largest trading partner was a further sign of a widening gap filled by mutual annoyance. The special relationship was suffering from systemic stress.

This bad patch was navigated safely as both Washington and Ottawa drew back from the brink and made adjustments in their treatment of each other. By the late 1970s and into the 1980s a reconvergence had taken place. Both sides had learned good hard lessons from the period of stress and understood better the political forces at work on their domestic scenes. From the United States' viewpoint, the reconvergence confirmed yet again that the economic forces shaping the contemporary world provided few options for the relationship. Enders observed accurately, if somewhat complacently, that Canada's "third option" had simply not worked. The trade links with Japan and the EEC "were not even marginally a substitute for the economic connection with the States." The lesson to be learned by the U.S. from the deterioration in the relationship in the late 1960s and early 1970s was to be more careful not to rouse Canadian sensibilities. Interestingly, in view of subsequent events, Enders concluded his analysis by warning that it would be unwise to proceed any further down the road toward freer trade because such a policy might stir up opposition in the United States (from protectionist interests) and in Canada (from the nationlist camp). Already, 80 percent of U.S. imports from Canada came in duty free. It seemed counterproductive to extend the margins of this when such action would lead to political complications. In this Endersian overview, the special relationship established during World War II remained intact. The difficult times had actually contributed to a strengthening of ties by forcing both sides to become more informed about the political forces at work on the other side of the border. The relationship was now more realistic, and therefore healthier than it had been in the more innocent 1950s.

This conventional American overview tended to pass over issues or periods that Canadian commentators would wish to look at more carefully. They would point out, for example, that the nationalist critique began to take hold in Canada in the late 1950s, and that it was not simply a byproduct of the Vietnam war controversy, although the war certainly intensified Canadian anti-American sentiment. They would point to American treatment of Canada during and after the Cuban crisis in 1962-63 to suggest that the United States intervened in an attempt to shape policy in Canada. They might argue that the combination of a continuing buildup of American trade and investment and protectionist pressures inside the United States forced Canada to seek a free trade solution that would open her even more to U.S. influence. In short, in contrast to Ambassador Enders rather benign reading of the record, a counter-case could be advanced which postulated that the United States had played a more pointed role in manipulating the relationship. To assess whether or not such a case holds up, it will be helpful to investigate two critical episodes in the modern relationship—the Cuban crisis and the related defense crisis of 1962-63 and the Free Trade Agreement signed in 1988. Without access to all of the documents, it is not possible to come to any definitive conclusions; but, based on the published evidence and scholarly interpretations, some reasonable points can be made on the issue of the United States' recent treatment of Canada.

The Cuban crisis is a key episode for getting at these questions, as it can be used to make the case that the United States did use its economic and miltary weight to make sure that Canada did not embark on autonomous policies that ran counter to U.S. interests. The Conservative government of Diefenbaker refused to arm Bomarc missiles in spite of the understanding at the time of purchase that they were to be armed by nuclear warheads. This disagreement over the Bomarcs became a crisis in 1962 when Canada failed to activate her forces. By failing to support the American stand against Cuba and the Russians, Canada appeared to be backing out of her defense commitments under NORAD. The rift between Washington and Ottawa became public as the issue was debated in the Canadian House of Commons. In the course of the debate, Diefenbaker made some points about the Bomarcs and about defense issues in general which were objected to in the United States. The State Department issued a press release on 30 January 1963 which took issue with Diefenbaker's version of the defense agreements, in effect implying that the Canadian Prime Minister was misleading the House and the people of Canada. In the subsequent general election, the Liberal party, led by Lester Pearson, received support from President Kennedy and his political staffers. Pearson's victory was warmly endorsed by Washington. One of Pearson's first public acts was to reaffirm friendship with the United States, not only in nuclear and defense matters, but on the economic front too. At Hyannis Port on 11 May 1963,

President Kennedy and Canada's new Prime Minister pledged themselves to "co-operation in the rational use of the continent's resources."[96]

A plausible interpretation of this sequence of events is that the United States was prepared to intervene when she feared Canada was abandoning the relationship of cooperative dependency. Such an interpretation can be supported from published documents on the American side. It is clear, for example, that from the time of Diefenbaker's election in 1957, the U.S. had been worried that his nationalist stance would lead to anti-American policies. In September 1957, at a meeting in London of U.S.Chiefs of Mission from northern European posts, the American Ambassador to Ottawa warned of this danger. The new Conservative government, Livingston Merchant told his fellow ambassadors and ministers, would try to reduce Canada's dependency on the United States. He pointed out that the Conservatives were "more nationalistic than the Liberals and more pro-Canadian which can merge into anti-Americanism." Merchant then set out some of the major issues that concerned Canadians, including the American wheat policy which undermined world grain prices by disposing of the U.S. surplus under the terms of the Agricultural Trade Development and Assistance Act of 1954. Canadians saw this as typical of American thoughtlessness, as Washington ignored the impact of U.S.trade policies on their northern neighbor. In this case Canada, historically a major grain exporter, was being hurt by congressional ignorance and lack of concern. Merchant also drew attention to the impact of U.S. investment in Canada. The "huge influx of capital investment funds from American sources" was beginning to give Canadians "a feeling that control of their economy was slipping away from them." These circumstances had created "major and growing problems with Canada" which would lead the Diefenbaker government "to try hard to reduce their dependence on the U.S."[97] Thus, at the very outset of the Diefenbaker regime, the U.S. Ambassador expressed open concern about the danger of Canada turning away from the post-war policies of close cooperation. Such evidence sustains the view that State Department actions in 1962-63 may have been part of a strategy adopted as soon as the Conservatives had gained power to weaken this troublesome Canadian regime.

But such a case does not stand up to closer scrutiny. The published American documents and the research of Canadian scholars show that there was no concerted attempt to undermine Diefenbaker and that the Canadian Prime Minister contributed in no small way to his own downfall. To begin with, Diefenbaker's electioneering rhetoric, which had set off alarm signals at the U.S. mission in

Ottawa, quickly dissipated once he came into power. In July 1957, he proclaimed in the course of a press interview that he would divert 15 percent of Canada's imports from the United States to Britain. This announcement was not the result of hard policy analysis but, as Robert Bothwell and his co-authors have suggested, seems to have "occurred to him during the course of the interview."[98] By the end of his first year in office, the policy of directing trade back into the old British channel was abandoned; and for the remainder of his term in office, Diefenbaker actually took measures which discouraged trade with Britain.[99]

During his presentation to the Chiefs of Mission meeting in 1957, Livingston Merchant had anticipated such an outcome. While warning of the possible anti-American direction of the Conservative government, he added that when the ministers settled into office and began studying economic realities, they would soon discover "that the range of options was limited." Merchant reminded the London group that in spite of the emergence of nationalist political rhetoric in Canada "they will continue as sound and reliable colleagues. Support for NATO is truly non-partisan. In general they tend to see the world through our eyes. They appreciate the geographical realities of their defense situation. They believe in free enterprise and we need have no fear they will abandon us."[100] Thus, even as Merchant expressed his views on Diefenbaker's anti-Americanism, he saw no threat deep enough to require a policy response. When the Conservative government itself quickly gave up on efforts to swim against the prevailing trade pattern, Merchant's forecast was confirmed. His ruminations in 1957 did not lead to a policy committment to intervene and make life difficult for the Diefenbaker regime. In fact, his message reassured the United States that she could live rather easily with the heightened nationalist feeling in Canada because the fundamental trends were running in favor of the U.S.

The nationalist interpretation of the 1962-63 defense crisis has encountered heavy weather even in Canada. The scholarship on the post-war decades has been cogently synthesized in *Canada since 1945* by Robert Bothwell, Ian Drummond, and John English, who give short shrift to the theory that the Diefenbaker government was maneuvered out of office by the Kennedy administration.[101] They point out that the evidence does not sustain the once fashionable view that the Liberal party was continentalist and pro-American, while the Conservative party was nationalist and worked to break out of the geographically defined trap that made Canada dependent on the United States. A startling confirmation of their argument can be seen with Diefenbaker himself. Shortly after coming into office,

Diefenbaker signed the NORAD agreement with the United States. The agreement committed Canada to a fully integrated, continental air defense system with its headquarters in Colorado. This major step was taken apparently without a cabinet meeting, during which all the implications of the agreement might have been explored. It was a repetition of the rapidity and ease with which the Ogdensburg Agreement had been concluded in 1940. But this time, the Canadian haste was less explicable because there was no overwhelming pressure from a world war. During the next two years, the Diefenbaker government entered into new defense production sharing programs with the U.S. (similar to the 1941 Hyde Park arrangements) which gave Canadian companies a further share in American military procurement. There was a sharp increase in American purchases of Canadian arms. As Bothwell and his co-authors acidly observe, "in this way the Diefenbaker government defended Canada against the horrors of continentalism."[102]

The crisis over Cuba forced the contradictions in Diefenbaker's position into the open. The Bomarc missiles had been based in Canada as part of the NORAD agreement but they were not loaded with nuclear warheads because Diefenbaker claimed he had not agreed to such arming. (The missiles were temporarily loaded with sandbags.) The Canadian Prime Minister contended that he had thought the missiles could be armed conventionally, but the specifications had been quite clear on this key point. Diefenbaker also raised the issue of control over the missiles. Secretary of State Rusk proposed in March 1962 that the United States would be willing "to work out arrangements for joint control consistent with national sovereignty," but the offer to negotiate was not taken up. By this time other cabinet members were becoming disturbed by Diefenbaker's course. Matters came to a head in January 1963 when the State Department issued the press release which was critical of statements Diefenbaker made during the Commons debate.

It was incidents such as these which convinced Diefenbaker that there was an American plot to ease him from power but, as we have suggested, the evidence is not compelling. Diefenbaker was criticized from within his own cabinet for his confused position on the Bomarcs and on his general defense posture with respect to the United States. The Liberal party, led by Lester Pearson, who had won the Nobel Peace prize for his role in defusing the Suez crisis in 1956, supported the American reading that Canada had committed herself to more cooperation than Diefenbaker was providing. (Although Pearson did say that, should he win the election, he would discuss the meaning and implementation of the defense agreements that did exist.) As we have noted, Pearson began his regime with a hearty endorsement of further cooperation. In response to Diefenbaker's criticism of the press release, Rusk replied that it was essential to correct the record with respect to the defense agreements between the two countries, once some aspects had been made public by Diefenbaker. Rusk added that the U.S. government regretted if the tone of the release had caused offense but insisted that the facts in the statement were accurate. No scholar or commentator has disputed this last part of Rusk's explanation. Obviously the United States wanted Canada to arm the Bomarcs with nuclear warheads and expected Canada to respond to the Cuban crisis according to the unified NORAD defense arrangements and the U.S. was, therefore, critical of Canadian behavior. The U.S. government responded to statements made in Canada and sought to influence Canadian opinion by issuing a press release, but this falls far short of a plot to intervene in Canada's domestic affairs. Once NORAD was signed, these kinds of issues were up for trans-border debate. As Bothwell and his co-authors sum up, the U.S. "did not compel Canada or try to compel it to do anything in particular and therefore did not infringe its sovereignty."[103] That is a level-headed assessment. Diefenbaker's confused course on defense since 1957 was the principal reason the Canadian government found itself in such a vulnerable position during the 1962-63 defense crisis.

The second important episode in the recent relationship worth examining is the signing of the Free Trade Agreement in 1988. This was the most dramatic development in Canadian-American relations since 1945, and it has all sorts of resonances—right back to the 1854 Reciprocity Treaty. To understand how it came about tells a great deal about the economic forces at work in North America. It is too early yet to have a complete picture of all the discussions that led to the agreement, but the published documents provide enough evidence to draw some preliminary conclusions about key aspects. The most striking feature of the process which led to the agreement is that Canada took the initiative in proposing a free trade solution. In a statement made to the Senate Finance Committee on 15 April 1986, State Department spokesman Kalb explained that the United States was responding to a proposal from Prime Minister Mulroney. "The Canadian Prime Minister," Kalb told the Senators, "has proposed that we negotiate a comprehensive trade agreement to promote freer trade between the two countries."[104] On 4 October 1987, President Reagan again publicly acknowledged that Canada had taken the initiative in proposing a far-reaching arrangement when he congratulated Mulroney "for the courage and foresight in seeking this free trade area."[105]

The Canadian decision to turn to this final, radical, free trade solution was driven by two elemental facts in her economic circumstances. The first was that the third option policy of diversifying Canadian trade into non-American channels had failed to significantly change Canada's trade dependency on the United States. The trade flow between the two countries was so powerful that Canadian efforts in Japan and the EEC could not reduce its dominating presence and influence on policy formulation. The second factor was a growing awareness in Canada that it might suffer from protectionist forces in the U.S. Congress. The U.S. administration did nothing to disguise these threats. In March 1982, for example, Assistant Secretary of State for Economic and Business Affairs Hormuts told a subcommittee of the Senate Foreign Relations Committee that there had been extensive discussion in Ottawa on potential reactions in the United States to some aspects of Canada's more nationalist economic policies. "The Canadian government," he informed the Senators," has a heightened awareness of U.S. congressional, executive branch and public concerns about the discriminatory and unfair elements of the NEP and FIRA."[106] These concerns, it was implied, might lead to pressures for retaliation in the form of protectionist measures which the administration might find hard to resist. Since so much Canadian trade was with the U.S., any protectionist measures would have an immediate and serious impact. Secretary of State for External Affairs Joe Clark made this cardinal point at a joint press conference with Secretary of State Schultz in October 1985. "The facts are clear," Clark explained,"there are some risks to Canada now from protectionist pressure in the U.S. We have a duty to take account of these risks, to try to put a better system into place." While appreciating that their thinking was being pushed in this direction by economic and political factors from outside Canada, the Mulroney government viewed free trade as a great opportunity for Canada. Since it was clear the American market was going to remain by far the largest market for Canadian companies, any improved access to that market would bring benefits to Canada. "There are some immense opportunities for Canada in the larger market," Clark told the press, and "we have an obligation to respond to the opportunity."[107]

In these circumstances there appeared to be no option of a full-scale free trade agreement. The duty-free trade between the two countries was already uniquely extensive and, in the calculations of the U.S. Trade Representative Office, would approach 90 percent by 1987 no matter what the respective governments did. The average American tariff applied to Canadian imports was only 1.3 percent and the average Canadian tariff on U.S. imports 4.3 percent.[108] With such figures it was difficult to construct a solution that did not proceed to free trade. The alternative was to turn to policies that would lead to protectionist outbreaks in the U.S. and nationalist restrictions in Canada, which would be damaging in economic terms to both countries, even more so to Canada because of its smaller, more export-dependent economy. A series of special sectoral arrangements was a possible option but was rejected because of the view that it would set off a series of intractable political wrangles as companies on both sides fought to preserve their turf.

Thus, while the Canadian government did make the decision to seek a free trade agreement, it is also evident that it did so because its choices were hedged in by rather limiting conditions. The political circumstances in the United States made the Canadians seriously consider the future direction of their relationship. The third option had proven to be a weak reed upon which to rely. The health of the Canadian economy continued to be tied to what was happening south of the border. There seemed no choice but to seek closer economic ties with the U.S. The decision was certainly molded by circumstances but all such decisions are of that nature. No government is presented with a blank page on which to write policy. The page on which the Mulroney government had to write was more crowded with text than usual perhaps; but, in the final analysis, the Canadian government, after considering all available information, decided it would be in the best interests of Canada to take the final step to free trade. Canada's exceptionally intimate economic relationship with the U.S. created the context within which Ottawa had to act but the Canadian decision was not forced by American policy.

In evaluating the American response to Canada during these years, from the defense crisis of 1962-63 to the Free Trade Agreement of 1988, the overriding impression is that American officials and cabinet members hardly thought it was necessary to have a policy for Canada. The constant refrain in Washington was that economic trends were naturally flowing in a direction advantageous to the U.S. and that the task was simply to keep things going in the right direction. This view was well expressed by Undersecretary of State George Ball in the course of a speech to the American Assembly in 1964. Ball included in his remarks a characteristically sharp reminder that while Canadians complained about the intensity of U.S. investment in Canada, they tended to forget, "on a per capita basis Canadians have invested almost twice as much in the U.S. as Americans have in Canada." He responded to the nationalist critique of the U.S. inside Canada by arguing that economic forces rather than any deliberate American policy were the determining factors. "For better or worse," Ball told the Assembly, "natural trends will lead in the direction of greater economic interdependence." The maintenance of "political independence," he added, "depends more on the state of the national will than on economic relations." Ball then noted that he made such statements "not as an expression of U.S. government policy but as a prediction of the natural evolution of economic forces in a time of vaulting technological advance." The task for both Ottawa and Washington was to manage domestic political pressures (protectionism in the U.S. and anti-American nationalism in Canada) that would press for destructive economic policies. The two governments should also continue to develop joint consultative agencies (such as the Permanent Joint Board on Defense set up in 1940 and the Joint U.S.-Canadian Committee on Trade and Economic Affairs established in 1954) to ensure that the integrative tendencies were properly managed. Ball's basic message was that these trends toward more economic integration were natural and, if wisely managed, would be beneficial to both countries.[109] A similar view of the relationship was evident in a joint report by Livingston Merchant who had served as the American Ambassador in Ottawa and A.D.P.Heeney who had been the Canadian envoy in Washington. They endorsed the need for a "specific regime of consultation between the two governments" and noted, "Canadian-American mutual involvement and interdependence grow daily more evident." The two ambassadors concluded that "for our part we are satisfied that the process can be as mutually rewarding as it is inevitable."

This sense of inevitability about the relationship was the characteristic American response to Canada throughout the post-World War II years. Ambassadors, Secretaries of State, Undersecretaries of State, and other American officials viewed American policy as largely determined by trends that politicians in either country could do little to change. It was necessary to work sensitively on a range of issues, such as acid rain, that had the potential to become major irritants to the relationship, but the overall course seemed self-evidently set. No fundamental policy thinking seemed to be required. Lawrence Eagleburger, Assistant Secretary for European Affairs summed up this frame of mind well during a speech before the Center for Inter-American Relations in 1981. "Living as we do with such a high degree of interdependence," he proposed, "our only reasonable choice is to make our relationship work to our mutual advantage." As he tried to sum up the modern American response to Canada, Eagleburger returned to President Roosevelt's speech at Kingston in 1938. "I would suggest that the Roosevelt formula—frankness, consultation, and concern for the common good—remains today as valid for

Canadians and Americans as it did in 1938." Eagleburger then added an afterthought which caught nicely the view at the core of the modern American response to Canada in the half century following Roosevelt's speech: "indeed, I would suggest that neither nation has much choice." [110]

Notes

1. Earl Grey to James Bryce, Ottawa, 1 June 1911, James Bryce Papers, MS, Bryce USA, 31, Bodleian Library, Oxford.
2. W.S. Fielding to James Bryce, Ottawa, 31 January 1911, Bryce Papers, MS, Bryce USA, 31.
3. J.L. Granatstein, *How Britain's Weakness Forced Canada into the Arms of the United States*, (Toronto: University of Toronto Press, 1989), 18.
4. Wilfrid Laurier to James Bryce, Ottawa, 10 October 1911, Bryce Papers, MS Bryce USA, 32.
5. Earl Grey to James Bryce, Ottawa, 7 April 1907, Bryce Papers, MS Bryce USA, 27.
6. Fred C. Slater to Huntington Wilson, 26 September 1911, SDDF 1910-1929, Box 5797, RG 59, National Archives.
7. U.S. Consul Singapore to Secretary of State Knox, 7 December 1911, SDDF 1910-1929, Box 5797, RG 59, National Archives.
8. H. Blair Neatby, *William Lyon Mackenzie King: A Political Biography*, 2 vols. (Toronto: University of Toronto Press, 1958), 2:176-95.
9. Auckland Geddes to Lord Curzon, Washington, 28 May 1920, Public Records Office (PRO), London, FO 414/126.
10. Idem., 3 June 1921, PRO, FO, 414/427.
11. Idem., 19 October 1923, PRO, FO 414/252.
12. H.G. Chilton to Austen Chamberlain, Washington, 26 November 1926, PRO, FO 414/258.
13. G.H. Ferguson to Secretary of State for External Affairs R.B. Bennett, London, 26 October 1931, *Documents on Canadian External Affairs* (*DCER*), 5, 37-38.
14. *U.S. Department of Commerce, Bureau of Foreign and Domestic Commerce, The United Kingdom: The Industrial, Commercial and Financial Handbook* (Washington: U.S. Government Printing Office, 1930). The report was prepared under the supervision of Hugh Butler, the American Trade Commissioner.
15. Ibid., 551-53.
16. Clarence T. Starr to Frank B. Kellogg, Washington, 26 January 1926, Frank B. Kellogg Papers, Reel 18, Michigan State University Libraries.
17. Auckland Geddes to Lord Curzon, 7 January 1921, PRO, FO 414/247.
18. Auckland Geddes to Eyre Crowe, Washington, 15 December 1923, PRO, FO 414/250.
19. W. Taussig, "The Tariff Act of 1922," *Quarterly Journal of Economics,* 37(1922): 1-28.
20. *The New York Times*, 26 June 1926; St. Paul Pioneer Press, enclosed in R.W. Callahan to Secretary of State Kellogg, 17 August 1927, Kellogg

Papers, Reel 27.

21. Albert Halstead to Secretary of State Hughes, Montreal, 18 February 1921, SDDF 1910-1929, Box 5798, RG 59, National Archives.
22. George M. Wrong to James Bryce, Toronto, 3 June 1921, Bryce Papers UB49, Bodleian Library, Oxford.
23. John Foster to Secretary of State Hughes, 30 December 1921, SDDF 1910-1929, Box 5798, RG 59, National Archives.
24. Memorandum of the Office of the Foreign Trade Advisor, 31 January 1922, SDDF, 1910-1929, Box 5798, National Archives.
25. Memorandum of the Office of the Economic Advisor, 20 February 1925, SDDF 1910-1929, Box 5798, National Archives.
26. W. McClure memorandum, 24 June 1927, SDDF 1910-1929, Box 5798, National Archives.
27. Henry Carter memorandum, 15 November 1929, SDDF 1910-1929, Box 5298, RG 59, National Archives.
28. Harry Hawkins memorandum, 12 November 1929, SDDF 1910-1929, Box 5298, RG 59, National Archives.
29. *The Burlington Gazette* [Iowa], 15 March 1927, enclosed in T.Y. Wickham to Secretary of State Kellogg, Kellogg Papers, Reel 25.
30. T.F. Bayard to Charles Tupper, 31 May 1887, PRO, CO 880/10/121.
31. Secretary of State Kellogg to William Phillips, Washington, 18 January 1927, Kellogg Papers, Reel 24.
32. H.G. Chilton to Earl of Balfour, 14 July 1922, PRO, FO 414/250.
33. A.H. Comstock to Secretary of State Hughes, 24 April 1924, SDDF 1910-1929, Box 2, RG 59, National Archives.
34. Alfred O. Crozier to Secretary of State Hughes, 7 April 1924, SDDF 1910-1929, Box 2, RG 59, National Archives.
35. Dorsey Newsom, U.S. Chargé, Ottawa, memorandum, 13 August 1928, SDDF 1910-29, Box 3, RG 59, National Archives.
36. Albert Halstead to Secretary of State Hughes, 10 January 1924, SDDF 1910-1929, Box 2, RG 59, National Archives.
37. Secretary of State Kellogg to William Phillips, 8 August 1927, SDDF 1910-1929, Box 2, RG 59, National Archives; Secretary of State Kellogg to William Phillips, 9 August 1927, Kellogg Papers, Reel 27.
38. Secretary of State Kellogg to William Phillips, 7 November 1927, Kellogg Papers, Reel 29.
39. William Phillips to Secretary of State Kellogg, Ottawa, 27 September 1927, SDDF 1910-1929, Box 2, RG 59, National Archives.
40. William Phillips to Secretary of State Kellogg, Ottawa, 21 November 1928, SDDF 1910-1929, Box 3, RG 59, National Archives.
41. Idem., 31 December 1928.
42. William Phillips to Secretary of State Henry Stimson, Ottawa, 5 April 1929, SDDF 1910-1929, Box 3, RG 59, National Archives.
43. Idem., 10 April 1929.
44. Wesley Frost to U.S. Legation in Ottawa and Secretary of State Stimson, 24 June 1931, SDDF 1930-39, Box 3178, RG 59, National Achives.
45. Ibid.
46. Benjamin Wallace, Office of Economic Advisor memorandum, 6 December 1931, SDDF 1930-39, Box 3178, RG 59, National Archives.

47. Ibid.
48. Richard N. Kottman, *Reciprocity and the North Atlantic Triangle, 1932-1938* (Ithaca: Cornell University Press, 1968), 89; Memorandum of Assistant Secretary of State Sayre on Trade Agreement with Canada, SDDF 1930-39, Box 3179, RG 59, National Archives.
49. Memorandum of conversation between W.D. Herridge and Secretary of State Hull, 8 February 1934, SDDF 1930-39, Box 3179, RG 59, National Archives.
50. Warren Robbins to Secretary of State Hull, Ottawa, 10 March 1934, SDDF 1930-39, Box 3179, RG 59, National Archives.
51. Warren Robbins to Secretary of State Hull, Ottawa, 21 November 1934, SDDF 1930-39, Box 3180, RG 59, National Archives.
52. Kottman, *Reciprocity*, 99, concludes, "there is no concrete proof that the United States used dilatory tactics as a political weapon."; Pierre de Boal memorandum, 21 September 1934, SDDF 1930-39, Box 3179, RG 59, National Archives; Norman Armour to Secretary of State Hull, Ottawa, 17 October 1935, SDDF 1930-39, Box 3182, RG 59, National Archives.
53. Secretary of State Hull Press Release, 22 November 1935, SDDF 1930-39, Box 3182, RG 59, National Archives.
54. William C. Bullitt to President Roosevelt, London, 8 July 1933, quoted in Kottman, 77-8.
55. Hanford MacNider to Secretary of State Hull, Ottawa, 19 May 1932, SDDF 1930-39, Box 3172, RG 59, National Archives.
56. Pierre de Boal to Secretary of State Hull, Ottawa, 21 February 1933, SDDF 1930-39, Box 3178, RG 59, National Archives.
57. Kottman, 121.
58. Hickerson's role in Canadian-American relations is concisely and cogently dealt with in Robert Bothwell and John Kirton, "A Sweet Little Country: American Attitudes Towards Canada 1925-1963," in Norman Hillmer, ed., *Partners Nevertheless: Canadian-American Relations in the Twentieth Century* (Toronto: Copp Clark Pitman, 1989), 45-47; I am grateful to Jack Granatstein for informing me of the relationship of Elliot to Trudeau about which more will be revealed in Granatstein's and Bothwell's forthcoming book on Trudeau's foreign policy.
59. W.Y. Elliot to John Hickerson, Cambridge, 27 February 1933, SDDF 1930-39, Box 3178, RG 59, National Archives.
60. Ibid.
61. W.Y. Elliot to President Roosevelt, Berkeley, 2 July 1935, SDDF 1930-39, Box 3181, RG 59, National Archives; Memorandum of conversation between William Phillips and W.Y. Elliot, 14 June 1935, SDDF 1930-39, Box 3181, RG 59, National Archives.
62. John H. Thompson and Allen Seager, *Canada, 1922-1939: Decades of Discord* (Toronto: McClelland and Stewart, 1985), 202.
63. W.D. Herridge to Secretary of State Hull, 14 November 1934, *Foreign Relations of the United States, 1934* (Washington, DC: Government Printing Office, 1935), 1:849-57; Warren Robbins to Secretary of State Hull, 22 November 1934, SDDF 1930-39, Box 3180, RG 59, National Archives; Memorandum of conversation between Secretary of State Hull and W.D. Herridge, 15 November 1934, SDDF 1930-39, Box 3179, RG 59, National Archives.

64. Francis Sayre memorandum of meeting at White House with President Roosevelt, Phillips, Grady, and Sayre, SDDF 1930-39, Box 3181, RG 59, National Archives. Roosevelt was especially concerned about the dairy farmers in New York, Pennsylvania, and New Jersey.

65. Pierre de Boal to Secretary of State Hull, Ottawa, 14 June 1935, FRUS 1935, 2:51.

66. Norman Armour to Secretary of State Hull, Ottawa, 17 October 1935, SDDF 1930-39, Box 3182, RG 59, National Archives.

67. Idem., 25 October 1935.

68. Wesley Frost to U.S. Legation in Ottawa and the Secretary of State, Montreal, 24 June 1931, SDDF 1930-39, Box 3178, RG 59, National Archives.

69. John D. Hickerson to L.D. Wilgress, Director of Commercial Intelligence, Department of Trade and Commerce, Ottawa, 19 November 1935, John D. Hickerson Papers, Reel 6, National Archives.

70. John B. Brebner, *North Atlantic Triangle: The Interplay of Canada, the United States and Great Britain* (New Haven, CT: Yale University Press, 1945), 304-328, titles his chapter on the 1932-42 decade "Maelstrom."

71. J. Pierrepont Moffatt to Norman H. Davis, 19 June 1936, quoted in Kottman, 8.

72. Grace L. Beckett, *The Reciprocal Trade Agreements Program* (New York: Columbia University Press, 1941), 91.

73. William S. Culbertson, *Reciprocity: A National Policy for Foreign Trade* (New York: Whittesey House, 1937), 76-7.

74. Ibid., 238-9.

75. H.C. MacLean to Leo Pasvolsky, 9 January 1940, Leo Pasvolsky Papers, Box 1, National Archives.

76. Leo Pasvolsky memorandum, "Outstanding Economic Events in the Last Twenty Years," 8 January 1940, Pasvolsky Papers, Box 1.

77. J.D. Hickerson to Secretary of State Hull, 13 October 1937, Hickerson Papers, Reel 1; J.D. Hickerson to William Phillips, 4 June 1936, Hickerson Papers, Reel 1. The 1938 negotiations are fully analysed in Ian Drummond and Norman Hellmer, *Negotiating Freer Trade: The United Kingdom, the United States, Canada and the Trade Agreements of 1938* (Waterloo: Wilfrid Laurier University Press, 1989).

78. J.D. Hickerson to William Phillips, 4 June 1936, 20 May 1936, SDDF 1930-39, Box 3182 RG 59, National Archives.

79. R.D. Cuff and J.L. Granatstein, *Canadian-American Relations in Wartime: From the Great War to the Cold War* (Toronto: Hakkert, 1975), 101.

80. Richard Preston, *Canada and Imperial Defence: A Study of the Origins of the British Commonwealth's Defense Organization, 1867-1919* (Durham: Duke University Press, 1967) and D.C. Gordon, *The Dominion Partnership in Imperial Defense*, 1870-1914 (Baltimore: The Johns Hopkins University Press, 1965) are the standard treatments of this subject.

81. James Eayrs, In Defence of Canada, 2 vols. *From the Great War to the Great Depression* vol. 1, *Appeasement and Rearmament* vol. 2 (Toronto: University of Toronto Press, 1965) describe the emergence of a distinctive

Canadian approach to defense policy during the inter-war years.

82. J. Pierrepont Moffatt to Secretary of State Hull, Ottawa, 8 August 1940, SDDF 1940-44, Box 4484, RG 59, National Archives.

83. J. Pierrepont Moffatt to John D. Hickerson, Ottawa, 22 August 1940, Hickerson Papers, Reel 5.

84. Ibid.

85. Adolf A. Berle Diary 1895-1971, 26 August 1939, Reel 1, Michigan State University Libraries.

86. Beatrice B. Berle and Travis B. Jacobs, eds., *Navigating the Rapids, 1918-1971: From the Papers of Adolf A. Berle* (New York: Harcort Brace Jovanovich, 1973), 365.

87. R.D. Cuff and J.L. Granatstein, *Canadian-American Relations in Wartime,* (Toronto: Hakkert, 1975), 69-92.

88. Ibid., 70.

89. Ibid., 88.

90. R.D. Cuff and J.L. Granatstein, *American Dollars, Canadian Prosperity: Canadian-American Economic Relations, 1945-1950* (Toronto: Samuel-Stevens, 1978), 65.

91. Memorandum by Assistant Secretary of State for Economic Affairs, Willard Thorp to Undersecretary Robert Lovett, Washington, 8 March 1948, *FRUS, 1948*, 9:406; John Foster to John D. Hickerson, 23 December 1947, SDDF 1945-49, Box 5884, RG 59, National Archives. Foster told Harrison, "I myself regard the difficulties at present as insuperable but I am the fellow who would have told Columbus the world was flat."

92. Lawrence Steinhardt to Secretary of State Marshall, Ottawa, 24 November 1948, SDDF 1945-49, Box 5884, RG 59, National Archives. In his recent analysis of the 1947-1951 years, Bruce Muirhead has argued, "the encouragement of a bilateral economic relationship with the United States was the only viable option [for Canada]." See Muirhead, "Perception and Reality: The GATT's Contribution to the Development of a Bilateral North American Relationship, 1947-1951," *The American Review of Canadian Studies*, 20(1990): 279-96.

93. William P. Snow to Julian Harrington, 8 December 1948, SDDF 1945-49, Box 5884, RG 59, National Archives.

94. J.L. Granatstein, "Co-operation and Conflict: the Course of Canadian-American Relations since 1945," in Charles F. Doran and John H. Sigler, eds. *Canada and the United States. Enduring Friendship, Persistent Stress* (Englewood Cliff, NJ: Prentice-Hall, 1985), 9-44, is a concise but authoritative overview of the recent relationship. Hellmer's *Partners Nevertheless* is a very useful collection of articles which also has an annotated bibliography.

95. Ambassador Enders speech, Stanford University, 3 May 1979, *American Foreign Policy Current Documents (AFPCD)* 1977-1980 (Washington: Department of State, 1983), 577-81.

96. Joint Statement by J.F. Kennedy and Lester Pearson, Hyannis Port, 11 May 1963, *AFPCD 1963*, 371-74.

97. Northern European Chiefs of Mission Conference, London, 19-21 September 1957, *FRUS 1955-1957*, 4(Washington, 1986).

98. Robert Bothwell, Ian Drummond, and John English, *Canada since 1945: Power, Politics and Provicialism (Toronto, University of Toronto Press,* 1981), 205.
99. Ibid., 205, 233.
100. Northern [European] Chiefs of Mission Conference, London, 19-21 September 1957, *FRUS 1955-1957.* see 171n.97
101. Bothwell, Drummond, and English, 242-52.
102. Ibid., 242.
103. Ibid., 248-50; Department of State Press Release, 30 January 1963 and Statement of Secretary of State Rusk, 1 February 1963, *AFPCD* 1967, 369-74.
104. Statement by Department of State Spokesman Kalb to Senate Finance Committee, 15 April 1986, AFPCD 1987, 286-87.
105. Statement by President Reagan, 4 October 1987, *AFPCD* 1987, 287.
106. Statement by Assistant Secretary for Economic and Business Affairs before a subcommittee of the Senate Foreign Relations Committee, 10 March 1982, *AFPCD* 1982, 712-13.
107. Joint Press Conference with Secretary of State Schultz and Secretary of State for External Affairs Joe Clark, Calgary, 28 October 1985, *AFPCD* 1985, 363.
108. Statement by Assistant U.S. Trade Representative before a subcommittee of the Senate Foreign Relations Committee, 10 March 1982, *AFPCD* 1982, 714.
109. Address by Undersecretary of State Ball to the 25th American Assembly, New York, 25 April 1964, *AFPCD* 1964, 436-39.
110. Address by Lawrence Eagleburger, Assistant Secretary for European Affairs, before the Center for Inter-American Relations, New York, 10 October 1981, Department of State Bulletin, No. 2057, vol. 81, (Washington, DC: Government Printing Office, 1981)

VI
ASSESSMENT

The questions to be answered in this concluding chapter remain those posed at the outset. Are there any permanent features or recurring patterns in the American response to Canada? Is it possible to identify an American policy toward Canada and, in particular, does it make sense to think in terms of an American imperialism directed against Canada? These questions are more difficult than they seem. There is so much encrustation on the American relationship with Canada that the underlying pattern is easily obscured. There have always been so many demographic, economic, and cultural interactions between the two countries; such a wide and complex range of official contact and un-official activity; and such an efflorescence of good neighbor rhetoric since the 1930s that the relationship can be reasonably portrayed in a variety of ways. One recent interpretation, argues that the contacts below the official level are so numerous and influential that they constitute the real relationship. According to this view, the "sub-system" or the complex of economic and cultural relationships below the level of government institutions in both countries contains the real forces that shape the contours of the American response toward Canada. On the other hand, it is plausible to present American economic expansion and American military and foreign policy influence as examples of the American empire at work in the modern world. And yet again, it is possible to concentrate on the evidence of institutional cooperation between the two countries since the establishment of the International Joint Commission in 1898 and cite this (in the manner of James Shotwell in the Carnegie Series) as confirmation that Canada and the United States have evolved a unique, exemplary collaborative relationship.

1.

The difficulties in determining what constitutes American policy can be well illustrated by looking at the background of the 1941 Hyde Park Declaration and the 1935 Reciprocal Trade Agreement, two markers at the beginning of the modern economic integration of North America. The Hyde Park agreement can be presented as an important element in a deliberate American policy of forcing the pace of economic integration. Since that integration led to the smaller economy of Canada adjusting to the needs of the larger American economy, the Hyde Park agreement becomes evidence that the United States was maneuvering Canada into a posture that made Canada less autonomous and pushed her into a dependent status. Yet one of the striking aspects of Hyde Park is that there was no prior planning by the State Department. Moreover, the draft agreement was drawn up on the Canadian side, and President Roosevelt simply accepted it. John Hickerson, who had been at the center of State Department planning on Canada throughout the 1930s, noted with some surprise these origins of the agreement. He explained to Pierrepont Moffatt, the U.S. Minister in Ottawa,

> the declaration at Hyde Park I now find was written by Clifford Clark, Jim Coyne and Hume Wrong. They drafted it as something which they hoped the Prime Minister would be able to get the President to agree to and the President agreed with a few slight changes in phraseology. No one in the State Department and, I am told, in our Treasury Department, had any advance knowledge of the statement.[1]

In the case of the 1935 trade agreement, the State and Treasury experts did play a central role, but it was a reluctant one. There was great fear of the impact of a Canadian treaty on American farmers. The final agreement was extremely narrow compared to the strategic planning proposed by W.Y. Elliott in his communications to Hickerson and Roosevelt. In the executive branch this reluctance was palpable. President Roosevelt's chief concern was to protect the dairy farmers in upper New York State. George Peek, Special Advisor to the President on international economic matters, was disdainful of the entire reciprocal trade program. He derided Secretary Hull as a member of "the school of international altruists." As Sir John Simon, who was the British ambassador in Washington at the time, observed, the reciprocal trade policy "is in fact the personal creation of the Secretary of State without whose devotion and care it could scarcely survive. The President has given it his perfunctory blessing rather than his active support and made no reference whatsoever to it in his recent message at the opening of Congress."[2] Notwithtanding this division and hesitancy on the American side, the Canadians pressed for the agreement. This was true of both the Bennett Conservative government and the Liberal one of King which came to power in the fall of 1935. Bennett, through the Canadian Minister in Washington and the American Minister in Ottawa, made desperate pleas for a trade treaty, and Prime Minister King took great pains to emphasize his desire to take Canada down "the American road."

Thus, during the 1930s and 1940s, when it is generally agreed that Canada made her decisive shift toward the United States in terms of economic integration, two centerpieces of the period turn out to be very ambiguous examples of American "policy." In 1941, the State Department was not even consulted. In 1935, the President was uninterested and the State Department hesitant. In both cases the pressure for action came from the Canadian, rather than the American, side.

If these two examples suggest some of the pitfalls in finding a readily identifiable American policy devised for Canada, a related difficulty is caused by the multiple levels at which there was an official, American response to Canada. An amusing example of this problem occurred in 1944, when a special report on strategic raw materials was published in the Army Service Forces Manual. The report noted that adequate supplies of nickel were available in Canada but warned "there is no guarantee that this source will be available in an emergency without military effort."[3] One of the features of the period from the 1914-18 war until the 1950s and beyond was the growing American interest in Canadian raw materials. It would seem reasonable to cite this report, which anticipated American military action in northern Ontario (where the Sudbury nickel mines were located), as an example of the aggressive or imperialist American way of thinking about Canada. But Lester Pearson, the future Prime Minister who was then a Counsellor at the Canadian Embassy in Washington, chose to make a jocular commentary on this Defense Department effort at analysis. He warned Hickerson, "the defense lines round Sudbury are practically impregnable and that any effort on the part of your Army to break through will be met by severe and bloody repulses." While maintaining this characteristically light approach, Pearson also added an edge of criticism. "I think it is an O_TR__GE," he continued, that a document of this kind should have been sent to the Canadian Embassy just at the time when our relations with the great republic to the south of us are becoming so firm and friendly. Nevertheless, in spite of the feeling created, we have decided, for the present at least, it is not necessary to barricade approaches to the Embassy.[4]

It would be absurd to take the manual as evidence of high level State or even Defense Department views but given the growth of American concern about strategic raw materials and the role of Canada as a source of supplies, such evidence forms part of a larger picture in which the United States tended to regard Canadian resources as exceptionally accessible because they were part of the continental hinterland. Certainly, this was exactly the long-term approach proposed by Professor Elliot of Harvard in his expert memoranda to the State Department in 1934.[5] If not evidence of an imperial policy, these kinds of views can be entered as evidence to convict agencies of the United States of insensitivity toward Canada as a sovereign power.

In the same vein, it would be possible to add to this type of official insult toward Canada the numerous congressional and political speeches made over the years by American public figures who called for an aggressive response to Canada. In 1867, the U.S. House of Representatives protested against the Confederation of Canada on the grounds that this strengthening of a British colony violated the Monroe Doctrine. In 1888, Senator John Sherman declared, in the course of a debate on trade relations, that any policy which would "tend to promote free commercial intercourse between these two countries, yes, anything that will tend to produce a union of Canada with the United States of America, will meet my most hearty support. . . . I want Canada to be part of the United States." And, of course, there is the notorious statement in 1911 by Champ Clark who, as we have noted, proclaimed, "he hoped to see the day when the American flag will float over every square foot of the British North American possessions clear to the North Pole."[6] The question facing the historian is what weight should be given to these examples of American rhetoric on Canada. Taken with the Department of Defense manual, they could add up to a substantial case for the existence of imperial attitudes if not imperial policy by the United States. However they are assessed, these kinds of spread-eagle statements add another layer to the relationship.

A further complicating element is introduced because of the strong regional variations in American attitudes toward Canada. We have seen this phenomenon in the American response to Canadian transportation policies in the nineteenth century. One line of analysis can be successfully pursued, with ample documentation, to show that Canada's improvement of the St. Lawrence route and the rapid construction of the transcontinental Canadian Pacific Railroad were regarded by American officials, congressmen and lobbyists as an imperially-backed strategy to siphon off American trade, even the U.S.-China trade, through Canada. But no American policy developed in response to this alleged Canadian commercial imperialism because the complaints were regionally based. It was the railroad and shipping interests in New York, Pennsylvania, and Chicago and their political representatives who took up this cry against Canada. The farmers of the northwest and New England businessmen and consumers welcomed the availability of the Canadian routes because of their impact on capacity and rates. Moreover, in New York there were so many American businesses engaged in the forwarding of bonded goods to Canada that any punitive action by the United States against Canada would have been opposed even by Republican businessmen, as President Harrison discovered when he scouted this option in 1892.[7] A further example of this phenomenon is the fact that in spite of all the American aggravation over the fisheries throughout the nineteenth century, no retaliation against the bonded trade was used as a method to bring pressure to bear on Canada. On this often vexing transportation question, while rhetoric seemed at times to be heading toward policy, the regional interests cancelled the possibility of any coherent American decision-making.

These features of American society and politics, of course, affect most aspects of American foreign policymaking. The size and complexity of the federal apparatus of power will mean that there is always a range of official views on any one country, and lobbies inside the United States representing particular economic interests or particular regional needs will press their cases with the White House, the State Department, and Congress. But the Canadian case is distinctive because there are so many geographical and economic points of contact. The St. Lawrence Seaway issue provides an excellent example of the intensity and interplay of these connections, and tellingly illustrates how regional factors prevented policy from emerging. The St. Lawrence project was the top priority when the United States opened the Legation in Ottawa in 1927, and it remained a high priority matter until the Seaway was constructed. In 1953, when the U.S. Ambassador to Canada, Stanley Woodward, reported on his mission, he reminded Secretary of State Dulles, "when I saw the President on the eve of my departure from Washington . . . he instructed me to devote my best efforts to promoting the St. Lawrence Seaway Project." Accordingly, continued Woodward, "during the past two and a half years I have regarded this as my principal task in Canada and it has been my constant pre-occupation."[8] From the 1920s, when the Seaway was viewed as a part of the solution to low agricultural prices, to the early 1950s, high-level American officials, including presidents and secretaries of state, made the case for the Seaway in terms of important national interests.

President Roosevelt, during World War II, emphasized the importance of the additional electrical power that would be generated from the Seaway project. "[It is] the race for production," Roosevelt urged, "that determines the rise and fall of nations" and the United States could not win that race without new sources of power. While Roosevelt's plea was made in the context of the war economy, he had been calling for additional power from the St. Lawrence back in the 1930s. In the post-war years, Under Secretary of State Dean Acheson added his considerable intellectual weight to the argument that the St. Lawrence project was significant for the continued health of the American economy. Returning to a theme that had interested Albert Gallatin as far back as the 1820s, Acheson related the St. Lawrence route to the economic well-being of the midwestern states. Acheson explained,

> Almost unique among the highly industrialized sections of the world, our middle western manufacturing areas have grown up far away from ocean transportation. . . . Since the First World War, this area has progressively grown into a surplus-producing area which now must ship its products not only within the United States but to foreign countries, and which must secure its raw materials not only from within the United States but increasingly from abroad. For all this, a water route to the sea is needed.

On the Defense Department side, similar strategic arguments were deployed. The National Security Resources Board drew attention to the usefulness of gaining better access to the iron ore in Labrador, and the Joint Chiefs argued that, from a national security standpoint, the United States could not accept a purely Canadian route into the heart of the United States.[9]

A plausible case can be made from this kind of evidence that the United States was pursuing a concerted policy on the Seaway in which Canada was treated as a mere adjunct to the U.S. economy—to help with domestic economic problems, to facilitate access to

Canadian raw materials, to improve the flow of American exports, and to keep foreign raw materials for America as cheap as possible. But no such policy was implemented because of domestic and regional opposition in the United States. Successive administrations through the 1930s and 1940s could not persuade the Senate to approve the project. Opposition came from American railroads, companies with a stake in the Mississippi route, the Atlantic ports from Baltimore to Boston, and private New York power companies who feared the impact of government-generated electricity.[10] Thus, the straightforward foreign policy thinking in the executive branch and in the State and Defense departments was completely blocked by powerful domestic lobbies. The geographical relationship between the two countries gave these domestic forces, operating through Congress, a direct and powerful impact on policymaking. In the end, it was the Canadian decision to proceed alone with the Seaway that broke the roadblock and forced the United States to commit itself to a joint project. In this instance, Canadian policy acted upon the United States, which had been prevented from acting because of domestic opposition. Contiguity and interconnections made such internal forces more prominent in American policy toward Canada, than was the case in any other bilateral relationship.

A final and pervasive, complicating factor that causes difficulty in assessing the fundamental American response to Canada has been the language and general tone of the relationship. In 1949, Lester Pearson, by then the Minister for External Affairs in Ottawa, made a speech in which he remarked that relations between Canada and the United States "have been characterized by the friendliness of the atmosphere of the back porch and the frankness of language on the bleachers."[11] This informality could easily create the impression of a friendly, issue-free relationship between two countries that shared a common outlook toward the world. Such an impression was directly created when good neighbor rhetoric was brought into play. This representation of the relationship first began to appear in the era of Anglo-American rapprochement before the Great War. Alfred Thayer Mahan, the naval and military historian, commented disapprovingly on the early manifestations of such idealistic formulations. He was moved to speak out by an editorial in *The New York Times*, 29 August 1914, which argued, "the unguarded frontier between the United States and Canada suggests the real reason why the United States has, for a century, maintained peace with Great Britain." *The Times*, of course, had its editorial sights set on the war in Europe and used the Canadian example to make a point that preparations for war led to war. Mahan was impatient with this ignorant view of North American history. The reference to the unguarded frontier "is one that is running trippingly from hundreds of pens at the present moment," but Mahan asked Americans to remember the historical record. The War of 1812, the border clashes in the late 1830s, the war scare over Oregon, and the tensions and incursions of the Civil War years showed the shallowness of such a view of the Canadian-American relationship.[12]

From these small beginnings before 1914, the unguarded frontier myth became fully mature in the 1930s. The Rush-Bagot Agreement which led to the removal of naval forces from the Great Lakes became the centerpiece of the mythology. When Norman Armour reported on his "opening gun" speech in Canada, upon taking his post as the American Minister to Canada in 1935, he noted, "in the course of my remarks I wanted to touch upon the Rush-Bagot Agreement—was ever any speech in Canada made without some reference to it."[13] As John Hickerson remarked in a 1930 memorandum, "the Rush-Bagot Agreement has come to have a great symbolical importance in our relations with Canada."[14] The State Department was slow to join this chorus of praise; but by the 1930s, there were numerous organizations propagating the undefended border and good neighbor themes. By 1937, the Chamber of Commerce of the United States sent John Hickerson a list of eleven nongovernment organizations which were active in promoting good relations with Canada. Among these was The Good Neighbor League, organized in 1936 at the request of President Roosevelt which, within two years, had branches in forty-eight states and a membership of 30,000. The Kiwanis Organization became a major force in this context. They described themselves as a "strictly North American continent organization" and they organized an annual celebration in the form of a Canada-U.S. goodwill week in April. In 1934, the Kiwanis first approached the State Department about erecting a plaque on the outside of the building where the Rush-Bagot Agreement had been signed. The initial coolness of the State Department to these developments (in 1938 J.C. Bonright of the Division of West European Affairs thought it best not to give official aid to the Good Neighbor League) gave way to hearty public endorsement. By the 1950s, Mason Wade, the Cultural Attache at the U.S. Mission in Ottawa, was organizing speeches by embassy officials to Kiwanis Clubs and advising his superiors that the annual good-will celebration was "a useful factor in maintaining the cordiality of the Canadian-American relationship."[15] By this time Presidents and Secretaries of State were issuing annual laudatory messages about the fine state of friendly relations between the two countries.

But this friendly rhetoric obscured as much as it clarified the relationship. Behind it there was a good deal of condescension and a realization that this kind of speechifying, while harmless, could usefully mask underlying goals that might be controversial. We have already seen, for example, that American cabinet-level officials had a set of specific economic and national security goals for participating in the construction of the St. Lawrence Seaway; but in public in 1952, when the joint project got under way, and again in 1959 when the Seaway was officially opened, all that was talked about was being good neighbors. The International Joint Commission which, since its inception in 1898, had held pride of place as an example of the special relationship, was often referred to in disparaging terms. During a discussion in 1948 between Julian Harrington and the Ottawa Embassy, and Lester Pearson on a range of matters, including the possible retirement of Prime Minister King, they thought that King might supplement his retirement income by appointing himself as Chairman of the Canadian Section of the IJC— "a job which pays well and does not involve much time or original effort." In 1939, John Hickerson ruefully told George Messersmitt, Assistant Secretary of State, "someone unkindly made the remark some years ago that in both the United States and Canada, the IJC has become a dumping ground for outworn political talent."[16]

On the American side, there was a related view that the praising of Canada was part of a necessary but tedious duty. In May 1945, for example, Lewis Clark, Counsellor at the U.S. Embassy, wrote to J. Graham Parsons complaining, "still bulking large in Canadian psychology is the childish desire to be publicly complimented and thought well of."[17] An actual instance of American officials pandering to this perception occurred three months later when the American delegates at the Potsdam Conference planted a story with the press to the effect that the Canadian delegation was the best one there. Hickerson confided to Ray Atherton, the U.S. Minister in Ottawa, "you doubtless suspected (and correctly) that this came from the U.S. press section who felt that a nice compliment of this sort coming at that particular time would do no harm. I don't think the Canadians knew where it came from. I kidded Norman [Robertson] about it and asked him how many copies of *Newsweek* he had to buy as his part of the deal."[18] American officials prided themselves in their presumed expertise in modulating these public responses to Canada. When President Eisenhower was due to visit Ottawa in 1953, for example, Ambassador Robert Stuart sent some pointers for the presidential speech. The Canadians "could be immensely flattered" by referring to the speech as "the Ottawa Declaration" it was mandatory to say, "we regard Canada as equal partners" and he warned Secretary Dulles to ask the speechwriters to "be brief about joint boards, etc." This last theme was becoming "threadbare because every American speaker says the same thing."[19]

It would be wrong to overemphasize the cynicism behind the rhetoric that was such a public hallmark of the Canadian-American relationship. Officials on both sides genuinely believed there was a special relationship characterized by frankness and friendliness. This can be seen in a revealing letter from John Hickerson about his friendship with Hugh Keenleyside. "I regard Hugh," Hickerson told George Hopper, the American Consul-General, in St. John's, Newfoundland, "as one of my best personal friends. . . . He is an honest, frank, square-shooter. It would be foolish to say that he and I always agree or always see things the same way. When we have disagreed we have been frank and completely honest with one another." The affection was matched on the other side. During a stay in Texas, Keenleyside wrote to Hickerson "after three days in Texas I understand and share your enthusiasm. It's a grand country. How about a new federation consisting of Texas and British Columbia. We could really go places."[20] Lester Pearson's jocular reply to the U.S. Army Manual's threat to invade Canada to secure her nickel supply is another example of this kind of easy, open communication that takes place more usually among friends than diplomats in their official roles. So Pearson was right about the "language of the bleachers." The common aspects of North American culture and the manifold connections between the two countries (including the fact that many Canadians, such as Keenleyside, had been educated in the United States) give a special tone to the relationship. It is important to gauge the impact of this tone whenever possible. It certainly had an impact on the writing of the Carnegie Series. But it is important not to give the good neighbor rhetoric too much weight. As Lester Pearson, when he was Minister-Counsellor at the Canadian Legation in Washington, perceptively noted in 1943,

> the very intimacy, informality and friendliness of our relations with the United States, though it has great advantages in many ways . . . does in another sense constitute a difficulty. The American authorities often tend to consider us as not a foreign nation at all, but as one of themselves. . . . They may make demands on Canada with a casualness that they would not dream of showing towards Brazil or any other Latin American state.[21]

This language of friendship, undefended borders, and good neighborhood is another encrustation that must be peeled away before the
fundamental shape of the relationship can be seen.

2.

The basic and enduring feature of the American response to Canada
was the goal of disengaging Canada from the British Empire.
Throughout the nineteenth century, Canada was viewed by the still-
developing United States as a troublesome part of the worldwide
British commercial and territorial expansion that often appeared
threatening to American interests. In the first forty years after
American independence, Canada was feared as a British military base
that threatened the fragile republic. The War of 1812 brought this
fearful phase to an end but the United States remained suspicious of
any signs suggesting the strengthening and expansion of Canada. As
long as Britain remained interested in Texas and Oregon, Canada was
viewed in this context. As late as 1845, Louis McLane, the U.S.
Minister in London, described British actions in North America as
designed "to encourage the novel idea of regulating and supervising
the balance of power on the American continent."[22] The acquisition
of Texas, the settlement of the Oregon question, and the winning of
California and the Southwest as a consequence of the Mexican War
finally put all these fears to rest. Moreover, with the collapse of the
old imperial trading system in the 1840s and the signing of the
Reciprocity Treaty in 1854, the United States thought that the British
Empire in North America had entered the final stage of dissolution.
Insofar as Secretary Marcy had any expectations of the 1854 treaty, it
was that freer trade with Canada would lead to a weakening of Empire
ties and a strengthening of North American economic integration.

Canada's role during the Civil War and the creation of an enlarged
Canada after 1867 were a shock to these American expectations. By
now the United States was powerful enough not to doubt her dominance on the continent, but there was an annoyance at Canada's
striving for "a second Empire." Republican administrations hoped, as
Secretary of State Blaine made clear in 1892, that their high tariffs
would bring Canada to its senses and force it to turn away from
Empire and sue for some kind of union with the United States.[23]

Canada's commitment to the imperial ideology in the 1890s and
her economic prosperity in the first decade of the twentieth century
suggest the failure of the Republican tack and the American policy
shifted back to the earlier pattern of attaching Canada to the United
States by freer trade. The goal of the 1911 reciprocity proposal was

to break the imperial orientation that had been revitalized since the 1890s. This policy did not work because of its rejection in Canada. The agricultural question in the United States during the 1920s and 1930s made any new approach to Canada difficult, but the impact of the Depression and of World War II quickly undermined the remaining imperial tendencies of Canada. By 1947, the Canadians were even discussing the possibility of complete free trade between the two countries, which would have dramatically consummated the shift into the American sphere. Free trade, which would permit common utilization of the continental market and continental resources and which would therefore knit the two countries together in the economic realm, was finally accepted in 1988. As Assistant Secretary of State Willard Thorp remarked during the abortive 1947 negotiations, such an outcome had been "an objective of U.S. foreign policy since the founding of the republic."[24]

A second basic feature of the American response to Canada was the view that geographical forces, if allowed to operate without artificial hindrance, would naturally draw Canada into a close and cooperative relationship with the United States. In the period 1783-1854, American administrations argued that British and Canadian trade restrictions blocked natural trade channels in North America and the West Indies. In the post-Civil War decades, Canadian transportation policies were criticized on the grounds that they created artificial east-west trade routes. American policymakers responded with formulations about the north-south linkages that ought to flourish if geography had its way. Israel Andrews in the 1850s referred to "the hydrographic basin" of the Great Lakes which both countries shared. In 1911, Osborne and Pepper talked about "contiguity and identity of interests" and "the natural channels of commerce." When asked to justify their Canadian policy, Taft administration officials explained it on this geographical basis. Osborne made the point that U.S. policy toward Canada "should be differentiated, even sharply and radically from that pursued toward European countries and the world in general." In a note to Charles Hilles, private secretary to Taft, Pepper observed, "the reciprocity agreement is desirable for geographical and other reasons which do not apply to Argentina, Australia, China, etc."[25] This conceptualization remained a major characteristic of American thinking as U.S. policymakers became aware of the vast store of natural resources in the northern part of the continent. In 1913, Canada accounted for 13 percent of U.S. raw material imports; by 1950, this had risen to 27 percent—a greater increase than any other country.[26] By the 1930s, background experts such as Professor W.Y. Elliot were preparing reports on long-term strategies to secure access to Canadian resources; and by 1935, Pierre de Boal had coined the phrase "a special contiguous country economic regime." Implicit in this phrase were the ideas propounded by Adams, Rush, and Gallatin in the 1820s; Andrews in the 1840s and 1850s; and Pepper, Hoyt, and Osborne in 1911 that contiguity and the north-south grain of the continent should be the basis for American thinking about Canada.

The goal of disengaging Canada from the Empire and the concept that geographical contiguity ought to tie Canada to the U.S. economy in a complementary way were present from the earliest decades of the republic. By 1911, these ideas had been transformed into self-conscious policy, and by the 1930s and 1940s, they had become routine statements in diplomatic correspondence. But to delineate the evolution of policy in this manner obscures as much as it clarifies the American response to Canada. The biggest single impact that the United States had on Canada was not by means of the policies proposed by the likes of Andrews and Pepper. The most fundamental impact was made by the tariff. In a revealing comment on this bedrock reality, former Canadian Prime Minister Arthur Meighen, as he assessed the challenge of governing Canada, noted that the American tariff had always been of key significance. "Give me control of the tariff policy of the United States for a period of ten years," Meighen declared, "and I can do more for the welfare of Canada than I could do for it as Prime Minister."[27] In 1886, 44 percent of Canadian exports went to the United States; by 1921, the figure was 46 percent; and, after a dip in the 1920s and early 1930s, it rose to 38 percent by the end of World War II and to 68 percent by 1982. The first American minister to Ottawa pointed out in an early report that U.S.-Canadian trade had doubled in volume every ten years since 1880.[28] But the American tariff impact on Canada was barely influenced by the State Department until Secretary Hull's reciprocal trade program began to have a limited impact in the 1930s. As William Culbertson, Head of the Tariff Commission, noted, "our tariff rates are a product of regional and political compromises and not planned and coordinated in the national interest."[29] In 1911, James Bryce pointed out that the easiest way for the United States to achieve its aim of breaking Canada's imperial ties would be to drop all tariff barriers. But tariff considerations in Congress cut against long-term, American strategic goals in the case of Canada. Some policymakers, such as Secretary of State Blaine, hoped the protectionist tariff policy would force Canada into being more accommodating. He explained to President Harrison, "we do not want any intercourse with Canada except through the medium of the tariff, and she will find that she has a hard row to hoe and will ultimately I believe seek admission to the Union."[30]   But Blaine and those protectionists who thought along the same lines were proved wrong. High tariffs hindered the achievement of the basic American goals. It took the twin shocks of depression and world war to undermine the unproductive American tariff stance and prepare the ground for the "comprehensive policy" identified by Andrews as far back as 1857. Beginning with the Reciprocal Trade Agreement in 1935, running through the economic and trade cooperation during the World War II period, and culminating in the Free Trade Agreement in 1988, American policy was dedicated to encouraging economic integration and facilitating the common exploitation of the continental market and natural resources.

This final American approach to Canada was solidly in place by the late 1940s and early 1950s. A confidential policy statement on Canada prepared in 1951 summed up the State Department's position. The first objective was to ensure recognition, in both the United States and Canada, of a special relationship that existed by reason of "geographical proximity, cultural and social similarity and economic and military interdependence." In terms of policy, the United States should work to remove as many barriers as possible. "The best integrated use of North American resources in people, materials and culture," continued the policy statement, "can only be achieved if obstacles to their free flow across the border are kept to an absolute minimum." Coordination of the two economies was an essential part of this integrative process. The economic difficulties of Canada in the post-war years and the crisis in Korea had "created a powerful impetus in the direction of further integration (including) large orders for critical defense materials such as nickel, zinc, copper. . . ."[31]   Two years later, U.S. Ambassador Stanley Woodward noted the accelerating pace of the steps "towards closer integration of economic policies between our two Governments." The cooperation on military procurement and production, begun during World War II,

> paved the way for closer coordination in these fields than ever before enjoyed in time of peace. . . . The past two years have witnessed rapid expansion and close integration of the economies of the United States and Canada. . . . Vast new natural resources of oil, iron and other essential materials have been discovered and are being developed . . . and the U.S. mobilization base has been extended to some degree into Canada.[32]

While giving first priority to further integration and coordination based on "geographical proximity," State Department experts were well aware (after the 1911 experience) of the danger that an overly aggressive pursuit of such goals would lead to a backlash of Canadian nationalism. Because of Canadian complaints during and after the World War II—often wickedly phrased in speeches by Lester Pearson—American officials in Ottawa and Washington well appreciated the problem. For example, Julian Harrington, the U.S. Minister in Ottawa, prepared a special report in 1949 on the "Development and Character of Canadian Nationalism." He made the case that Canadian nationalism was a complex phenomenon because of different views of Canada held by English and French Canadians. Strong regional differences, along with the ambivalent relationship with Britain, compounded the problems for "the creation of a positive national spirit." But Harrington warned that the beginnings of such a modern nationalist spirit could be detected in reaction to "Canada's increasingly marked orientation towards the United States. The Nationalists," continued Harrington, "worry particularly over cultural and economic penetration by that country [the U.S.]." Harrington argued that this kind of nationalism "does not seem so far to have penetrated beyond intellectual, artistic, political and governmental circles" to the great mass of ordinary people.[33] Nevertheless, the State Department took this development seriously and the 1951 policy statement was emphatic in the need to respect Canadian sovereignty. "It is our policy," the Department report stated, "to avoid meticulously any action which might be construed as an infringement of Canadian sovereignty or a disposition to ignore or over-ride legitimate Canadian interests. . . . As a matter of policy the Department should be continually alert to detect and ward off any proposals which might wound Canadian susceptibilities."[34]

These warnings by American officials proved to be prophetic. Through the 1950s, the economic cooperation went on apace and was accompanied by wide-ranging American influences on Canadian society and culture. During the 1960s and early 1970s, there was a formidable Canadian nationalist reaction to increasing American influence on Canada, spearheaded by the New Democratic party (a development Harrington had anticipated back in 1949 when the NDP was still the CCF). A range of counter-measures was undertaken to protect Canadian cultural and educational institutions (including regulation of content on radio and television).[35] But in the midst of this resurgence of Canadian nationalism, which incorporated many of the old, nineteenth-century Canadian attitudes toward the expansionist United States, the main objectives of American policy continued to be met. Canada's attempts to diversify her trade options by increasing exports to Japan and the European Economic Community did not change the fundamental pattern of her economy. The signing of the Free Trade Agreement in 1988 and the subsequent victory in Canada of Prime Minister Mulroney's Conservative party were effective signs of the success of American policy in spite of the nationalist movement in Canada.

3.

The question remains whether these American policies and attitudes constituted an imperialism toward Canada. In seeking an answer, some easy solutions must be avoided. It is too simple to use all the effusive oratory by American politicians in the nineteenth and early twentieth centuries. This was directed to a domestic audience and usually reflected traditional anti-British attitudes more than a policy toward Canada. But, it is not so easy to dismiss the informed observations of American officials writing at a time when a planned Canadian policy was in place. In 1951, for example, Don C. Bliss, the U.S. Minister in Canada, reported to Secretary of State Dulles, "Canada is in effect helpless to follow economic policies incompatible with ours although Canadians dislike to admit this self-evident fact and it should not be proclaimed in the United States."[36] This American diplomat took it for granted that Canada had become an economic adjunct of the United States, which serves adequately enough as a working definition for an imperial relationship.

But self-evident truths are often trickier than they seem. There are significant characteristics of the American response to Canada that make imperialism a misleading term to apply. The first point to make is that the United States' powerful economic relationship with Canada came about so easily that policy hardly entered into the outcome. Thomas Hotchkiss, the U.S. Consul in Ottawa, pointed out in his 1886 annual report that, in spite of U.S. tariffs and Canadian tariffs, Canada's trading orientation was continuing to shift away from Britain and toward the United States. The slippage in imports from Britain was partly explained by the increase in Canadian domestic manufacturing, but Hotchkiss was "certain that her preferences for the supply of very much which she is compelled to purchase abroad were with Americans and for merchandise of American manufacture."[37] Hotchkiss' reading of the trends was confirmed by the trade figures for the next hundred years, as the following table illustrates:

190

Canadian Imports 1886-1982 [38]
(in Percents)

Year	U.S.	U.K.	Other Foreign	Total
1886	44	41	15	100
1906	60	24	16	100
1926	66	17	17	100
1946	73	10	17	100
1967	72	6	22	100
1982	70	3	27	100

The trend was formidable irrespective of tariff policies and other issues that affected relations between the two countries. Even at the height of the protectionist tussle, from 1880 to 1911, as American Republican administrations built their walls and as the Canadians responded with their national policy, the pattern was unmistakably clear for anyone who cared to look at the figures. Britain's steady and finally dramatic decline as a supplier of goods to Canada is also abundantly clear from the 1914-18 war to the present. The rise in other foreign suppliers in the 1960s and 1970s is a sign of Canadian efforts to stimulate another option to the American one. But, in spite of these efforts, the dominant fact remains that almost three-quarters of Canada's imports came from the United States. When the figures for Canadian exports are examined, the pattern becomes even more overwhelming. In 1886, the United States took 44 percent of Canadian exports; by 1951, she took 59 percent; and in 1982, the United States bought 68 percent of Canada's exports. These powerful, bilateral trade flows have been a fundamental shaping force of the relationship since the confederation of Canada was created in 1867.[39] Their direction made American policy a question of drifting with the current, rather than charting a course.

A second way in which matters were made easy for the United States concerns Canada's relationship with Britain. In 1948, when Willard Thorp was getting excited about the prospect of finally breaking Canada's link with the British Empire, John D. Hickerson, the Canadian expert at the State Department, understood that the question was no longer critical. Hickerson pointed out that Britain's military and economic decline since 1914-18, especially as a consequence of the World War II drain on her resources, meant it was now an empty objective to weaken the Canadian link to Britain. In fact, Hickerson lamented Britain's decline because the United States would benefit from a stronger Britain in the dangerous post-war world. "God knows, I wish the British well," Hickerson confided to Ray Atherton, the U.S. Minister in Ottawa, "It is in our interest that Britain be strong both from the economic and military standpoint. I am, however, far from hopeful."[40] Thus, if one looks only at the Thorp evidence, there is an argument for a self-conscious American determination to make a final break between Canada and the Empire but inside the top levels of the State Department it was well understood that this old nineteenth-century game was no longer relevant. It certainly had been a traditional goal, as Thorp correctly pointed out, but it was a goal achieved more by Canadian than American efforts. The history of Canada since the achievement of responsible government in the 1840s had, as one of its main themes, the disentangling of Canadian national interest from that of Great Britain. In the 1850s, the Union of the Canadas placed tariffs on British imports; and, although English Canadians rallied round the Empire in the 1890 to 1918 period, the historical trend was for Canadian leaders to press for an articulation of the Empire relationship that would allow more autonomy for Canada and the other British settlements. By 1931, that autonomy had been achieved and, in contrast to 1914, Canada made her own declaration of war in 1939. Although the issue was occasionally controversial in Canadian domestic politics, the direction taken by modern Canadian governments was toward reducing the colonial relationship with Britain (culturally as well as institutionally) and presenting Canada as an independent, North American nation (albeit with an international outlook and a continuing commitment to the British Commonwealth). The repatriation of the 1867 British North America Act to Canada in 1982 marked the final stage of this Canadian distancing from the Empire. Here again American policy was pushing at a door being pulled open by the Canadians.

A third factor to bear in mind when assessing American motives is the tone of the relationship encouraged by the Canadians during the two decisive decades of the 1930s and 1940s. Under the stress of the Depression and the war against Germany and Japan, the crucial decisions came so easily. The Prime Minister of Canada took the extraordinary step in 1935 of turning up on the doorstep of a surprised U.S. Minister in Ottawa to assure him that Canada wanted "to take the American road." The Ogdensburg Agreement and the Hyde Park Declaration, during the first two years of the war, came without public debate or hard bargaining from the Canadians. As Pierrepont Moffatt, the U.S. Minister in Ottawa, reported on 22 August 1940, the one aspect of Ogdensburg that might cause problems in the future was that the agreement "came at a time when circumstances forced every Canadian to approve it rather than at a time when it was adopted just because it was the wisest thing to do and Canadian opinion could freely debate its merits and reach this satisfying conclusion."[41] Canadian historian Donald Grant Creighton, in his later work, identified Prime Minister King as the villain who had sold out Canada to the United States in the 1930s and 1940s. Creighton's criticism is too tendentious because it was not a one-man show, and the underlying economic and military driving forces behind the changes were very strong. Moreover, it is clear that Mackenzie King did not take Canada naively down the American road. His government criticized many American initiatives and proposals during and after the war, and he blocked the 1947 free trade negotiations because he understood there would be a Canadian nationalist reaction. He was also as fawning to British leaders as he was to Americans.

In a recent collection of essays J.L. Granatstein has exposed the weakness of the view that Mackenzie King was responsible for the shift of Canada into the American sphere. Granatstein points out that the international context, especially the weakness of Britain, was the molding force that most powerfully affected Canadian-American relations during this critical period.[42] Looking at it from the American evidence, it is clear that U.S. policymakers were committing themselves to an integrationist policy even before Mackenzie King returned to power in 1935. On this point, the memorandum written by Benjamin Wallace in 1931, which was devastatingly critical of the traditional protectionist approach and proposed a policy of comprehensive collaboration with Canada, is critical for showing that American policy was not a response to King's sycophancy. Still, Creighton has a point. Everything came so easily and quickly to the Americans, in spite of the sometimes sharp debate over details. They were assured so frequently by King that Canada was an "American" nation now, that it is hardly surprising that Washington officials looked forward to further economic and military integration as a matter of course. The tone adopted by King helped American policymakers (in any case preoccupied with more dramatic world crises) to avoid thinking hard about what they were doing with Canada. They thought they were accepting a situation that was evolving naturally in their favor rather than imposing a policy.

In this context, an even broader argument can be made that throughout most of the period covered in this book (beginning in 1849 when Britain abandoned the old imperial trading system), Canada was pushing to extend the economic links with the United States. It was the Canadian colonial administration, backed by London, who pressed for the Reciprocity Treaty in 1854. Canadian governments in 1866, 1869, and 1874 sought a renewal of this freer

North American trading system. Even Macdonald's Conservative government approached the Harrison administration in an attempt to negotiate a trade agreement in 1892. As John Osborne, Chief of the Bureau of Trade Relations in the State Department, pointed out in 1908, all "the overtures came in each instance from Canada." The Liberal administration of Laurier in 1911 was pleased with the reciprocity offer from the Taft administration. During the agitation for reciprocity in the late 1880s, the Marquis of Landsdowne, the Governor-General of Canada, acknowledged, "in the strictly commercial aspect . . . there appears to be no room for doubt that commercial Union would be greatly to the advantage of the people of the Dominion. . . . The different sections of the country are geographically so widely separated from each other and so closely connected with adjoining portions of the United States."[43] During the 1911 reciprocity debate, the Governor of Newfoundland wrote to James Bryce, the British Ambassador in Washington, "whatever comes of it now, I do not think that two countries with such a long common frontier . . . will very long remain without reciprocal arrangements of some kind."[44] Canadians worked for economic and trade cooperation for most of the period since 1935 and took the iniative in proposing the comprehensive free trade agreement of 1988. In short, all Canadian governments, from 1849 to 1988, worked for closer economic ties with the United States.

Reading even the secret memoranda from the critical period of integration does not provide telling evidence for imperialism. In May 1950, Julian Harrington, Minister at the U.S. Embassy in Ottawa, submitted a memorandum to the Policy Planning Staff reviewing "Basic Factors in United States Relations with Canada." The memorandum reflected American views of the trends since the 1930s, in that Harrington was clearly convinced that the Canadians were anxious for more integration. After apologizing that the Department might already be well aware of what he was about to say, Harrington opened by emphasizing "that closer economic integration with the United States has become a major objective of the Canadian Government." He then summarized his assessment of attitudes toward the United States. "All Canadians," he continued, "are conscious of the tremendous power, influence and economic preeminence of the U.S.; few, if any, honestly fear imperialistic designs. High ranking Canadian officials have privately expressed to me the inevitability of eventual economic union with the United States." For its part the State Department policy staff must bear in mind "the inescapable fact that we are dependent upon Canada for many strategic materials." Harrington ended in a somewhat deflated manner by noting, "problems elsewhere in the world" might detract from working up a policy in Washington, but he repeated his core point, "we have . . . a situation in Canada in which an international economic boundary is confidently expected to vanish in the course of time."[45]

American officials, then, even in their internal correspondence, viewed themselves as heading in a direction natural to the economic forces, and one that was approved of by Canada. The American view of their response to Canada was even more clearly set out by William P. Snow, Assistant Chief in British Commonwealth Affairs, in a 1950 memorandum.

> The American attitude is quite uncomplicated and easy to describe. Perceiving no reason to fear or envy the Canadians, we have the friendliest of feelings towards them as neighbors and as partners in various international endeavors, including the cold war. We have no designs on their territory or their sovereignty. In fact, we are not as a rule deeply interested in or well-informed about Canadian affairs. As for harmonious relations, we are inclined to take these for granted, having too many compelling troubles elsewhere in the world to search for more beneath the surface of U.S.-Canadian relations.

Snow noted that Canadians expected to open up further the trading relationship between the two countries and in general, to open up U.S. trade with the rest of the world as the engine that would keep the international trading system in a healthier state. "They think we should turn the trick," Snow remarked, "by adopting the role that Britain played during the nineteenth century, opening our markets to the world on liberal terms. In their desire to see it achieved, they do not always realize the time and effort that would be required to bring about this fundamental change in U.S. national policy." Snow went on to describe a more complex Canadian attitude toward the United States. They resented being treated as "camp followers"; they were sensitive about their newly gained autonomy. ("They even attach significance to the fact that Canada did not declare war against Hitler until ten days after Britain did.") This "political touchiness," as Snow described it, was "not unnatural under the circumstances," and U.S. officials should take great care to be aware of Canadian susceptibilities.[46]

These memoranda show that American officials who worked on Canadian matters were not saints. They were insensitive to Canadian concerns about sovereignty, and they were slow to appreciate the significance of the debate in Canada about the impact of American economic and cultural forces north of the border. They were sometimes condescending as they described the need to accommodate

Canadian "political touchiness." They assumed that a continental economy in which the United States would be the most influential actor was well on the way to completion. As Snow complacently put it: "Both sides must learn to live with the fact that as between the two countries the natural advantages are mainly on the U.S. side and that the political boundary divides into two competitive areas what would otherwise be a continental economic unit."[47] But do complacency and insensitivity constitute imperialism? The British Ambassador in Washington, Roger Makins, did not think so. In a 1955 report to Harold Macmillan, the British Foreign Secretary (described in London as "a valuable and striking view of the Commonwealth through American eyes"), Makins reviewed all the economic and military-strategic forces that were drawing Canada more closely to the United States. He thought, "no conscious national effort is made by the United States to encourage this absorption . . . [and there was] no desire on the part of U.S. policymakers to absorb Canada."

A good insight into how Americans viewed their Canadian policies was provided in 1947 by Andrew Foster from the British Commonwealth Affairs Division of the State Department. As he assessed the course of events on the last day of the year, he readily acknowledged that the United States was actively pursuing its own national interests, but he thought that Canadians were gaining advantages too and that there was a sharing of beneficial outcomes. There were benefits to both countries from the increasing integration. Foster explained that his report was not intended "to prove we are on the side of the angels. Whatever benefits and advantages Canada gained from the U.S. relationship in 1947 were given in our own self-interest. It is my purpose however to emphasise that the overall picture shows that Canada did all right in 1947."[48] In spite of tensions and periodic crises, Canada continued to do "all right" in the twentieth-century world of nation-states. The United States certainly pursued its own self-interest, but no other nation behaves differently in that respect. Because the United States economy is much larger and more complex, American interests often set the agenda, and Canada must work hard to protect her own national goals. But the United States and Canada are two advanced capitalist powers who share a similar view of North American and the international economic environment they want to live in. American policy has not caused a stunted development in Canada in the same way as imperial intervention, in the view of many scholars, has had a deleterious impact on third world economies.

On the other hand, if there is considerable doubt as to whether an imperialist policy existed, the evidence is overwhelming that an incipient imperialist ideology with respect to Canada has existed in the United States since the end of the War of 1812. Its core belief is best summarized in a phrase used by John Quincy Adams in a letter to Richard Rush back in 1818. Adams wrote of "our natural dominion in North America."[49] This view, that the United States had the right to dominate the continent, informed the entire range of American thinking from the bellicose expressions of Blaine to the reasoned and carefully phrased policy statements by officials from Pepper in 1911 to Bliss in 1951. But in this case, an imperial ideology did not translate into an imperial policy because so many of the goals sought by the United States were also sought by Canada. U.S. expansion undermined the societies and economies of the North American native peoples but did not undermine Canada. On the contrary, the economic growth of the United States was the most significant factor ennabling Canada to become a prosperous modern society with a prosperous modern economy. In spite of all the periods of tension and misunderstanding, Canada benefitted from the rise of the U.S. to the status of a global power. Canada was strong enough in terms of its institutions and political traditions to benefit economically from neighborhood with the expanding U.S., while still preserving her territory and integrity as a state and a society. At every critical stage of the increasingly integrated relationship, Canadian governments led by freely elected, experienced, and well-educated politicians, advised by competent officials, chose to follow the path of cooperation with the United States. With so much overlap in terms of intention it is, in the final analysis, unproductive to classify American policy with respect to Canada as imperialism. The study of imperialism is already a complex subject as scholars attempt, by a variety of approaches, to delineate the relationship between western commercial and industrial powers and the rest of the world from the sixteenth century to the present. Trying to work Canada into the field of analysis does not produce illuminating results. The historical pattern of the relationship and the contemporary evidence simply do not support those Canadian scholars who portray Canada as the victim of American imperialism.

This conclusion takes us back to the point made by Charles Pepper, as he drafted the reciprocity policy in 1911, that the Canadian case is distinct because of geographical contiguity, because of the similarity in stage of development, and because of the pattern of north-south continental regions. Whenever American officials and experts thought about Canada they thought in these terms. Israel Andrews in the 1850s assumed that lowering the trade barriers would lead to Canada's economic absorption by the United States. Pepper, Hoyt, Osborne, and Knox in 1911, all argued that reciprocity would break Canada's Empire orientation, give the U.S. access to Canada's grain and, in general, make the Canadian economy complementary to that of the United States. American officials in the 1930s, 1940s, and 1950s thought along the same lines of creating a special contiguous-country economy that would fit with American needs in terms of markets and especially raw materials. The State Department officials of the 1940s and 1950s were simply elaborating and making systematic the insights of Andrews a hundred years previously. Indeed, there was a remarkable continuity in the views of those Americans who thought about Canada from the middle decades of the nineteenth century onward. Domestic political forces inside the United States, rather than Canadian or British counter-policies, were the most persistent obstacle to the achievement of American goals. From 1866 to 1935, protectionist forces were powerful enough in Congress to prevent the State Department from implementing an integrationist policy. In 1911, the peculiar political conditions in Congress, the need for the Republican administration to make some headway on tariff reduction, and the fear that the British imperial consolidation movement might become successful led to the one great exception, the Taft reciprocity offer to Canada. But protectionist forces returned in strength and lasted through the 1920s, until the shattering of the old political world by depression and war enabled a systematic American approach to emerge. By that time the ultimate goal was coming about so easily that American policymakers thought that the increasing pace of economic integration was the result of natural developments believed in by a succession of Canadian governments from 1934 onward.

Canadian policymakers had a much harder task than their American counterparts; they had to construct policies that would derive benefits from the proximity of the United States without permitting American influence to gain too strong a hold on Canadian economic and foreign policy. The compelling theme here is Canada's attempt to construct and maintain a separate nation-state in North America in spite of the division between Quebec and the rest of the country, in spite of strong regional diversity, and in spite of the powerful pull of forces emanating from the American leviathan. At the moment that struggle appears to be a success although the internal constitutional debate presents a more serious challenge to the existence of Canada than any U.S. policy ever has done. Even with the high level of North American economic integration, Canada possesses vital literary, artistic, and educational cultures and a national identity on the world stage that keeps her distinct from the United States. Vigorous efforts are made at the federal and provincial levels to provide effective support for the continuance of this distinctiveness. Canada usually plays a constructive role at the United Nations and takes the lead in the British Commonwealth and other international arenas to maintain a posture with respect to international relations that can be differentiated from the other North American state.[50] As J.J.S. Garner, the Acting British High Commissioner in Ottawa observed in 1948, "the traditional aim of Canadian policy has been to avoid Gleichshaltung either with the United States or the British Commonwealth. . . . Canada therefore is likely to continue in her attempt to defy the laws of logic and geography."[51]

4.

The great nineteenth-century French historian Jules Michelet remarked that in the beginning history is altogether geography. In the early stages of human history, the fundamental features of the landscape—mountain ranges, river valleys, areas suitable for hunting and cultivation—determined patterns of human settlement and permitted the coaxing into existence of particular sequences of human development. As humans learned to influence and manage their environment, social formations and then polities emerged that sometimes worked with these geographical features but eventually became strong enough to imprint the human pattern over them. Geography turned into history. If we look at the history of European North America in these terms, the critical period in the American relationship with Canada was not 1935-1988 but 1763-1812. In the seventeenth and first half of the eighteenth century, the French colony of Canada developed in harmony with the geography of North America as it pushed out its traders, soldiers, and missionaries along the great river routes of the interior—up the St. Lawrence to the Great Lakes, down the Ohio and Mississippi rivers to Louisiana. The conquest of Canada by the British in 1759-60, the extension of the American border up to the Lakes in 1783, and across the continent at the 49th parallel after the War of 1812, sealed off Canada from the natural grain of the continent. To be sure, the nature of the northern terrain, the river routes running out from the Hudson's Bay, and the river highway of the lower St. Lawrence still provided a base for development, as numerous Canadian historians have argued. But there is no getting away from the fact that it was a stunted base. Canadian administrations since the 1820s (when the Welland Canal was constructed around Niagara Falls) have tried, by canals and then railroads, to build a successful northern economy. The creation of Confederation was an essential step in that endeavor. This new transcontinental dominion was a surprising challenge to the United States and its growth and development, as we have seen, annoyed Americans. But even a successful Canadian Confederation could not alter the fact that the United States was the dominant continental power. The remorseless course of continental economic integration was told in the trade figures. In 1878, John A. Macdonald, the leader of the Conservative party, invented the national policy to build a distinct northern economy on an east-west axis; in 1988, the Conservative government of Brian Mulroney staked its political life on a free trade agreement with the United States in recognition of the north-south pull of trade and investment. In North America, geography is winning out over history.

Toward the other end of Pennsylvania Avenue from the Old Treasury Building, on which the historical marker commemorating the Webster-Ashburton treaty is set, stands the new Canadian Embassy. It is the only embassy on Pennsylvania Avenue. Its position between the White House and Congress is fitting, for Canada has always stood in a special relationship with the United States, as it shares the northern part of the continent. The fact that the Embassy is nearer Congress than the White House or the State Department is also appropriate. The great game for dominance in North America has long been won by the United States. The State Department policy has easily been set—encouragement for economic integration and military cooperation without causing problems by appearing to interfere with Canada's sovereignty. Because of the high level of integration, Canadians will be affected by congressional legislation more than the people of any other foreign country. Canadians have always been as much affected by congressional legislation as by American policy emanating from the White House and the State Department. The placing of the Embassy nearer to Capitol Hill than to the other end of the avenue is symbolic of this reality.

The embassy building on Pennsylvania Avenue aptly recognizes Canada's exceptional relationship with the United States. That relationship is unequal because Canada has always been the weaker party. Canada has a smaller population, a less powerful economy, and less military strength which means that the agenda and pace of change is more often than not set by the United States. Canada has had to adjust her policies to the fundamental fact of U.S. dominance of the continent. But throughout the nineteenth and twentieth centuries, from the Reciprocity Treaty of 1854, to Ogdensburg in 1940, to NORAD in 1957, and to the Free Trade Agreement of 1988, Canadian leaders have always viewed a collaborative relationship with the U.S. as essential to Canada's national well-being. Because Canada presents no threat to the U.S. and because Canada is the smaller power, Canadians often grumble about their treatment by the United States— either on the grounds that Canada is taken for granted or on the grounds that American influence undermines Canadian national goals. But such suffering is a far cry from imperial exploitation. Victims of American imperialism cannot afford to build state-of-the-art embassies on Pennsylvania Avenue.

One last point is worth making about the Canadian-American relationship, which is so often singled out as perhaps the most neighborly and peaceful one modern history has witnessed. The final shape of this relationship was decisively determined by war. The American War for Independence and the War of 1812 ensured that Canada would be kept out of the continental heartland and that the U.S. would become the great power of the region. The Union victory in the Civil War confirmed that the United States would be the dominant continental and hemispheric state. The two world wars of the twentieth century were the most powerful factors forcing Canada to become integrated so quickly and easily into the American "empire." The economic and fiscal forces set in motion by the Great War and World War II were so strong that American policy simply followed in their wake.[52] In these circumstances American policymakers were never challenged by the Canadian question; their goals were achieved with a minimum of effort and with a considerable degree of support from their Canadian counterparts.

Notes

1. John D. Hickerson to J. Pierrepont Moffatt, 30 April 1941, John D. Hickerson Papers, Reel 5, National Archives; Memorandum of Conversation at White House by Francis Sayre, 3 July 1935, State Department Decimal File (SDDF) 1930-39, Box 3181, RG 59, National Archives; Clark was Canada's Deputy Finance Minister, Hume Wrong was the Minister Counsellor at the Canadian Legation in Washington, and in the following year became Assistant Undersecretary of State for External Affairs; Coyne was Governor of the Bank of Canada. J.L. Granatstein who has written most illuminatingly on this matter, emphasizes the international context within which the agreement was made. The decline and near collapse of Britain in 1940 made it impossible for Canada to avoid a significant realignment fiscally and economically with the United States. See R.D. Cuff and J.L. Granatstein, *Ties That Bind: Canadian-American Relations in Wartime from the Great War to the Cold War* (Sarasota, FL: Samuel Stevens, 1977), 71 and Granatstein, *How Britain's Weakness Forced Canada into the Arms of the United States* (Toronto: University of Toronto Press, 1989) For the dominant sub-system thesis, see John H. Redekop, "A Reinterpretation of Canadian-American Relations, "*Canadian Journal of Political Science*, 9 (1976): 234-40, 242-43.
2. Sir Robert Lindsay to Sir John Simon, Washington, 29 November 1934, 25 January 1935, Public Record Office (PRO), London, FO 414/272.

3. Army Service Forces Manual (M104)—Strategic and Critical Raw Material (Washington: Department of Defense, 1944). The best overview of the United States' need for Canadian raw materials remains Bernard Goodman, *Industrial Materials in Canadian-American Relations* (Detroit: Wayne State University Press, 1961).

4. Lester Pearson to John D. Hickerson, Washington, 4 May 1944, Hickerson Papers, Reel 6.

5. W.Y. Elliot to John. D. Hickerson, Cambridge, 27 February 1933, "Summary of Trade Proposals Affecting American Mineral Policy," SSDF 1930-39, Box 3178, RG 59, National Archives.

6. Keenleyside, *Canada and the United States: Some Aspects of their Historical Relations* rev and enl. ed. *(New York: Knopf, 1952)* 256; Tansill, Canadian-American Relations, 409.

7. These contradictory responses were first evident in the rival Hatch and Taylor report on the 1854 Reciprocity Treaty and reappeared in various congressional hearings in the latter part of the nineteenth century. These are summarized in Gordon T. Stewart, "An Overview of America's Canadian Policy," *Diplomatic History* 6(1982):342-43.

8. Stanley Woodward to Secretary of State Dulles, Ottawa, 13 January 1953, SSDF 1950-54, Box 2773, RG 59, National Archives.

9. Franklin D. Roosevelt Message to Congress, 5 June 1941, *U.S. Cong. Sen. Rept.* 810, 80th Cong., 2d sess., 43 and Dean Acheson to Senate Subcommittee on St. Lawrence Seaway Project, 30 October 1946, 100-1; Report of the National Security Resources Board, 24 April 1950 *The St. Lawrence Seaway Manual: A Compilation of Documents on the Great Lakes Seaway Project, U.S. Congress, Sen. Doc.*165, 83d Cong., 2d sess. 47-9, 54-5.

10. In addition to these understandable domestic lobbies opposed to the St. Lawrence Seaway, there were wilder categories of opposition which revealed the persistence of old, nineteenth-century attitudes. During the 1934 debate in the U.S. Senate (which ended in rejection of a draft treaty), Senator Lewis of Illinois declared he was against the Seaway because it would provide "a military highway through the United States for Great Britain." Sir Robert Lindsey to Sir John Simon, Washington, 9 February 1934, PRO, FO 414/272; Leo Pasvolsky noted about the opposition in 1941:"it is the usual line up, railroads, railway labor and utilities on the one side and about everybody else on the other; but concentrated special interests can very often beat a majority." Beatrice B. Berle and Travis B. Jacobs, eds., *Navigating the Rapids, 1918-1971: From the Papers of Adolf A. Berle* (New York: Harcourt Brace Jovanovich, 1973), 371.

11. Julian Harrington to Secretary of State, Ottawa, 21 January 1949, SDDF 1945-49, Box 5884, RG 59, National Archives.

12. Robert Seager II and Doris Maguire,eds., *Letters and Papers of Alfred Thayer Mahan* (Annapolis: Naval Institute Press, 1975), 3:542-43.

13. Norman Armour to William Phillips, Ottawa, 14 October 1935, SDDF 1930-39, Box 4003, RG 59, National Archives.

14. John D. Hickerson Memorandum, 12 May 1930, John D. Hickerson Papers, Reel 1.. National Archives.

15. Charles Stelze (Executive Director of the Good Neighbor League) to Secretary of State Hull, New York, 1 October 1937, J. Pierrepont Moffatt to Ben Field, Washington, 28 May 1938, Edwin Hill to Clinton E. MacEachran, Chicago, 30 July 1934; SDDF 1930-1939, Box 4003, RG 59, National Archives; Mason Wade to Secretary of State, 29 April 1953, SDDF 1950-1954, Box 2773, RG 59, National Archives.

16. Julian Harrington to J. Graham Parsons, 10 February 1948, SDDF 1945-1949, Box 5884, RG 59, National Archives; John D. Hickerson to George Messersmitt, 12 May 1939, Hickerson Papers, Reel 1.

17. Lewis Clark to J. Graham Parsons, 2 May 1945, SDDF 1945-49, Box 5883, RG 59, National Archives. Parsons was Assistant Chief in the Division of British Commonwealth Affairs.

18. John D. Hickerson to Ray Atherton, 4 August 1945, Hickerson Papers, Reel 4.

19. Robert Stuart to Secretary of State, Ottawa, 8 October 1953, SSDF 1950-54, Box 2773, RG 59, National Archives.

20. John D. Hickerson to Herbert Bussley, 2 February 1945, Hickerson to George D. Hopper, 25 January 1944; Hugh Keenleyside to Hickerson, Laredo Texas, 2 February 1945, Hickerson Papers, Reel 5.

21. Memorandum from Minister-Counsellor Lester Pearson, Washington, 18 March 1943, *Documents on Canadian External Relations*, vols. 1-10 (Ottawa, Information Canada, 1970-) 9:1138-42.

22. Lewis McLane to Secretary of State Buchanan, London, 1 December 1845, in William Manning, *Diplomatic Correspondence of the United States: Canadian Relations, 1784-1860* vols. 1-4 (Washington, DC: Carnegie Endowment for International Peace, 1940), 3:986.

23. Ibid., 126-129.

24. Willard Thorp to Undersecretary of State Robert Lovett, Washington, 8 March 1948, *FRUS 1948*, 9:406.

25. Charles Pepper to Charles D. Hilles, 19 June 1911, William Howard Taft Papers, Reel 399, Case 543, Michigan State University Libraries. Back in 1826, John Quincy Adams made a similar point when he observed, "the relative geographic position and the respective products of nature culti-vated by human industry had constituted the elements of a commercial intercourse between the United States and British America, insular and continental, important to the inhabitants of both countries." John Quincy Adams Message to Congress, 5 December 1826, *American State Papers. Foreign Relations* vols. 1-6 (Washington, DC: Gales and Seaton, 1859), 6:207.

26. Goodman, 9-10.

27. Pierre de Boal to John D. Hickerson, Ottawa, 15 April 1933, SDDF 1930- 39, Box 3179, RG 59, National Archives.

28. William Phillips Memorandum, Ottawa, 27 March 1929, SDDF 1930-39, Box 3, RG 59, National Archives.

29. William S. Culbertson, *Reciprocity, a National Policy for Foreign Trade* (New York: Whittesy House, 1937), 93. This is, of course, only a par-tial view. American tariffs had an important impact on American eco-nomic relations with the rest of the world, and they were used to adjust foreign trade in ways that favored U.S. growth (for example, the

reciprocity policy toward South America in the late nineteenth century). But the initial push for tariff protection emerged for sectoral and regional reasons in the United States. Since Canada had so many economic points of contact, American tariff policy was not finely tuned for a Canadian policy (as was dramatically demonstrated when President Nixon imposed his emergency tariff in 1971). See Tom E. Terrill, *The Tariff, Politics, and American Foreign Policy, 1874-1901* (Westport, CT: Greenwood Press, 1973).

30. Secretary of State Blaine to President Harrison, 23 September 1891, in Charles C. Tansill, *Canadian-American Relations 1975-1911* (New Haven, CT: Yale University Press, 1943), 435-36.
31. Policy Statement on Canada (Green Booklet), Dept. of State, 19 March 1951, SDDF 1950-54, Box 2773, RG 59, National Archives.
32. Ibid., Stanley Woodward to Secretary of State, Ottawa, 13 January 1953.
33. Julian Harrington to Secretary of State, Ottawa, 5 July 1949, SDDF 1945-49, Box 5884, RG 59, National Archives. A recent book has made the case that the anti-American nationalism in Canadian intellectual and political circles does not extend to the great mass of Canadian people. See Peter Brimelow, *The Patriot Game: Canada and the Canadian Question Revisited* (Toronto: K. Porter Books, 1986). Brimelow's thesis has had a mixed press in Canada but it does bring out a viewpoint that was widespread in the State Department.
34. Policy Statement on Canada, Department of State, 19 March 1951, SDDF 1950-54, Box 2773, RG 59, National Archives.
35. There is an extensive literature on Canadian nationalism and the United States in the 1960s and 1970s. A good starting point is Stephen Clarkson, *Canada and the Reagan Challenge: Crisis in the Canadian-American Relationship* (Toronto: J. Lorimer, 1982). As always J.L. Granatstein is indispensable—*Canada 1957-67: The Years of Uncertainty and Innovation* (Toronto: McLelland and Stewart, 1986). See also A. Rotstein, *Essays on Economics, Technology and Nationalism* (Toronto: New Press, 1973) and *The Prospect of Change: Proposals for Canada's Future* (Toronto: McGraw Hill, 1965) as well as the collection of essays by Hillmer, ed., *Partners Nevertheless:Canadian-American Relations in the Twentieth Century* (Toronto: Copp Clark Pittman, 1989).
36. Don C. Bliss to Secretary of State, Ottawa, 23 April 1951, SDDF 1950-54, Box 2773, RG 59, National Archives.
37. Thomas Hotchkiss, Annual Report, 15 January 1886, Despatches from U.S. Consuls in Ottawa , Reel 2.
38. Figures compiled from M.C. Urquhart and K.A.H. Buckley, eds., *Historical Statistics of Canada* (Toronto: Cambridge University Press, 1965) and U.S. Bureau of Census, *Historical Statistics of the United States—Colonial Times to 1970* (Washington, DC: U.S. Government Printing Office, 1976) as well as periodic Canadian official publications such as "Canada and World Trade" in *Canada Today*, 19(1988/3).
39. A fine assessment of the modern economic relationship is Richard G. Lipsey, "Canada and the United States: The Economic Dimension," in Charles S. Doran and John H. Sigler, *Canada and the United States:*

Enduring Friendship, Persistent Stress (Englewood Cliffs, NJ: Prentice Hall, 1985), 69-108.

40. John D. Hickerson to Ray Atherton, Washington, 2 March 1945, Hickerson Papers, Reel 4; John D. Hickerson to Nelson T. Johnson (American Minister to Australia), Washington, 9 October 1944, Hickerson Papers, Reel 5.

41. Pierrepont Moffatt to John D. Hickerson, Ottawa, 22 August 1940, Hickerson Papers, Reel 5.

42. Donald G. Creighton, *The Forked Road: Canada 1939-1957* (Totonto: McClelland and Stewart, 1976); J.L. Granatstein, *How Britain's Weakness Forced Canada into the Arms of the United States*. The work of Granatstein and Bothwell on twentieth-century Canadian-American relations makes a compelling case that it was the two world wars which were the crucial determinants in pushing Canada into a dependent relationship with the United States.

43. John B. Osborne, "The Commercial Relations of the United States and Canada," U.S. Congress, *Sen. Doc.* No. 862, 61st Cong. 3rd sess., 55.

44. Ralph Williams to James Bryce, Government House, Newfoundland, 4 March 1911, MS Bryce USA, 31, Bodleian Library, Oxford.

45. Julian Harrington to Secretary of State, Ottawa, 12 May 1950, Policy Planning Staff 1947-1953, Box 13, RG 59, National Archives.

46. W.P. Snow to Ernest Perkins, 8 March 1950, SDDF 1950-54, Box 2773, RG 59, National Archives.

47. Ibid.

48. Roger Makins to Harold Macmillan, Washington, 2 November 1955; Roger Makins to Sir Ivone Kirkpatrick, Washington, 14 April 1955, PRO, FO 371/114384 and 114386.

49. John Quincy Adams to Richard Rush, 20 May 1818, in Manning, *Diplomatic Correspondence*, 1:268-69.

50. Stephen Clarkson, ed., *An Independent Foreign Policy for Canada* (Toronto: McLelland and Stewart, 1968); John Holmes, *Life with Uncle: The Canadian-American Relationship* (Toronto: University of Toronto Press, 1981); W.T.R. Fox, *A Continent Apart: The United States and Canada in World Politics* (Toronto: University of Toronto Press, 1985); Andrew Axline, *Continental Community: Independence and Integration in North America* (Toronto: McClelland and Stewart, 1974) all set out these issues.

51. J.J.S. Garner to Phillip Noel-Baker, Ottawa, 6 March 1948, PRO, DO 35/3115.

52. Granatstein, *How Britain's Weakness Forced Canada into the Arms of the United States*, passim.

Selected Bibliography

A. Primary Sources

1. National Archives, Washington, D.C.

a. State Department Decimal File, RG 59

<u>1910-1929</u>

Box 5794	611.4231/38-269
Box 5795	611.4231/270-401
Box 5796	611.4231/402-546
Box 5797	611.4231/547-687
Box 5798	611.4231/688-425/54
Box 5804	611.429/1012-611.4331/19
Box 1	711.42/24-711.4237/104
Box 2	711.42157SA29/137-345
Box 3	711.42157SA29/623

<u>1930-1939</u>

Box 3179	611.4231/781-904
Box 4003	711.42/103-711.4231/230
Box 3189	611.4231/2471-2680
Box 3182	611.4231/1270-1479
Box 3172	611.4225/250 611.423/380
Box 3178	611.423/391-611.4231/780
Box 3180	611.4231/905-1050
Box 3181	611.4231/1051-1269

<u>1940-1944</u>

Box 4504	842.4061/360-842.50/158

<u>1945-1949</u>

Box 5883	841.5151/1-145 - 842.00/12-3146
Box 5884	842.00/1-147 - 842.00(W)/12-3149
Box 5886	842.00PR/1-148 - 842.012/12-3149

<u>1950-1954</u>

Box 4821	842.00/1-1350 - 842.00/5-2853
Box 2773	Political Rels US/Can

b. Policy Planning Staff 1947-1953, RG 59 (Room 6E)

c. John D. Hickerson Papers

d. Leo Pasvolsky Papers

e. Notes to Foreign Legations

f. Despatches from U.S. Consuls
 Ottawa (1880-1902)
 Montreal (1850-1906)
 Halifax (1833-1906)

2. Public Record Office, London

Foreign Office
 FO414
 FO800
Colonial Office
 CO880
Dominions Office
 DO35/3115

3. Bodleian Library, Oxford

James Bryce Papers (Bryce Papers and MS Bryce USA)
Alfred Milner Papers

4. Michigan State University Library

Joshua Giddings-George Julian Correspondence
Andrew Johnson Papers
William H. Seward Papers
Grover Cleveland Papers
Benjamin Harrison Papers
Theodore Roosevelt Papers
William Howard Taft Papers
Frank B. Kellogg Papers
Adolf A. Berle Diary 1895-1971

5. Printed Sources

American Foreign Policy. Current Documents (Washington, DC: Department of State, 1959-)
American State Papers. Foreign Relations (Washington, DC: Government Printing Office, 1859).
Berle, Beatrice A., and Travis B. Jacobs, eds., *Navigating the Rapids: From the Papers of Adolf A. Berle* (New York: Harcourt Brace Jovanich, 1973).

Blaine, James G., *Political Discussions Legislative, Diplomatic and Popular 1856-1886* (Norwich: The Henry Bill Publishing Company, 1887).

Cunningham Jr., Noble E., *Circular Letters of Congressmen to Their Constituents 1789-1829* (Chapel Hill: The University of North Carolina Press, 1978).

Documents on Canadian External Affairs, 10 vols (Ottawa: Information Canada, 1970-).

Manning, William R., *Diplomatic Correspondence of the United States: Canadian Relations*, 1784-1860 4 vols. (Washington, DC: Carnegie Endowment for International Peace, 1940-1945).

Nevins, Allan, ed., *Letters of Grover Cleveland 1850-1908*. (Boston: Houghton Mifflin Company, 1933).

Seager, II, Robert, and Doris Maguire, eds., *Letters and Papers of Alfred Thayer Mahan. vol. 2, 1902-1914* (Annapolis, MD: Naval Institute Press, 1975).

U.S. Department of Commerce, Bureau of Foreign and Domestic Commerce, *The United Kingdom: An Industrial, Commercial and Financial Handbook,* [edited by Hugh Butler] (Washington: U.S. Government Printing Office, 1930).

U.S. Department of State. *Foreign Relations. United States (FRUS),* 1934 (Washington, DC: Government Printing Office, 1951).

———. *FRUS*, 1935 (Washington, DC: Government Printing Office, 1952).

———. *FRUS*, 1948 (Washington, DC: Government Printing Office, 1974).

———. *FRUS*, 1955-57 (Washington, DC: Government Printing Office, 1986).

Williams, C.R., ed., *Diary of Rutherford B. Hayes* (Columbus, OH: The Ohio State Archeological and Historical Society, 1924).

Congressional Papers

There is one set of Congressional papers that must be singled out because it is extraordinarily useful. The Senate Finance Committee in 1911 prepared a massive three-part report which included all previous Congressional reports on American relations with Canada as well as lengthy extracts from House and Senate debates at various critical periods in Canadian-American relations. Reciprocity with Canada. Compilation of 1911, *Sen. Doc.* no. 80 (three parts), 62d. Cong., 1st. sess., 1911. Included in Part One are such items as:

Reciprocity proceedings in the House of Representatives, 1850-1854. [9-65]

Report of the Senate Committee on Foreign Relations (Canadian Reciprocity), 11 July 1854, 394-434.

Report of Israel T. Hatch on working of 1854 Treaty, 22 March 1860. [633-57]

Report of James W. Taylor on working of 1854 Treaty, 2 May 1860. [663-72]

US Congress, Reciprocal Trade with Canada, *Sen. Ex. Doc.*, no. 114, 52d. Cong., 1st sess., 1982.

US Congress, Senate, Report of the Select Committee on Relations with Canada, *Sen. Doc.* no. 1530, 51st Cong., 1st sess., 1890.

US Congress, Report of Israel D. Andrews, *Sen. Ex. Doc.* no. 23, 31st. Cong., 2d sess., 1851.

US Congress, Report of Israel D. Andrews, *Sen. Ex. Doc.* no.112, 32d. Cong., 1st sess., 1852.

Secondary Sources

The standard literature in the field is covered comprehensively in the relevant sections of Richard Dean Burns, ed., *Guide to American Foreign Relations Since 1700* (Santa Barbara: ABC-Clio, Inc., 1983). Howard Jones, "The Canadian-American Boundary, 1783-1872," 263-89; Lawrence Gelfand, Scott Fowler and Scott R. Hall, "Anglo-Canadian-American relations, 1867-1914," 387-91; Robert S. Bothwell, "Canadian-American Relations Since 1941," 1055-74.

J.L. Granatstein and Paul Stevens include a section on "Foreign and Defence Policy" in their useful annotated bibliography *Canada Since 1867: A Bibliographical Guide* (Toronto: Hakkert, 1974), 33-55. And Norman Hillmer's "Further Reading" section in his *Partners Nevertheless: Canadian-American Relations in the Twentieth Century* (Toronto: Copp, Clark & Pitman, 1989), 319-22 is a knowledgeable summary of the present state of the modern portion of the field. Charles F. Doran and John G. Sigler, eds., *Canada and the United States: Enduring Friendship, Persistent Stress* (Englewood Cliffs: Prentice Hall, 1985) is a collection of papers prepared for a 1984 American Assembly conference and provides a benchmark in the scholarly treatment of current issues.

The Carnegie Series volumes are still essential reading for the information they contain and for their extensive references to official and Congressional documents. All titles are listed in the final volume, John Brebner, *North Atlantic Triangle: The Interplay of Canada, The United States and Great Britain* (New Haven: Yale University Press, 1945), 386. For this study the most useful volumes were: Lester B. Shippee, *Canadian-American Relations, 1849-1874* (New Haven: Yale University Press, 1939), Charles C. Tansill, *Canadian-American Relations, 1875-1911* (New Haven: Yale University Press, 1943) and L. Ethan Ellis, *Reciprocity 1911: A Study in Canadian-American Relations* (New Haven: Yale University Press, 1939).

Published at the same time as the Carnegie Series, but not part of it, is a one-volume treatment of the entire period from independence to the establishment of direct diplomatic relations in 1927, James Morton Callahan, *American Foreign Policy in Canadian Relations* (New York: The MacMillian Company, 1937). It is rather a difficult read but its severely chronological approach provides a helpful guide to Congressional debates and publications on Canada.

For the period up to 1871 all previous monographic literature is superseded by Reginald C. Stuart's masterly and comprehensive *United States Expansionism and British North America, 1775-1871* (Chapel Hill: The University of North Carolina Press, 1988). Stuart also includes a seventeen page bibliography. Modern writings on Anglo-American relations such as Howard Jones, *To the Webster-Ashburton Treaty: A Study in Anglo-American Relations* (Chapel Hill: The University of North Carolina Press, 1977) and Bradford Perkins, *Prologue to War: England and the United States, 1805-1812* (Berkeley: University of California Press, 1961) and *Castlereagh and Adams: England and the United States, 1812-1823* (Berkeley: University of California Press, 1964) provide essential background for appreciating American attitudes toward Canada during this period. And J.C.A. Stagg's influential, *Mr. Madison's War: Politics, Diplomacy and Warfare in the Early Republic, 1783-1830* (Princeton: Princeton University Press, 1983) has drawn attention to the looming presence of Canada in the minds of those who managed American administrations in the early republican era.

For the nineteenth century as a whole Kenneth Bourne's remarkable *Britain and the Balance of Power in North America, 1815-1908* (London: Longmans, 1967) gives a clear-headed assessment of British plans for using Canada to check the rising power of the United States. Robin Winks, *Canada and the United States: The Civil War Years* (Baltimore: The Johns Hopkins University Press, 1960) is still the best treatment of that important topic. Alvin M. Gluek's *Minnesota and the Manifest Destiny of the Canadian Northwest* (Toronto: University of Toronto Press, 1965) shows the regional dimension to American expansionist drives. Donald F. Warner, *The Idea of Continental Union: Agitation for the Annexation of Canada to the United States, 1849-1893* (Lexington: University of Kentucky Press, 1960) is still a reliable guide to the various annexation movements that periodically made themselves heard. Robert C. Brown, *Canada's National Policy, 1883-1900: A Study in Canadian American Relations* (Princeton: Princeton University Press, 1964) is a detailed and authoritative account of Canada's major response to American protectionism. Carl Berger's, *The Sense of Power: Studies in the Idea of Canadian Imperialism, 1867-1914* (Toronto: University of Toronto Press, 1970) is fundamental for an understanding of Canada's evolving relationship to the British Empire. Edward P. Crapol, *America for Americans: Economic Nationalism and Anglophobia in the late Nineteenth Century* (Westport: Greenwood Press, 1973) is very useful for understanding American resentment about Canadian development. Finally, Richard Preston's *The Defence of the Undefended Border: Planning for War in North America, 1867-1939* (Montreal: McGill-Queens University Press, 1977) is a characteristically thorough analysis of the military factor in Canadian-Ameican relations.

In dealing with the modern period since 1914 all roads lead to the work of J.L. Granatstein, Particularly two books written with R.D. Cuff:—*Ties that Bind: Canadian-American Relations in War Time: From the Great War to the Cold War* (Toronto: Hakkert, 1975), *American Dollars, Canadian Prosperity: Canadian-American Economic Relations, 1945-1950* (Toronto: Samuel-Stevens, 1978) and Granatstein, *How Britain's Weakness forced Canada into the Arms of the United States* (Toronto: University of Toronto Press, 1989). The work of John Holmes, *The Shaping of Peace: Canada and the Search for World Order, 1943-1957* (Toronto: University of Toronto Press, 1979-82 [3vols]) describes the aspirations of Canadian policymakers during the years of integration and James Eayrs' work provides an account of developing Canadian concepts of external relations in the inter-war years, *In Defence of Canada* (Toronto 1964-65 [5vols.]). The best single volume coverage of the critical World War II years is C.P Stacey's Arms, *Men and Governments: The War Policies of Canada, 1939-1945* (Ottawa: Queen's Printer, 1970). See too on this subject S.W. Dzuiban, *Military Relations Between the United States and Canada, 1939-1945* (Washington, DC: Office of the Chief of Military History, 1959). The work of Charles Doran and Norman Hillmer has already been noted above but special reference must be made to Ian Drummond and Norman Hillmer, *Negotiating Freer Trade: The United Kingdom, the United States, Canada and the Trade Agreements of 1938* (Waterloo: Wilfrid Laurier University Press, 1989) which deals more fully than previous works with these key trade talks in the 1930s when the United States responded to the empire trade threat. This should be read in conjunction with Richard Kottman's *Reciprocity and the North Atlantic Triangle, 1932-1938*, (Ithaca: Cornell University Press, 1968). Bernard Goodman, *Industrial Material in Canadian-American Relations* (Detroit: Wayne State University Press, 1961) is a solid starting point for this important topic which occupied an important place in American thinking on Canada in the twentieth century.

Index

The American Response to Canada since 1776

Copyeditor: Martha Bates
Designer: Michael Brooks
Indexer: Ellen Link

Typestyle is Garamond throughout.

Printed by DATA Reproductions Corporation
on 55# Glatfelter Natural
Bound in Roxite "B" Linen

CANADA

2¢

XMAS

"WE HOLD A VASTER E